T0168609

SOUTH AMERICAN JOURNALS

UNIVERSITY OF

MINNESOTA PRESS

MINNEAPOLIS

Allen Ginsberg

SOUTH AMERICAN JOURNALS

JANUARY-JULY 1960

EDITED BY

MICHAEL SCHUMACHER

Photographs on page 2 courtesy of The Estate of Allen Ginsberg. Photograph on page 96 copyright *El Comercio,* Peru. Photographs on pages vi, xiv, 113, 176, 240, 276, and 279 and all drawings by Allen Ginsberg courtesy of the Allen Ginsberg Papers, Stanford University Archives and Special Collections.

Published by the University of Minnesota Press
111 Third Avenue South, Suite 290
Minneapolis, MN 55401-2520
http://www.upress.umn.edu

Printed in the United States of America on acid-free paper

The University of Minnesota is an equal-opportunity educator and employer.

28 27 26 25 24 23 22   10 9 8 7 6 5 4 3 2 1

*

Library of Congress Cataloging-in-Publication Data
Ginsberg, Allen, 1926–1997, author. | Schumacher, Michael, editor.
South American journals : January–July 1960 /
Allen Ginsberg ; edited by Michael Schumacher.
Minneapolis : University of Minnesota Press, [2019]
Includes bibliographical references.
Identifiers: LCCN 2019007797 (print)
ISBN 978-0-8166-9961-2 (hc/j)
ISBN 978-0-8166-9962-9 (pb)
Subjects: LCSH: Ginsberg, Allen, 1926–1997—Diaries.
Ginsberg, Allen, 1926–1997—Travel—South America.
South America—Description and travel.
Classification: LCC PS3513.I74 Z46 2019 (print) | DDC 811/.54 [B]—dc23
LC record available at https://lccn.loc.gov/2019007797

CONTENTS

EDITOR'S INTRODUCTION

vii

A NOTE ON EDITING ALLEN GINSBERG

xv

SOUTH AMERICAN JOURNALS

Chile, Argentina, Bolivia

3

Peru

97

SELECT BIBLIOGRAPHY BY
AND ABOUT ALLEN GINSBERG

327

May 1960

Macchu picchu Dreams

60-06

SA
Notebook
6

PATRIA
MARCA REGISTRADA

CUADERNO
AMAUTA

PERTENECIENTE

A

and peruvian Typed

Improvisations

VARGAS DIAZ Hnos. S. A. Ltda.
CUZCO
Mesón de la Estrella No. 128
Teléfono 2630 — Apartado 150

INDUSTRIA PERUANA

60 H.

6170

EDITOR'S INTRODUCTION

Allen Ginsberg began keeping journals in his youth. The early journals were little more than diaries, with entries recording his day-to-day activities and opinions. Ginsberg, embarrassed by the egotism and naïveté these journals contained, insisted that they not be published until after his death.

The quality and depth of his journal writings improved exponentially when he attended Columbia University and met Lucien Carr, Jack Kerouac, William S. Burroughs, Neal Cassady, and others associated with the group of writers eventually known as the Beat Generation. These writers sought a new vision for American literature, and they used their own lives as the grist for novels and poetry that would have a lasting influence on contemporary writing. They found ways to document and even celebrate the lives of those normally overlooked by writers of the day. Ginsberg's journals at this time became more sophisticated alongside his hopes of becoming a major poet, though they paled in comparison to the journals he would keep later.

His life and mental landscape changed dramatically and permanently during the summer of 1948, when he was just twenty-two years old and still a student at Columbia. He was staying at a friend's apartment in Harlem, reading the works of William Blake, St. John of the

Cross, Christopher Smart, and other visionary writers and mystics. One evening at dusk, while staring out an open window and pondering the handiwork of the craftsmen who had designed and built the cornices at the rooftops of nearby buildings, he heard a voice in the room—an auditory hallucination he interpreted to be the voice of William Blake— reciting "Ah! Sun-flower." This, Ginsberg averred, was a *vision* of great importance, a voice speaking through the ages, instructing him to heed a vocation of poetry. The experience, Ginsberg insisted to friends and family, was real; it had not been imagined. Other visionary flashes followed, including experiences that occurred when he was out in public. Ginsberg spoke of these visions to anyone who would sit still for it (see his poem "The Lion for Real" for one account), but he found that he had few supporters. His father, Louis, was particularly concerned: Allen's mother, Naomi Ginsberg, had been tormented for much of her adult life by paranoid schizophrenia, and eventually she would be institutionalized. Louis Ginsberg feared that his son might be heading down a similar path.

Ginsberg's attempts to reconstruct his visionary experiences, published in *The Gates of Wrath*, were largely unsuccessful; words obstructed, rather than clarified, the experiences. Obsessed with expanding his consciousness, Ginsberg tried to do so by experimenting with different drugs, including marijuana, peyote, heroin, nitrous oxide, and lysergic acid, but these blurred the answers he was seeking and proved to be elusive. Many of these experiences were recorded in his journals or in poems written while he was under the influence.

As he was learning, one couldn't just will spiritual breakthroughs into existence.

Ginsberg's quest coincided with his breakthrough as a poet. He had struck up a friendship with William Carlos Williams, who had been unimpressed with Ginsberg's early rhymed imitations of works taught in the academic community. "In this mode," Williams wrote Ginsberg after sampling some of these efforts, "perfection is basic."

Rather than becoming discouraged by Williams's observations, Ginsberg changed directions and developed at a remarkable pace. His journals *became* his poetry. He broke prose passages in his journals into short lines resembling poetry, much of these efforts contained in *Empty Mirror,* a collection of poems published well after his establishment as a nationally recognized poetic presence. Williams was thrilled by these new poems. "How many such poems do you own?" he asked his young protégé. "These are it."

Thus encouraged, Ginsberg fished through his journals and pulled many new poems from the prose within. This shift, though perhaps subtle to the casual observer, represented a new, dynamic direction toward using idiomatic language and the rhythms of everyday speech Williams had already perfected; Ginsberg followed his example and found it liberating. His poem "The Trembling of the Veil" was closer to depicting the visionary experience than any of his previous rhymed attempts. Concrete images, rather than flowery speech, along with the longer lines he admired in Walt Whitman (an early hero) and the prose of Jack Kerouac, guided him in the next decade's poems.

By the time he was packing his bags for his trip to South America in 1960, Ginsberg had established himself as the major, if controversial, new voice in American poetry. "Howl," "Sunflower Sutra," and "America," from his first slender volume of poems, *Howl and Other Poems,* forced a strong, occasionally heated discussion on the direction contemporary poetry was taking; the sales of work by Ginsberg, Kerouac, Ferlinghetti, and others, in numbers previously unheard of in the serious, academic-driven literary community, had altered the discussion of literature. And because these newcomers were writing about their own lives, or the "beat" members of a "generation destroyed by madness,"

Editor's Introduction

the argument grew to include *subject* alongside the idea of literary merit.

Ginsberg still hoped to crack the code to widening what was usually accepted as ordinary or average consciousness. This was on his mind in January 1960 when he boarded the plane for Chile. He hoped that one drug, highly recommended by William S. Burroughs, might act as a beacon illuminating his questions about life, death, consciousness, God, and eternity. He intended to honor his obligations in Chile, and then proceed to Peru and the remote regions of the Amazon.

In 1954, Ginsberg had spent his first extended period outside the United States, in the Yucatán, where he explored the Mayan ruins at Chichén Itzá. He was befriended by Karena Shields, a middle-aged archaeologist who took him in as her guest and helped acquaint him to the region. Ginsberg's adventure led him to memorable experiences, including feeling the earth trembling around him during a seismic shift in the unstable region, followed by his rediscovery of a cave long believed to have disappeared owing to the passage of time and earthquakes. True to form, Ginsberg recorded the finest details of his journey in his journals, eventually published in *Journals: Early Fifties, Early Sixties*. He also wrote "Siesta in Xbalba," his first modestly successful long poem, about the purgatory between life and death, as part of his meditations during his wanderings in the Yucatán. As with his previous Williams-influenced journal poems, he caught the lightning of the visionary experience without consciously trying to set it to poetry. It wasn't planned; it just happened.

His visionary poems written throughout the 1950s, including "Laughing Gas" and "Lysergic Acid," were attempts to move forward with the aid of drugs and experience. In "Laughing Gas," he was administered nitrous oxide by a dentist, and as he sat in the dentist's chair, a notebook in his lap, he tried to record his state of mind the moment before he lost consciousness. This and other drug-influenced poems contained flashes of a different consciousness, but they ultimately failed to answer the questions Ginsberg wanted to address. He hoped the strong powers of ayahuasca, or *yagé,* would lead him to success. For this, he had William Burroughs to thank. Burroughs had traveled to South America in 1953, not long before Ginsberg had ventured to Mexico, where Burroughs had taken ayahuasca, which he declared "the ultimate fix."

But vision, Ginsberg learned from Burroughs, did not arrive without a price. Taking ayahuasca was not a pleasant experience, and the visions could be horrific. In an April 15, 1953, letter, sent from Bogotá and eventually published in *The Yage Letters,* Burroughs described the effects that a single dose of ayahuasca had on him. "In two minutes a wave of dizziness swept over me and the hut began spinning," he wrote Ginsberg:

> It was like going under ether, or when you are very drunk and lie down and the bed spins. Blue flashes passed in front of my eyes. The hut took on an archaic far-Pacific look with Easter Island heads carved in the support posts. The assistant was outside lurking there with the obvious intent to kill me. I was hit by sudden, violent nausea and rushed for the door hitting my shoulder against the door post. I felt the shock but no pain. I could hardly walk. No coordination. My feet were like blocks of wood. I vomited violently leaning against a tree and fell on the ground in helpless misery. I felt numb as if I was covered with layers of cotton. I kept trying to break out of this numb dizziness. I kept saying over and over, "All I want is out of here."

Ginsberg's own experiences with ayahuasca, described at great depth in these journals, were similar, but with differing effects on his writing. Burroughs wrote prose, usually in short, episodic bits that he used to entertain Ginsberg, Kerouac, and others, some of which were published in *Naked Lunch*; he probed the way ayahuasca fractured his perception.

Editor's Introduction

By the time Ginsberg left for South America, Burroughs had begun his "cut-up" writings found in his most experimental work. He created new ideas by joining two different thoughts into a new one, not unlike the visions he had seen under the influence of ayahuasca. Ginsberg, on the other hand, was much more interested in the spirituality in his poetry, which was made more personal in its leaning.

These journals act as a bridge between Ginsberg's earlier writings about widening his consciousness and his *Indian Journals,* written while he and Peter Orlovsky traveled to India and stayed on the subcontinent for more than a year. In India, he sought out holy men and spiritual seekers, told them of his Blake visions and his subsequent attempts to broaden his perceptions, but he found that these men had little interest in the use of drugs in the quest. "If you see something beautiful, don't cling to it. If you see something horrible, don't cling to it," they advised.

Ginsberg's visions in Peru gave him both to consider.

ACKNOWLEDGMENTS

Allen Ginsberg, of course, is the first person to thank. His initial decision to publish his journals was nothing less than an act of generosity, a gift to scholars for generations to come.

Peter Hale, overseer of the Ginsberg estate, has been very helpful in my editing of Ginsberg's journals, whether it involved assisting in lining up contacts or simply offering encouragement. With Peter at the helm, Ginsberg's legacy is in good hands.

The overwhelming percentage of Allen Ginsberg's papers (journals, poetry, letters, clippings, etc.) are housed at Stanford University, and the staff in the rare books and manuscripts library were very generous with their time and assistance, especially in providing me with tran-

Editor's Introduction

scripts and photographs that I didn't already have in my collection. My thanks to all.

I've leaned heavily on Gordon Ball, editor of Ginsberg's *Journals: Early Fifties, Early Sixties* and *Journals Mid-Fifties,* for guidance in the editing process. Gordon had worked closely with Ginsberg on the two books he edited, and he was invaluable in advising me on how Allen would have done things.

Bob Rosenthal, author of the wonderful *Straight around Allen,* a memoir of his time working as Ginsberg's office manager from 1972 until Ginsberg's death in 1997, has always been very helpful, and I'm glad to call him a friend.

Jeff Posternak, Ginsberg's representative at the Wylie Agency, handled the business details in ushering this book into print.

Finally, I owe a debt of gratitude to Erik Anderson and Kristian Tvedten at the University of Minnesota Press. Both are first-rate editors with exceptional instincts, and I appreciate their enthusiasm and guidance throughout the work on this book.

Editor's Introduction

First Nite Notes

Ready Wire-Glo

No. W-271   Pocket Notes

A NOTE ON EDITING ALLEN GINSBERG

Allen Ginsberg was fond of his South American journals, and he spoke of his hope of eventually seeing them in print. He talked to me about it on a couple of occasions, and I have no doubt that, had he lived and somehow found the time, he would have overseen their editing and publication. My first obligation in editing this book was to him, and I worked on the manuscript as if he were still alive, using his exacting eye to judge my efforts. It was no small burden to know that future Ginsberg scholars might be using these journals as references in their own work—in my view, there was no margin for error.

One does not edit Allen Ginsberg (or any other writer, for that matter) without making a lot of decisions. Writers are very protective about the words they publish—or they ought to be—and there are unwritten rules one faces when publishing words that weren't originally intended for publication.

The reader should keep the following in mind:

1. Ginsberg's spelling could be spotty, especially in the case of proper names. It was not uncommon for him to use two or more spellings of a proper name. I silently corrected what I knew to be misspellings, knowing that he would have done the same. When in doubt, I main-

Laugh Gas ~~Jan~~ 5, 1960: 4:45 PM

60-14   (1)

"You're fighting problems that are
outside your control ~ in this
business (Dentistry) - you gotta
outguess the factors that are involved"
Meaning: my patients never brush
their teeth properly.

_____

the muzak has a thin
sophisticated violin sound,
ancient and nostalgic even to
a child's ear. When a Gypsy makes his
violin cry. Because it comes from
very far away. Continuous flow of
calm, melancholy old favorites.
    "I would never drill the wrong
tooth!"

tained his spelling. (This also applies to his spellings of Spanish words.) I left intact obviously intended misspellings ("stept" instead of "stepped," "mexcity" for "Mexico City"), just as Allen had in work published during his lifetime; there's a charming playfulness to this.

2. I retained most capitalizations exactly as Ginsberg wrote them in his journals, though I made silent corrections in some cases. It's possible that he might have corrected some of them, but I doubt it, given the quirky capitalization found in the journals published while he was alive to supervise the editing.

3. I silently inserted a punctuation mark on a rare occasion, but only if the prose became unreadable without it. Ginsberg wrote in bursts of mental energy, his words sprawling out onto the page as quickly as he thought, and the unpunctuated passages give the reader an indication of the workings of his emotions and mind.

4. The reader will note the occasional question mark within brackets: [?]. This indicates a missing word. Ginsberg's handwriting was usually legible, but every so often a word would be scribbled in such a way that even he himself could not determine what he had written. Those transcribing the journals years ago had no more answers than I did, so, rather than cut a line or paragraph containing an illegible word, I inserted [?] to indicate a missing or illegible word. As a general rule, the loss of a word did not affect the overall meaning of the passage.

5. I indicated the excising of a longer passage with bracketed ellipses: [...]. In most cases, this was simply a matter of cutting brief passages that were repetitive or, I felt, unnecessary. On a rare occasion I cut a passage that had so many missing words that it would have been confusing to the reader.

6. Readers will note that I inserted two of Ginsberg's letters into the text. I believe they add important information absent in the journals

Editing Allen Ginsberg

or clarify what Ginsberg chose to include. Ginsberg was always careful to note that his work, whether poetry or journal entries, was not autobiography in the strictest sense because he was only recording what was on his mind at a particular moment. Significant events, he would say, had been glossed over or ignored entirely. The letters included in the book are my attempt to fill in the blanks.

Editing Allen Ginsberg

SOUTH AMERICAN JOURNALS

Ginsberg in Panama, on the way to Chile

Chile,
Argentina,
Bolivia

In November 1959, Allen Ginsberg and poet and City Lights publisher Lawrence Fer-linghetti were invited to participate in an international poetry conference in Chile in January 1960. Although both men were already overburdened by work, they enthusi-astically accepted. They would travel separately.

Ginsberg needed no encouragement to travel; his relentless curiosity and engaging personality made him a natural at it. He'd spent months in Mexico exploring the Yu-catán on his own in early 1954, had journeyed to Tangier with William S. Burroughs in 1957, and, even more noteworthy, had lived in Europe, with Paris as his headquarters, for a year and a half in 1957 and 1958. For his trip to South America, he would have preferred to roam with Peter Orlovsky, his companion and lover since 1954, but Orlovsky lacked a valid passport and Ginsberg once again would be a solo traveler.

He began his journey on January 14, uncertain about what lay ahead. The confer-ence at the University of Concepción was largely a means to a different end: Ginsberg wanted to head north when the conference ended, see the Andes Mountains, and, with any luck, venture to the ruins of Machu Picchu, which in 1960 were largely ignored and not the tourist trap they would eventually become.

Ginsberg blocked out two months for his visit to South America. He would stay much longer.

TO S.A.

Newark Airport Noon Thurs Jan 14 1960

Sleet whizzing on the
   concrete runway,
as the lane turns to move.

18,000 feet

   Cape May is small, seen the first time—many Clouds—the Eastern
Seaboard is Dotty—Isles & Sandbars & glistening little houses—
   The old man from Paterson returned from Wrights with only 80 a
month pension, 65—tho he gets Social Security and Paterson's Comp—
he was up in a balloon in France in 1917—never been in a plane before—
had fine teeth.
   Okeechobe late afternoon a lake of night—Pond a sea.

   Sun overhead in the haze
down there the back swamp
   round sun shining under
     the surface
Sun moving along the
   surface
   like a shining Disc
Horrorsun swifting across
   The water.

In Miami—Sudden
rotting tropical ocean
   smell—
dark streets with palms,
   a canal
a broken pianoplayer
      in a
   Modern Bar

The moon
   Eating Turkey Patiently
over the Caribbean

The green fires are the towns
of Cuba
   —Imagine that Country
in the hands of Revolutionaries

Panama Airport
   Boy it feels funny
—the balmy rot smell
in the night,
   Palm trees,
      a shoeshine boy
An aztec eagle on the
      Terminal floor
         and my beard
in the 25c photo machine
looking like 1940 Communist
      Terrorist refugee in police files

Chile

Morning—riding along coast of S.A.—Brown's South America—looks like Clouds or mists [in] distance on left—apron at seashore irregular—at Lima Airport the shit has the smell in the air again. Below Lima the Desert stretched like brown rubber apron from Shore inland to mountain. After that a floor of cracked clouds down south. Later out of window at left, a blanket of white cloud stretched out to the horizon where —the mountain—Andes run continuously—themselves small from afar, and sandwiched under another higher layer of cloud.

2PM Jan 15, 1960

Waves of land rising toward the mount—slow motion earthcrust—holocaust

----

Santiago

    Met by thin litterateur with Programs

    To Hotel Panamerica—

Downstairs in the bar, the assembled Argentineans, Panamanians, Chileans, and us—

    I drank Vino Undurraga (white) and sat on leather sofa slightly tipsy, bored, waiting to take off for the flat Roofs I see from my hotel room with Balcony.

Osormigeo

    In Santiago zoo

       Anteater:

i.e.—animal developed

Chile

to eat ants—
    all his Karma is ants
Shaped to sweep them to his
    hose mouth
his whole head a funnel
    of bones & flesh and fur
To snift up hoards of Ants,
Pure Karma of bitty
   (he'll be reborn an ant?)
And seeing him surrounded by
            Doves
In a wire enclosure in
    The dirt
Surrounded by the subtler
    bodies of the llama and
    the Camel
I saw his fate at once,
his humble ego
    stinking of formic acid

So that the Tigers and the
    man eating birds
leave him to Pad in peace
    and—
   his ridiculous victory
    over the sun & moon
is to be
    Ant-Eater
Made of sentient fur,

Chile

a joke on the Cosmos
pure first saint
of South America.

[. . .]

More Anteater
Es Tan obvio
Es Tan obvio
He's so obvious
    like a fairy
waving his hand at a mirror
        or a Cock—
Es tan obvio
    What he's doing here on earth—
Does he cry?
            when he doesn't get
        enough Ants to eat?
Oh he must love the ants
His very existence is centered depends
            on them
Like a dope fiend or a Cocksucker—
He must dream Ants
and does he think it is strange
    to devour a whole
            Ant-Colony?
His long thin tongue took thousands
    of years to grow
and his ancestors devoured

millions & millions of
       Ants
to nourish that fortunate long body
built to seek only Ants.

Who would be a Seraph?
   Who would be a giraffe?

In an instant
   when I glimpsed the
Ant Eater waving his nose
   down below in his Cage
I understood not merely
   Charles Darwin
   & the theory of Evolution
I understand the history of
   All sentient beings
and their
   Poor Trapped souls
       (Traphoods)

For we're all ant eaters by
      Nature
Proud of our noses, not suspecting
What we're built for—
him to eat ants—me to
   write poetry
and god sits and laughs
   at all His forms,
Surprised by Himself—

God is an ant,

      too—

God eats god, a good efficient

    anteater like himself—

And the Marxists are

     anteaters

And the Capitalists are ant-

     eaters

And you, Chilenos, sitting

    All night in El bosco

Discussing Literature

    So proud of yourselves—

Remember your Ant-Eater

  up on San Cristobal hill,

alone amid Cries of Purple

    assed baboons,

(Tigers and straw-legged

       birds

    with long thin whistles,)

who waves his long nose

back and forth at the full

       Moon.

It's not his fault, he was born

    that way.

Sunday

    8 AM up & ride out to Valparaiso—stopt for new champagne—on road, bought cough-medicine in local pharmacia, and Continued to the Bay—like Napoli—a ride in boat to the sea—old rusty tanks sitting w/

seaweed to the waterline—then sat at Club Naval—a small side room with banquet chairs for 12—"chicken-eaters"—like ant eaters—arguing about literature w/ chicken bones flopping about plates under their absent minded hands with knives.

Alone in Santiago

Preparing to go asleep
outside my Balcony
    the shadow of Andes
in the Southern blue—
a bell rings twice on the plain,
an airplane beacon winks
            in red—
I am an extraordinary personality
alone with god in another
            continent.
—I feel sad again,
            Peter's[1] in N.Y.
And what good is Death
                able—
to pierce thru the Dullness
    of the wall
—there're literateurs arguing
    Marxism over lamb—
these beggars in hoods

1. Peter Orlovsky, Ginsberg's lifelong companion.

Chile

collecting garbage
—even the ant-eaters
sense of humor
is obvious—
to a lark in the Kosmos—
much less to extraordinary
self which is disappearing—
Goodnight, Southern Stars
Goodnight, evil little
bell of Santiago,
Goodnight, memory of Peter
Goodnight, Allen, too, his
elbow on the pillow
in the bed, aching
as we scribble
out our schizophrenia
of Lonely Death—
Goodnight, Codeine, Amigo,
Clare, Goodnight shirt
and holey socks
Goodnite, Don Allen,[2] in N.Y
anthologies of
our poems—
Must we Perish?
All the Poets
are sleeping in this Grand Hotel,
and I must sleep too soon,

2. Donald Allen (1912–2004) edited *The New American Poetry 1945–1960*, an influential anthology that included many works by the Beat Generation.

audio stinkfinger
Serious one,
                Machu Picchu
    Palaverer & Prayer
    under pyramids
        years ago,
            forgot—
an ant Crawls on a Green leaf
    6 years ago
and passes my retina
    Is there forever—
Loose bones Jack books,
            Love leaves,
Oh! that after the
    Turmoil of Nothingness
        Crying aloud to itself
            in years—new years—
I wake up much later
    in the universe still
    Neal,[3] Alone,
more real than I can Imagine
        what to do
except complain
God,
Show me up, in out.

3. Neal Cassady (1926–1968), central figure in the Beat Generation, fictionalized main character (Dean Moriarty) in Jack Kerouac's *On the Road*, Ginsberg friend and lover, later a figure in Ken Kesey's bus of Merry Pranksters.

Chile

b. June 3, 1926
d—4 A.M. Encore
Bong Bong Bong Bong

As the nite bell rang on Junk-
Juice, w/ Peter and we heard
Time, in the stillness
    echoed in heaven
    over the TV antennae
here—Cockcrows, the street—
    light shades cast, the
    glance of human dogbark
Wakes in la noche for a
    Cry of S.A. pain
I am the Lone Watcher
    in Santiago
one of a million eyes
    awake of asleep
near Aconcagua's ripple
    in the Southern Dark
—high Mts. In the sky
    glimpsed flying over
    clouds—silver
        presences—
[?] box of books of
    queerer consciousness
      than most
Sans images—
    Gulp, Bamboo
    Crane, Betray

Chile

Begone, Arctic
 Vam, Void—
Voodoo Mama
 up North
"Nevermore"
 Nap, Poe—me
Me now, Me Penguin
 No Me, Anteater,
No me, no ants
 Me Bee
many many tree me,
 trip trap
up Jaguar
 Slash, wound
Blood, Field
 Burn, Cocaine,
Burn body opio
 Boom Me Bastard
Wa Wa Whoopie
Carl Sandburg
 oops, Eliot, James
  Save the Buddha too.
 Bone,
  Dream
dead city itch
  Bah, Damn
   Codeine
Wop fat belly
 me goof

Chile

Monday's
       Dead City Itch
Left Santiago 3 PM—
The Panamericans got my
       number—"Bourgeois"—

A hundred mile field
  of white cloud
Fly has visions on the plane
          Window
Clinging as big as

Notes for Speech
    Plato—When Mode Changes[4]
    Williams idea—when a form is broken, as atom, new energy is
released.
    Poesia—is invencion continue, una revolucion permanante—

All this is after the fact, frankly. I don't know how we write. I'm generalizing once the creation is completed.

Composition as creation, *Discovery* as in Gertrude Stein.

[. . .]

4. Allen Ginsberg's essay "When the Mode of the Music Changes, the Walls of the City Shake."

Chile

America! America

I've traveled many places
    & seen you from
afar
looked down from the
north pole at your
        radar echo
And seen you from under
        the Southern Cross
I see you falling in the nite
    like a shooting star
in constellation, [...]
—I see you wandering
    a lone road to the Madhouse
        night
            like my mother
    Naomi
Not knowing your fate
I see you go mad,
            America
& Die in the world's
        madhouse
Another nation fallen

Everyone knows we will
        The Next war
Can't beat Russia & China

Chile

Those Chinamen entering our
    gardens & apt houses
with gasmasks & bayonets
    spearing grandmother
      and adolescents
ordering everyone around
    forming communes—

Concepcion, Chile—January 1960

LATUS   Coranormal cough medicine
TUPA   Nicotinia

Poetry is a shoe that fits the mind.

Trip to town of Coal Mines—going around the shoe corner for ciga-
rettes the Banquets are eclipsed fast—I hardly remember one dinner af-
ter another except as a fast dream.

    The Miners Scrambling out of the dripping black iron elevator like
dirty animals—crouched together while the different stages of the ele-
vator are unloaded—a platform of miners substituted for a platform of
coal on the elevator.

LITERARY CONFERENCE

    One Argentinean speaker so boring that I saw a thousand people
sitting in silence, smiling to themselves, tapping their fingers, playing

Chile

w/ their mustaches "en el annio 32 in *mi* patria" crossing their legs, sighing, leaning forward, yawning, closing their eyes w/ their hands, clearing their throats, scratching themselves, sitting with blank eyes—

Letter, Allen Ginsberg (in Santiago, Chile) to Peter Orlovsky (New York), January 24, 1960

Dear Peter:

Came down here to Concepcion, sat part way in front pilot's seat in control cabin and saw the Andes far away on left. The Conference lasted a week and ended yesterday. I seem to be the only bearded man in Chile, so my photo was in all the newspapers—and children on the streets thought I was Fidel Castro's representative. Most everybody at Conference was un-poetic but one thing was most interesting, all the communists seemed to take over enough to make the whole week a big argument between pro and anti political writers. Everybody from every country got up and made fiery speeches about the workers. Everybody wanted revolutions. I delivered an address also on Wednesday—in broken Spanish, English, and French—and had translated and read them Wiener's query poems, Lamantia's[5] "Narcotica" and Gregory's "Bomb" —plus a long lecture on prosody, jazz, drugs, soul, etc. It was a big mad interesting speech and they dug it—I think it was probably the best of the speeches. Then 2 nites ago Ferlinghetti and I read—he did well but my reading was without real feeling but had some force. So I was depressed afterward tho the audience seemed to enjoy it. But was unhappy not to deliver the lamb to the communists. But anyway withal we were

5. Surrealist poet Philip Lamantia (1927–2005) read at the Six Gallery reading in San Francisco in 1955.

Chile

big hit and now Beat Generation is considered great new American poetry and all the professors will bring it back to Uruguay and Argentina and perhaps Colombia.

At same time there are some interesting people here like in Tangier—the best friend I've had here is a strange roly-poly philosophy professor at the university who talks English and is called Luis Oyarzin. Luce (lu-cha) (little light) is a big telepathic botanist, naturalist, fairy, astronomer and poet (tho not a great poet—too shy)—he's like a small Ansen but funny. He has various queer friends including an old man named Hyde who has a house here and is very brilliant and lost like an old lady with books. Also a young couple of lovers, boys, whom they all know—so there's a whole semi-hip queer secret society here. Oyarzin is also a big head of the Fine Arts School and is leaving for China in a week. He says he will get us invited (expenses paid by Chinese) to visit China—everybody here visits China. He sends you regards.

I've slept with nobody and masturbated twice. The land is like California. Tomorrow I'm taking a 3rd class train south towards an island called Chiloe fish and maybe finish *Kaddish*. Then return here, fly to Santiago, take a round trip bus ride across Andes, return and fly to La Paz Bolivia—see Machu Picchu—then to Lima Peru for a week. Then to Panama City for a week. So I will be here about another month or month and a half and then be back.

How are you and Lafcadio[6]? From here it seems you must be in a labyrinth of his worries. Tho I have been in a labyrinth of communists which is just as bad.

Also I went to a Jazz festival & heard a beautiful Uruguayan trumpeter play a genius like 1920 horn last nite.

One of the things we did was go to a town by the sea called Lota, to

6. Lafcadio Orlovsky, Peter's brother.

Chile

see the Miners there who work 12 hours a day for $1.20. Mines are along tunnels undersea. The political writers organized the trip to impress us with the sufferings of the workers here. Everybody's talking Revolution & Workers etc.

I have not received mail & won't till I get back to Santiago in 1 or 2 weeks. Did you ever get the Check from Ferlinghetti? I expect some money from Fantasy and Ferlinghetti says he owes me more & is printing another 10,000 copies [of *Howl and Other Poems*] (that makes 50,000) when he gets back.

My writing here is simplified down because I am so used to talking simple Spanish. I feel as if I were translating everything to basic explanations. I have been a little lonely but feel good anyway. The unfinished book [*Kaddish and Other Poems*] bothers me so I may try it here more. I hope you are not feeling trapped in N.Y.C. Perhaps we can all go to Mexico later in the Spring or further on. Is Lafcadio showing any signs of independence and feeling?

My plane ticket is good for side trips to Bolivia so it's very cheap for traveling.

Another person I like is Nicanor Parra,[7] a poet about 45 years old who is always falling in love with Swedish girls, writes intelligent and sincere poetry and is also a big mathematics professor who studied in England and U.S.A. He too went to China last year and believes and accepts Mao Tse-tung's Yenan literature theory. City Lights just put out a book of his translations—not bad, at least readable. I'm sorry you did not, could not, come—you'd have been the most amazing person here.

Well OK for now—I haven't written anyone but you and I should send

---

7. Nicanor Parra (1914–2018), a Chilean poet and mathematician, befriended Ginsberg during his stay in Chile. The two later reconnected when Ginsberg was in Cuba in 1965.

postcards to everybody so I will today. I am generally confused, by the communists and by being alone, but it feels good to be wandering solitary in South America. No cocaine yet but still have to get the Chilean Yage-like drugs and try them.

Love,
Allen

When Russia invents a super rocket the USA sets off a secret bomb.

The major point of Michelangelo's Vision of heaven and hell as commanded by the Vatican is the Vision of himself in all the false panorama as an empty skin.

[. . .]

Jan 27, 1960
    My train from Concepcion to Teraico 3rd class—6 AM, drank posole & farina & water—
    Peace to the white horse standing by the seawall at Bio Bio. In our car, young kid selling huge Chaplinesque fish, singing beggar, a lady sitting on bench over the fish—2 vendors of nations (handkerchiefs, knives, needles) (whistles)—Vendors of bread, bitter peas, peaches—
    And how nice to sit in the market at some town in Chile and stare happily at a table full of flies.

[. . .]

Chile

January 29, 1960

Valdivia—a big room w/ 2 front windows and a bumpy old bed with soft hugs cold blankets—wakened in the morning at 7 by the police making investigations of my privacy.

Dream last nite:

A supercolossal Prophetic symbolic Movie of life is being made in the City Futuristico—glimpses of the Diabolist's apartment—his gnomes are turning over huge pots on pits filled with human backs, and against the wall is a lineup (in the red glare) of archaic hunchbacked knights and Monsters and Madmen of old—a hideous scene that only a small part of the great movie of life.

Across the grand plaza to the supercolossal apartment house to visit the celebrated mysterious figure Dr. Magicus who is the Sage of Earth—

Up the elevator, press his buzzer & he appears at the door startled, unshaven about 35 & experienced with a sport jacket & slacks & clean neat shirt—a friendly professional, remote figure.

He is a little dismayed & startled by our appearance in the elevator (I am with a bowlegged newspaper boy or something?) and has a frown on his face.

"Pretty soon I'll have to move, I can't handle all the business that comes my way—but excuse me, I'm tired, I don't know if it was friend or god knows who."

He is not exactly paranoiac but seems apprehensive that the Mad Forces are congregating around him. He had opened the elevator door to his apartment himself to make sure.

Seems equal to any occasion, invites us in, quite cheerful, there is a party going on, people listening to music—he has a slightly sad face, but quite open—a good man with sense of beauty—I'm delighted to find that Dr. Magicus is a good guy & not at all extraordinary—his magic seems to reside in his entire experience of Central reality—probably a vision-

Chile

ary of some sort, who is not completely successful, an unsuccessful visionary about as good as he can get.

Against a book case, I notice he is smoking long thin stick of tea, several in ashtray, but does not make a tsimmus about offering it—it's just there to use if anybody wants to pick up—

Finally time for the end of the Picture—we go outside the entire cast is assembled—the city with its interior luminescence, vast metallic steps and serried serialized skyscrapers begins to move forward in unison—all the characters, all the actors, on foot, on bicycles, taxies & buses (mostly empty) proceed to one direction down a main street—before the invisible camera—I see a middleaged neurotic friendly poetess or actress in the bus—she & I wink at each other as if to say, "This is really a corny spectacular—second rate—where's all the real Secrets of the Future?" but it's only for the public. However, not so ugly.

At that point the movie is over & I'm downtown Los Angeles with Peter[8] & Phil Whalen[9]—where to go? To see my relatives? Whalen seems to have some idea of the city—tho no sense of direction at the moment—and I invite him to Aunt Tillie's house—then I say, "Ah, this is the second time we've been in Los Angeles together, isn't it?" and he says yes—he had used to live there before, too—and knows the way around the big band of the main street to downtown from our residence —which leads back to some old dream of being loose in some imaginary Newark, downtown, and not knowing how to return to the main corral Logfence huge—vast avenue of dirt—wandering round downtown looking for a pension.

8. Peter Orlovsky.

9. Philip Whalen, poet, Buddhist, Ginsberg friend, and one of the participants in the historic Six Gallery reading in San Francisco.

Tinilhue (sea weed similar to Cockayuyo)
Chamico—Karl Vogel—Pharmacia La Union
Hugo Gunkel Botanist in Corral

Valdivia—2nd day—boat ride to Corral & other town, back at sunlit, rouged clouds over vast S.A. sky.

♥

Leucimelia Activa
    (Lacrilegas) (family)
Found by Father Athanasio in Nueva Imperial
Found in Volcan Chosacuenco

January 30, 1960
    On boat outside Valdivia going to Corral, the light blue afternoon sky, green bumpy clouds with tall Van Gogh trees, the mounds of earth crawling with sentient life—
    I sat on a box of melons, Crack, it broke—
    The Water of the Channel as bright as Switzerland—
    What will happen?
    The stars already happen but we see them late.
    Our deaths which have already happened in the future will arrive to us in the present soon—like the light of stars.

Jan. 31, 1960 Valdivia, Chile
    Enormous loneliness lack of connection—today at the pier in Valdivia watching boys swim, some kids naked, one 14 years old dark skin with

Chile

small wool trunks & a hard on standing stretching to dive, in the sun; sat an hour.

Walked around band stand Plaza Park, Sunday, paranoiac in my beard & getting old, holding in my belly to be electric.

To the market to see the fish & smell around.

An old dark restaurant bar, waiting for a pork chop.

Depressed 2 days, sad alone in Valdivia.

Dream—I lost Peter going between two towns with Spanish acquaintances—I left him behind, remembered late, went back—to find him—afternoon dream feeling I neglected him.

Feb 1, saw Montgomery Clift in Raintree County movie in English—he too looks sad.

Dream Play

Characters:

    Kerouac the Dream Writer

    Tom   the fairy

    & Payne   lovers

    Pozo—the Villain, a fat Hungarian

    Crapp—his mad assistant

Various personages, cops, angels, soldiers, streetcleaners, cops

Time outside the gates of a play within a play

The Play of Jealous Lovers

    Characters:

        Doc—the Lover, Paul Muni

        Ameralda—the Beloved, Bette Davis

        Maid—Judith Anderson

        The Rival Lover—the Gardener, Van Johnson

Chile

—Because of a confusion of loves, they all kill each other, while the rest of the cast watches outside the garden gate of the big house & pities them.

Kerouac meanwhile spouting lamby poetry about Suffering, Death, redemption which nobody but me believe—all Buddhist—

Scene opens with a murder by Pozo over the Jewels—killing Tom

Terry Payne is sorry to see Tom gone but waits—

A scene of extraordinary beauty as we see, thru the eyes of Tom, the world as it is.

(Crapp still trying to get the Jewels off Payne who offers them up secrety in the night while he sleeps.)

But meanwhile the rest of the world is shooting each other up with balloons & water pistols. Each shot tires them more & more till they are nearer & nearer death & they continue living but weaker, after being hit by soldiers with balloons in neon uniforms. These are angels of divine vengeance—which is Time, wearing everybody out slowly.

We see that inside, tho their bodies get slow motion, their souls are unchanged.

Finally the other Jewel thieves murder everybody, Payne Pozo, Crapp, Kerouac.

Tom was upstairs waiting all the time.

The actual murder scene shows Pozo in bed & Crapp in bed being murdered with strange guns that turn them luminescent for a minute then their souls leave their body.

They all file downstairs.

Tom & Payne are restored to each other Tom says, "I thought you'd never get here. I thought you'd forget."

Payne—"I just waited till the drama was over like I was supposed to, I knew we'd meet again anyway & there was nothing to be lost."

Chile

Crapp—"Those dirty bastards murdered me! Why didn't you stop them, Pozo, you saw them, they got you first."

Pozo to the audience—"Well, I much apologize for Crapp, he's the type ahem that would probably—well, he'll offend the reader, be offensive to the reader, as they say"

Tom & Payne clasp & kiss, farewell to life and hello to heaven as they file out.

Meanwhile the inhabitants of earth are slowly killing each other with balloons.

Feb 2 Al Volcan Osorno

Sun across the lain from the train Vaster each time I look. Old lady with a White Shawl, Stuid mount! Diminishing head! Arms outstretched in power over the Andes. Sunlight now on the Crown Each side a broken inferior mount, Puntagudo's broken Cock, Calbuco's snowless nearly rags—Brother andes ranged behind black in the afternoon or Snow cragged too

I promised I wouldn't waste my life as others did but now I see a wrinkled Indian face that's full of hair and know all's melded in the gold of Age.

Boy on a train with his
   wife
(who looked like a broken peach
   with new baby—2 days old—
      and long soft brown
         hair)
but the boy I loved, after sitting

on the next bench 6 hours
Next to Volcanos
Because he had fair beardless
  skin—almost feminine,
and large, clear eyes, O maybe 19
and a clean shirt—still able to
  Come on her with love,
unlike the old wise gold of age—
It's Christ crucified here,
        as he sees his baby die,
his wife grow old,
  and works in a factory
        80 hours a day
for responsibility to delicate flesh,
or lets himself get fucked
  by an old Allen for Money
—Ugly tho I thought him
        First
he's the most beautiful boy
  I've seen in Chile—
And now stares wordless out
  the train window
waiting for Puerto Montt

Osorno over the trees on icecream Cone as big as the moon

Read Shakespeare Sonnets before bed
Dream—Calbuco Feb 4, 1960
  Some rich young fairy gives me the key to his apartment forever, to
enter at will.

This is a fragment the dream began in the old world and was continuous.

I was downstairs in the foyer with some new kid love—I had an elegant fair coat—left it downstairs & went up & rang the bell—no one answered—so I used my key to get in thru the wall of the back bedroom—

Opening the wall Curtain there was Jack naked in the bed being fucked up the ass by the young eager host—Jack had apparently decided to fall in love and accept all & try this—it was his first time & he was eager & embarrassed, blushing, but open & tender so.

My mistake to open the wall and see, because everybody in the party with us saw it and was amazed, laughed, and also I interrupted the host & also Jack's first affair.

But also I thought, ah if Jack lets him he'll also let me, & we'll be sweet loves again like before.

Then I remembered my coat downstairs, now that I was really in the apartment for good—but I was half naked, from the waist down, as was Jack, so I sneaked down the main stairway to get it.

But there were some old ladies on the landing in the foyer who saw me—I hid behind a pillar—but they were wise—so I rushed—passed the doorman—& grabbed up the huge sable coat—and put it on to cover my nude ass—

Then I realized I had to pass these observers, tho the front door to the at was closed—to get back in thru the back wall—as thru a theater—

So I began singing a distracting theatrical song the accent of Ethel Merman the accent of Libby Holman to them & to the doorman, to cover my exit—

Up each step, another verse, mounting progressively—as I went out one side up the main back stairway (instead of the elevator)

Becoming more & more open in my blues as I reached the top to

Chile

enter the theater—till as I actually entered the door I was chanting a religious blues chorus, improvised.

Sort of a French art song which opened up at the end in a surprise Spiritual with full heart force to God.

This was my way of distracting and convincing the ladies that

"smile for the ladies

come from hell"

it was all for real, the theater of live, with my nakedness—covering it up with Godsong, as if I belonged in the rich apartment they were the old ladies of.

(I saw Montgomery Clift in Raintree County movie 2 nites ago) (he lives with Libby Holman)

Woke, & felt my life was torn in 2, as last nite dream of Phil Whalen in Alaska—

No longer pure & sincere, too much literary world, not enuf pure spirit love, the world of broken politic entering in. Jack lost his Cherry, drinking, we no longer sacramental lovers.

Hard to admit. What is hard to admit.

I don't write like the Springtime like Shakespeare.

♥

Next day, Answer, New Dream

Feb 4

Dream—Me Escandulo

In NY, in the Village at small theater with Ferlinghetti in a road-show, for charity to help some literary follies we fill in as singers in one set—I remember in the first night's performance I feel a little his (interruption)—hysterical paranoiac—self Conscious—humiliated—to be found dead in a single prosaic chorus line—secretly want to "steal the show" (as yesterday I wrote Phil Whalen I had done with the international literary conference) but in our short set there's not much time to do—

The first performance, onstage, the audience—Ferlinghetti (whom I envy because he read well at Concepcion and I read badly) and I bustling onstage—I don't remember what I did—something that goofed the audience—electrical—& went off with much applause from the astonished & admiring audience.

The second show was another scene, we sang a popular song, and the main singer ended with a weird note, Ferlinghetti jazzed a one note response and I ended capping his with a piercing alto human-cry, opening my soul for an instant—that again, by virtue of a single note, brought down the house.

Between shows, out to meet Eugene & Louis, them giving me many attentions, in a car, even Uncle Max was there, and then Aunt Judy with her new soft handed dopey daffodil schoolteacher-Doctor husband arrived—with a car full of fat Jewish relatives from the Bronx—to catch my act—envious since she was as youth onstage—and I acting indifferent to all this attention, embarrassed meeting the strangers—then returning to the theater, to be shown off the 3'rd show—this time a new format, I to read poetry—perhaps Kaddish—for the first time in N.Y.C., the whole Kaddish including Caw Caw—wonder if it's not too long, if Ferl had heard it before, if I can struggle thru the length of the whole thing without embarrassment & deliver a lamb to audience again—time to go on, small Living Theater or Circle in Square audience waiting—woke—

Realized immediately clearly for the first time (strangely) that the whole secret of my poetry & career as poet and presently beard id egotism—astrologer's prophecy that I be successful on darkened stage before multitudes—L.C.'s[10] warning about vanity—all mad self display and need for a hideous sort of exterior show of Divine Selfhood & Incarnation in *Me* of all people.

For a minute almost shaved off beard. What to do, go into Monastery? Since I vaunt death of Self, only now discovering this surface of myself? Write to Peter for permission to Shave Beard? Or act heroic & shave it off like stroke of suicide? Or let things lie & think till Inia what to do with this Allen?

Meanwhile at San Augustin (opposite Calbuco) with Hugo Zambelli as guest for a few days—in morn at 6 AM up riding in launch buying fish from fisherman.

Later yesterday climb a hill to see the Panorama—Islands, houses, cows, Andes from Osorno to 200 miles or more south through slightly haze.

Today a walk thru Calbuco Town—ending at park overlooking beach & rock pool—Clearer day, 17 mountains stretching South covered with snow among the hundreds of other peaks to be seen, a few sailboats in the nearer water below, a party of visitors on the promontory a little rock, having their pictures took—

10. Lucien Carr and Allen Ginsberg met during Ginsberg's first year at Columbia, and Carr became very influential in Ginsberg's early "Beat" ideas. Carr, from St. Louis, introduced Ginsberg to William S. Burroughs and Jack Kerouac. This group of friends discussed what they called a "New Vision" for prose and poetry, which became the foundation of Beat Generation writing.

A moan, groan to my left, as if someone singing, I turn & see it's a man with a camera holding down another as if fighting squeezing his head—it's an epileptic fit in front of the panorama of the Andes. He gets up later w/ his pants full of white calcium from the path and confusedly goes thru his pockets finally gets his pesos out of his watch-pocket & counts them.

    —February 5, 1960

Siesta in Chile

in the mirror
    Beautiful Man!
My hair long as the wind
     Swayed upon my head
            From my dreams
Black beard like Conrad, Lawrence, Lone.
    Eyeglasses broken
White clear eyes dark pupils
    Aedad 33
A fly buzzing round my Crown—
Now in the middle of my life again.
Rawbone face, I'd love myself
If I were not me,
        A work of art,
    A solitude with great eyes
Lacking nothing, romance or humor
    But
What voice "calls from the sea"

That I destroy this beauty
        in the mirror.

This after dream:
   In a corridor in a gym,
   The Ball is being thrown
        up thru a chute
        from the basement—
My lover, a boy larger than me
   blond, hairy, smelling of sweat,
      naked, grapples me
   in a mock combat
   bends me against his strength,
I smell his armpit as we
   wrestle, but can't see his face.
He's pushing me on the balls of
   my feet—to the right spot—
   with love—to catch the ball.
A wrinkle—sensation in my
   neck, a kiss in the
      neck, I wake,
there is a sensation in my neck,
   my flesh crawls,
A fat 33
   I am half-way to Death now

Outside a great sun shines on the
   Rocks of the Andes, Covered with snow
   100 miles distant

and shines
    on the calm-chopped aqua
        Azul of the fish lagoon.

Jan [*sic:* should be February] 6, 1960
Nights—a compound of anxiety
    about the Swiftness of time
        my age 33 ½ life over—
        among the silvery mountains
The sense of having missed out
    found a false face, a beard
        and poetry and boy—
And not a Female and Progeny
        as nature—late Shakespeare
            Sonnets—
and the realization of the evil life of
        the poor as per
        the Communist poets,
So read Neruda last nite.

Two dreams in one nite—
(1) Some kind of nightmare old nurse-helper in scientific laboratory, it's dangerous to work there we are experimenting on project which turns organic life into Cannibal-flower inhuman—got a substance can inject—so everybody in lab got to be careful not to get contaminated—this old librarian-lady assistant suddenly takes me aside with witch-like sexual female domineering auntliness and suddenly behind my back I feel the pinch of a needle—she's been transformed & is injecting me—I shudder away just in time—maybe.

Chile

(2) Making a fine Chopped fruit salad for all my friends to enjoy—when it comes time to add the dish of pears & peaches—it's up in a hotel room over the city—by the window—with this person who's helping me translate the fruit into Chopt Salad (the man who translated Wieners[11] into Spanish) I look for the dish of pears & find on the big windowsill instead, a small razor blade packet with a little cocaine left in it—the Cops are coming & will find it—I think of throwing it across the other roof on the street into an alley, lose it, but he—the translator—is probably a cop & sees the evidence—but if a cop he's planted the evidence himself—so no skin off my teeth—I taste it & hesitate not knowing what to do, whether Cops will come or not, suspecting him in his suit—in this high hotel room—wondering what happened anyway to the fruit salad.

[...]

Dream—Neruda, young sporty man 40 or so, 36, 38, in white jacket, I meet him as per schedule in apartment I'm staying in in Santiago—try to show him my poetry, he is very polite—I try to impress him but with language barrier is difficult—showing him a book of Howl (awful ugh quack).

[...]

Feb 10
Walk along road on top of Calbuco Island—Tiyuki birds Scree-scree-scree—wild blackberries so many I passed the laters by, every bend in

11. John Wieners (1934–2002), poet friend of Ginsberg.

Chile

the road a new turn—on to Volcano or channel or neighboring Island precipice, fences made of new branches, or old barbwire—a pebbly beach where 3 boys swim, all ugly with big stomachs, one slipped on a rock—yet brown skin belle—a little girl practicing playing rowing a boat, women washing laundry in the shade of trees nearby.

I am a bearded stranger on their shore.

Santiago for Herbs
Libreria orientalista
    Front of Congress—For
        Calle Catedral

Noscapina
Dionina
Codeina

Feb 10 Calbuco

Coming, again, in a strange country, at night alone, 10—or 15 years later I think of your face & torso, and our first love then, Neal[12]—of the bed in Harlem, and the night in Vicki's pad—and what love followed, and the years of change and sweetness and all my desire, and your hand, and our pilgrimage with $20 from Denver to Houston to die—the ocean after that & the beginnings of growing old—that I am here now, remembering the vibrancy of our sympathy then & its choked up love and knowledge.

12. Neal Cassady.

Chile

So in all of my existence this wells up again in memory in all its old studiousness and nostalgia and truth forever—the wager of love is won

My semen handkerchief on the open page of Donne in the bedroom's lone darkness.

Dream

Lafcadio in Restaurant in San Francisco—we go in—a restaurant a part of City Lights but old, new faces, & new Chic, with a menu & an old tough pro-gangster type Maitre 'd—

He shows us in with special bows for me—I look, the menu is expensive—choose a table—go to can—back, Lafcadio has changed the place, is now sitting at the fish bar—& has chosen & ordered (wisely) a cheap good dish from the plat du jour—a fish or veal stuffed w/ sausage—I agree & comply, a little upset by his change of plan but amused & all's well.

Then he says, "Can we eat on the roof?" as we once did—I inquire, the man says "6th floor" but Lafcadio means on the Fire Escape—

Then he moves over so I have no place to sit—then some people come & make us sit with them—or Lafcadio moves to their table before they get a chance to sit down, then he suddenly moves the table on them— they notice—I get mad & hit him on head with ice—a girl gasps and faints—disorder—they whisper & want to go—I suggest we move—

Earlier, we are driving car (I am driving happy) across America & stop over in one city with a family, rent a cheap apt with them for the nite—"I feel excited about my new life."

[. . .]

Picasso's Blue Boy—crowned with misty pink flowers—Bouquets in imagination back round the downcast thin romantic face—a youngster —teenage idol—Rimbaud Gerard Phillips, Jimmy Dean—French &

Spanish both—the capacity to be a Christ—or flop, like Rimbaud a mad businessman in Africa—male youth of XX Century—Certainly not Responsible—with a newfound pipe (gift of an elder Welsh farmer stuffing his pipe with stubby fingers)—he holds it strangely, effeminate—so capable of homosexual passion too—giving himself to some ugly virile senior, or junior—if loved a handsome man'd be a narcissist, Melancholy eyes, tempestuous affair with some great Doll—who digs him but won't fuck—or some chubby circus doll who idolizes him too—as did Picasso—creating archetype modern mouth. Still universal, serviceable for America or 21st Century too—maybe—on the wall in Calbuco, Chile.

And now Castro in Chilor
   sitting at bar, stuck
with pushy schoolteacher
   from Santiago
who done me out of a free room
      by hanging round,
Who done me out of a nite's
      solitude
   by hanging round yakking
who gonna sleep in the next
   bed to me.
      hanging round
and who'll put his sticky
      hands under my blanket
   looking for my cock
I'll have nightmares tonite.
He's got a Cap and a wool Cloth

and talks continuously
  about his travels thru Chile.

In a Field in Chiloe—

  The Universe is an Infinite Being.

Walking in the field, open, high over Chiloe—across the bridge thru
town with the houses on matchsticks su bord do Rio—up a dirt road to
a high field over the town—could see the vast graveyard, crosses inside
a white wall, next to the huge hospital, in front of which was a Sta-
dium crowded with voices faraway shouting Calbuco verses Castro and
the long schoolhouse next to that, and the town perched high on a cliff
over the canal—vast canal like a river—across the way more fields and
precipices covered with green—then crossing to this open little plateau
where I'd wandered disconsolate after a restless unhappy lone siesta,
thinking my trip here worthless since I'd missed all the sightsee buses
to strange towns—lakes, echoes, mounts, lagoons—on the field saw the
panorama, took off my hat to feel the open sky over my head a few sec-
onds—looked at the sun—vast light moving now in afternoon midway
to the hill of West—Mounts & granges covered with shrub & faraway
antlike horses—the Sun in its way over the earth generating light which
falls on every grassblade & casts a shadow this sun then in intimate or-
ganic relation with every thing living on the planet—constantly supply-
ing solar light and energy to the Myriad minutiae of the field, from little
jumping flylike mites to infinite invisible bacteria—enlarging again to
the million daisies and yellowflowers, or cottontufts scattering seeds to
the wind in this field—so that as the bacteria and bloodcells in a man
also make up his organism & maybe soul—so also the million bacterial
horses & elephants of the world with their interrelated rows and fields
of hay make up with the sun & single integrated living organism of fan-

Chile

tastic proportions—in our world nearly infinite to the mind, that it can't comprehend at once all the stalks of trees on one hillside with its natural inhabitants of flies and birds—as the wall of trees on the hill opposite where I now sit—looked up and it was a vast giant hill faraway I'd forgotten in the writing—with new rainclouds sliding up over the sun—coming toward me, and the wind freshening and blowing the spikey plants in waves—the waterfall below still falling like a well oiled part of the machine.

All the being—origin in our sun—but there are a million suns all brothers and thinking light together in a million worlds—so that the universe is one infinite being

Feb 15, 1960

Dream: Peter, tall and naked sticking his ass out to be washed. Our infantilism together. The president of the U.S. wants to have a conference with me. I go to the Summer Palace in the mountains. The others are jealous.

The stars are jealous

a long walk
to the top of the hill
a dead green beetle

In Anoud long walk past the Normal School to a part of town I hadn't seen—Cliff, rocks & bathers below, and then up rolling field to the top of a hill to see the mouth of the Pacific, Islands, the town and steeple, a rooster crowing below in Anoud, and a dead hush of a beetle. The birds make noise in pairs.

Feb 16—

One day in Anoud—Walk with the Journalist of Southern Cross (Cruz del Sur) and later that nite to the Electric power plant—high stacks of wood, of branches and split trunks, a great wall of broken trees stacked against the factory, the electric factory, then talked to the worker inside—worked there 15 years, since a kid—grew with Fire & Dynamo— makes 876 pesos a day (87c present US) & costs him 20 days work for his room & board—what dark black room & watery soup?—for a month —can't get married, rather nice looking, covered with soot, & friendly— invited me in to look. So I decided there is something wrong with the Economic system here—what is the use working all day for money if you don't even get money? Some kind of factory saint. My hotel bill for nice hotel & food plus extra lunch was $4,000 pesos or 5 days work for him.

So far the facts are

1.) Low pay for labor
2.) High taxes on imports
3.) 26% of taxes go to army
4.) *Possibly* much Capital goes out of country to U.S. hands & pockets & capitalists

"Chupa la Sangre"
We suck the blood of Chile

Maullin. Dr. Otto. Latus is Atropine

Our prayers to god sound like the crackle of live lobsters in the sink.

Chile

Tonight shot 2 Eukodol in vein—suddenly in auto-vein shots Always depended on Bill[13] before Garver[14] or Burroughs.

"Salvation" (whatever it is) lies not in redemption of—a transient form,
God will hear our prayers when we hear the prayers and know the griefs
of the insects.
When we hear the prayers of lobsters and Hark to the supplication of
the lambs under the knife
and know the infinite griefs of the insects.

Till then God (which is within us) cannot be awakened—he is put to
sleep by an indifference to the call of all sentient beings.

Are we, am I, ready to hear the griefs of the insects?

But I live as if indifferent to the sufferings of animals and men who
die and groan to feed me and make my house warm and bright—as if
shielded from their sufferings, from knowledge & share of theirs by my
tricky beard and wit.

So that my poetry is all a half-celestial con, worth nothing to the
bloodshot eyes of Physical sufferers in the mines & factories & fields.

My original vow to help mankind in its sorry world fate. On the boat
to Columbia, is now being tested.[15]

Can I as the Marxists claim remain aloof from the "final conflict" to
bring bread & love to the masses?

13. William S. Burroughs (1914–1997), prolific writer, author of *Naked Lunch*, central figure in the Beat Generation.

14. Bill Garver was a friend of Burroughs and Ginsberg, a substance abuser who died young.

15. Ginsberg's original intention when attending Columbia University was to become a labor lawyer.

Chile

In reverie middle of night, pulled down my shorts under the covers & stroked my belly & cock voluptuously imagining it was Peter's hands, and came, and woke from reverie with still dry hard-on—the come was imaginary—several times.

Hanging round Calbuco a couple extra days—the doctor no bring more dope.

Only execrable thoughts—hitherto impossible to be conscious of—my hideous new belly, corpulence of lassitude and self disgust, indulgence in inertia and potatoes.

Tonight Zambelli, with the rough Italian worker—capitalist ex fascist (chauffeur to an Italian general) and Carlos Ramos the ex communist young doctor, and the wop's kid wife, and the Juez—Judge and George Washington Mendez who is thin boned and frightens me with his drunken sincerity—like being in love with a murderous flamingo— all drinking till 11 PM, then they leave & I sit down to talk to them, Hugo comes back in, the doorbell rings, Mendes is back, drunk, Inez cries, throws a scene, I retire—hiding in bed in the dark hoping all this Spanish tragedy will pass over in a few minutes & leave me alone.

Thinking of the golden crab with the spider legs and orange specks on the shelf in the closet in the kitchen, still alive moving around in the dark, one leg over the shelf in the void, feeling for a place—the crab in the dark, desperate, rattling around next to a big piece of goat cheese.

The fish in the boat, noble sierras with broken jaws, flapping tails around the bottom of the boat, shivering and palpitating, the stream of life still running thru their bodies for an hour after being fished out of the water & clubbed by an ignorant Chilean

The delicious super-crabmeat, nutty flavored, I [?] supper.

The petrancas or babe Penguins swooping in the clear water after schools of silver fish, sardines darting in the green.

All creation eating itself alive

The suffering of all this sentience must be relieved (redeemed) by some transcendent Idea which justifies its indifference to mortal death as a joke of illusions.

Feb 17, 1960

Extraordinary Dream on the Verge of a Nightmare

I

With L.C.,[16] need to go downtown to mail Poet Card to old girl friend who is sick, has given me the card but I've neglected to mail—to Barbara who has Leukemia or Cancer in hospital—

His mother also is sick—as youth he used to hate & be afraid of her—but now he is able to go to Dr. to get a change of cunt for her—a long fish—oyster pole threaded with clams—to stink up her cunt as replacement for rotten tissue—he is the man of family now and goes in car downtown to get some cunt-stick, I go with him, intimate friend.

"Your nature & work's improved," he tells me.

"No, I simply started by 'giggling slyly' and all the rest has risen from that," I say.

"Shit, Ginsberg, you even stole that from Kerouac," he says.

I feel guilty & embarrassed, remembering Kerouac had used the same expression in Town & City for Levinsky.[17]

16. Lucien Carr.

17. In Jack Kerouac's novel *The Town and the City*, Levinsky was a character based on Ginsberg.

"Well, he used it, it's true, but it's me & I've developed from that—and I've done something different with it—my own."

This seemed to satisfy him, or at least avoid further penetration.

Similar to Conversation forbidding me to encourage use of his name in secret works.[18] By Jack. The Emotion of this dream.

Meanwhile we are still love-friends a drive downtown past Times Square

II

By the Naval Club of the Territory (of Chile) on a Boat.

Burroughs has returned—sits reading the Maritime Journal for weather reports He asks me for information—he once mentioned he wished I could keep account of daily weather occurrences for his use in theory.

I confess I've neglected to keep them—thru slovenliness, he sniffs I rebuke him—after all, Bill, I assumed—I promised to keep a daily report when you were in love with me as part of propaganda to make you like me in your state of shall we say deluded mentality caused by excessive indulgence in narcotics—now you're cured. Just wanted to be nice to you.

"And for that matter after all it's no loss, you can get all the daily weather statistics you want in the—"

"Ah, yes, in the Classified Column"—

"Yes, there are the annual yearbook or the Telegram Almanac."

"True enough—you're right—no point your knocking yourself out for nothing—I was shall we say too far out to attend to these details at the time."

18. Lucien Carr absolutely forbid Ginsberg from using his name in his work. Kerouac, who wrote fictionalized autobiography, used his friends in his work, using thinly disguised names, but could be testy about Ginsberg or others using his name.

Chile

"Besides," I add, "I simply hate to keep daily Journal records, it's just a drudgy task I've never been able to abide—makes me nervous & bored with the pen."

At this point, in the Club, I am looking for a seat—someone ahead in the second seat on the Left Isle, had been sleeping there, the windows are open in a crack to admit a draft, I try the seat behind him but can't see—he gets up to go away so I steal his seat.

It's an old distinguished family friend of L.C.—this is an aristocratic chamber—But many years empty & the club decadent—this old eccentric fellow has a huge package he carries permanently on his shoulders on a pole—a huge torn package 42 years old, full of old clippings & flowers & books—a friend of L.C.'s—Bill Becker or Kenny Love—each respected—I steal his seat. Never changes the package—rather interesting to see him so spry & talkative with his eccentric old package on back.

In one side on the stage is the Monkey Isle—on the other is a boat full of U.S. sailors.

In the swimming pool in between—it seems that one of the monkeys had gone mad & killed a little girl who was swimming on that henceforth the monos were restricted to their pigeonholes as in the isle—years ago—now slowly the race of monos has become decadent & rachitic—lost all their old customs & health & Beauty—now only a handful of desperate midget deformed members of the race survive.

They challenge their captors to a last sad duel—three of the worst deformed Creepy monkeys to be beaten up by one healthy sailor.

The sailors at first refuse out of fear & disgust with the dying race of monkeys—but some sense of pride forces the monkeys to insist & finally the three degenerate beasts—one all pure silver bone & deformed spine like a husk of a foetus—trembles forward out of his pigeonhole, followed by 2 other cripples—to be beaten up by the sailor.

Just at this point, there is an invasion at the balcony in the high window by our Friends—

Chile

Ava Gardner & the Powers from Art & Hollywood accompanying a troop of huge prophetic apes—from afar—come with medicine to cure the dying race & change the rules of their captivity. It's all been a stupid political arrangement that's killed the monkeys—on the balcony I see the huge Bull apes—they come down to smear the surviving monos with a black Jam made from none other than Latue, the racial secret herb—that had been denied them.

Ava Gardner turns me on, she comes over & puts me into a feelie-phonograph machine with the latest sexy record.

It's a hysterical chick who sucks your finger & moans & screams hysterically in your shoulder—crying that she's madly in love with you & that you don't love her.

"How do you like that?" asks Ava "I don't like it," I say "Who needs that sweet-toothed hysteria?"

Her face clouds.

"But it's so sweet, let's see how how hot it gets if I can come:—

This seems to satisfy her.

"I mean it's sure meant to be sweet & is" I add—or have said.

Meanwhile the monos are smeared with Jam Latue & are saved.

A strange old photo—of McCarthy as a young almost adolescent, the day or days he first arrived to be head of the isle, to be the governor here. Horrible his face—like over-long lips, very effeminate—and eyes too big, cheeks too girlish—but the mouth long & smeary & sensual—I look close & see it's a double exposure that makes him look like a fruity Latouche, i.e. Lesbian Liberace young pampered, neat. I point out he has 3 lips not the usual 2.

Meanwhile producer is playing my record & I wonder how he likes me—but then I realize I shouldn't worry, of course they all like me. I'm Frank Sinatra.

Chile

[. . .]

Feb 20—Wrote Neal, danced the Cubos all nite with Huge & Luce the
administrator of the city of Calbuco.

    When I look up at the stars thru binoculars it is as if I share a secret
with the universe.

What if I thought that death
with all its cranks & grave
Were only a new rude wheel
and I its skeleton slave.

Original Sin has built its
       palace in my bones
And All is lost unless Christ comes
       (with miracle, a save)
I eat the gnat, the mouse, the
       lamb most brave
The swan the turkey and
       the cow
I chew the bones of grasshoppers
And cook the defeated crow

Frogs grak under my bed
       lamenting their lost legs
& million flies emerged from the
       wall to march
Every mosquito I had ever killed
       clouded the room
Outside the thousand crabs

Chile

oysters clams and octopi
I'd eaten crowded the water with
      their sentience.
Great hoards of feeling fish, Sardines &
   tuna, Sierra & Salmon—Pices &
Flounder, pike and trout gazed
      up in hostile curiosity
         & indifference—sea urchins—
at the death of my innocent
         Soul,
and the bleating of fields of lambs
      rose up from my dinner
of lambchop, a hoard of pigs
rushed squealing in my sigh,
great hoards of cows and bulls,
a whale swam up for that
one slice of his side I chewed,
and one horse, neighing for the
   slices of his thigh I'd cooked for
         Chinese stew—
All beasts I murdered followed
   by the cocks, the hens,
the turkeys, large and small,
The doves & sparrows & the
      few scarce pheasants,
several armadillos and tepesquentlas
grieving & groaning in my sight

And I could no longer find sin
   in my heart

To blame them for the selfishness
of their diet of each other
and turn in my blood, the
    Corpuscles of my Death
eaten by my friendly brothers
    The millions of called critters
      devoured for my health—
and back to that first triumph
      when my sperm
beat out the hoard of either
      sperms
and entered the womb & closed
      the door of Life
on a million brothers that
      waited & swam & died in the slime
of my mad mother's
      womb
What sentience had the
    vegetables, what life
the fruits & nuts & seeds of
    plants
I'd mashed & digested in
    my teeth—
Why horror of the Spider
    waiting on his web?
What millions grassblades
    I mowed
Bloom in no heaven?
    Original Sin,
Blood of beasts & flowers & men

Chile

That I am steeped in
and the human beings who have
        labored in the mines
and seas and fields to bring me
        death for supper?
Every rose I pluck's a babe
        that dies
that Crown of daisies in
        my hair
in 1933 was a chain
        of skeleton slaves
of my pale humor's return—
and every beggar that I pass
I fuck him up the ass—
By not giving all my clothes to him.

If I have no feeling for those
        whom I ate
Whose blood I sucked, whose bones
        I chewed
Whose livers and hearts and lungs
        I relished in stew
or fried with screaming onions,
Who'll Pity my soul when
        it dies? Who'll love me
        then
As I lie on a deathbed in an
        indifferent universe?
Only the Sweet Secret Creator and Being
        of all these

Smiling over a mountain of
    his own bones
Building a vaster mountain of
    New souls in his Mind.

Because the other day, yesterday
    morning, they bought
2 young turkeys, "Terniers"
    underage—
and I said, "They're too young
    to die"
but ate them that
night as soup and
    Broiled with potatoes.
I could have stopped their
    Death?
And what good that nite,
    To buy two ragged urchins
Tickets for the Smalltown
    Chilean Calbuco
Amateur Musical Comedy
    To give them a
        Merciful thrill
And make me feel like a
    Secret Benevolent
        Prince?
And Conspirator for mercy
    for the lowly?

Chile

I eat the lowly
Where do we end the mercy?
    With the rock in the fields?
        The iron bedded in the Deep?
How live without causing
                Death—
and leave the rest of the created
        Universe alive
—a strange spectacle on
        this planet
    as strange as undersea—
a film of cancerous growths
        on the surface
animate creatures that
    depend on other animate
        creatures for food
So that only the water we
        drink is innocent
        & without a living soul
    to mourn its change
        & death.

How ugly to the innocent
        eye of the rock
This manifestation of
        life spirits writhing
        and digesting
            in the jungle
Over the surface of the globe

Life Spirits, Transient
      Phantoms
Consuming each other screaming
      for permanence
      and divinity.

Pork Chops? Pork Chops? Pork Chops?
    I'm sick of Cannibalism!
Not water in the tap, a television
    Set—I'm sick of Capitalism
    exploiting Chilean iron
          miners
Coal miners, copper miners,
    woodsmen, wheatmen
        shoeshine boys & fishermen.
I am living on the blood of
       other human beings
getting a fat belly & long beard
      and excellent reputation
        as a poet
      and even plenty of money.

God has one eye that
      bulges like an
         octopus's eye—
and sees the billion
    deaths at once without
a blink?
    or is Death Sweet,
The sweet release of phantoms

Chile

from their dream
of murder?
Summary of Calbuco fantasies
& Chilean Meditations—
After the Communist Shocks
to my American innocence.

Calbuco, Feb 21, 1960

The Spirit is not
in cooked meat.

Sunday at Breakfast

Fog rolls in the Canal
Roses put forth their green against the fly-buzzed window
Sunday morning table in Chile, with a cigarette
A barefoot servant with long hair and a babe
drinking coffee in the kitchen
And I smoke and drink and eat honey—
the taste of bread and sweets
The Same as in the Bronx
15 years ago—
There Elanor[19] was wont to rise at ten or twelve
and set the Lox and toast and Jam
around the cereal, cooked or raw,
with Bagels, seeded rolls, sweet butter, whitefish too

19. Elanor Frohman was Ginsberg's maternal aunt.

Chile

and eat a long and dainty meal with Uncle Max and me,
      Listening to new records on the phonograph
          or WQXR, or Six Songs for Democracy
—I sip my Coffee and remember Melville in old age
         Demanding his Bohee—
The old nostalgia of old times!
        Aunt Elanor was thin
And had a rheumatic heart; and Uncle Max the same,
              Tho much more fat
So that they rose late every day—but Sunday she
       in special invalid Leisure
Listening to mellow socialist music
       And ended drinking tea
   with milk at noon,
Time to turn
 on the opera—and sit on the couch
reading the Sunday Worker and the NY Times
    All thru the winter's day, and talk
      high up in the Bronx
         over a decade ago.
Thus childless, in their 40's, the long Sunday passed away
   that seemed eternal to my student eye—

I think of Max now, lone in the Bronx
    Eating his Sunday breakfast, lorn of Elanor
opening a letter from me, from another world
    and wonder if the Lox and tea and Jam
and NY Times are there, and the card table spread with white cloth in
   the kitchenette
as when Rosa Poselle, retired for many years

still sang in his living room her aria, Castra Diva,
or lifting her eyes to the Jewel Song, the phonograph still turns
near the painted dragon bowl of Russian wood.

    Calbuco, Chile Feb 21, 1960
        Sunday at Breakfast

Calbuco Feb

No more crying, no more sighing
Your lovers come back
and he'll never go away
No more dreaming, no more scheming
he's six feet black Perfect
    Billie Holliday

Billy Holliday! A name
Incredible a dyke of Loss
Circus Lesbian
The little fat man killed
   with a blue hat
      and red stars
and a whip to tame white horses
      and a midget Flag.
Holliday in Reality—drunk
      on morphine or whiskey
with a pet dog
      in criminal nightclubs
I loved you Billie Holliday
      with all my lesbian soul

Because you took morphine and moaned
Because your love was never sure
Like any saint seeking perfection
Cry no more sigh no more Lady.
Day comes when we no longer Send
for Whiskey, even Morphine has an End
outside the law, might forever Shaday

Because you loved and did record your groan
with Rose in hair and dog tongue up your dress

Chile—1960—Feb Mar etc.

This tree has an enormous
    hard on
branch a foot thick stuck
    out of its crotch
and chopped off two feet long—
above rise the rest of the arms
    in a vast wave at the clouds
        in the wind—
blind stubby knob of
    love
Pointing outward at the road
to the fields of old cut wheat
    and the shiny lake beyond
    Sign manifest out of the void
   that love is Blind—
What Cares this Cock who knows it

or who bangs on the trunk & kisses
      its broad mouth?

Feb 22 Volcano Osorno

The Choicest barriers on the bush
of all the fresh cold berries of the morn.

Todas Santos
Vn. Printagudo
Co. Techado
Co. Troneador

Blackberries blossom on the slopes of the Andes

Feb 23
5:61 PM entered Argentina
"Viva" etc. Weak Cheers.

    Riding in car for instant the large trees' perpendicularity in front of me was larger mandala image of the more distant tree high on the mountain's smaller perpendicularity—

    Flashed on mind a mandala of correspondence, caused by accidental conjunction of different phenomena with the observer's eye.

    Earlier—a handsome youth with wool cap, worn brown leather jacket, camera & [?] & motorcycle—sitting at rest in front of landscape—I imagined him without the sore of worry on his face—a man for an instant transparent—an ageless eye one with the mountains observing phenomena.

    Later in car saw the correspondence of nature forms and wondered

Argentina

"Was this created by intention to serve for symmetrical correspondence to a mind's eye? Or is the correspondence accidental?"

But in the original plan of the universe, that hermetic instant of my perception of Correspondence was also scheduled.

Thus great massive rocks heavy as 1000 years of flood & volcano serve a universe as light as a feather of my observation & perception.

Pluralistic universes as in laughing gas—scheduled from the first Word.

I can't explain the sensation.

The trees arms bent down for an instant—that instant—to shelter the passing auto from future rains.

Now all the bare trees on the rockface mountainside are pointing upward—to signify—to indicate—

Upward—the heavens are clouded to signify—symbolize a block in my consciousness.

The winds rise to manifest the disturbance of my thought.

If it rains, it will be on purpose to stop this meditation.

The instant in which the Universe appears as a mirror of some inward thought of mine is the purpose for which the universe was created—to contemplate itself.

All the volcanos serve this eye

God eats himself.

Barriloche The dedos (dice) fall on the table with a hard noise.

"—And many a ground nesting flycatcher spied—"

Argentina

Old rain, dotted in the dust

Cragged mountains yield
     the Law—
Hymn to Light
Tho I have wearied and been
      long forlorn
and now my powers fail
I have been wed to light
     For 15 years
And still look upward
      at my virgin groom
in whose white breast
   I want to lay my head.

A carved Walkingstick on the moon—1944

Feb 24, 1960

Dream the other Nite—Last nite
    Ferlinghetti dies of cancer, or unpleasantly—I get a feeling of hor-
ror—I depend on him—now where will money come from—I see his wife
Kirby, helpless & crying—unhappy—the store in ruin, or going to rot—
my affairs crumbling & going to rot—and the taste of real Death in Fer-
linghetti's like the death of a father on whom the whole family is de-
pendent—who now will take care of them? They feel lost, the world
changes for them—

Argentina

What myriad thoughts I had yesterday—all forgotten.

Burroughsian Satire—the high class tourist hotel in watering spot in Argentine Andes—masculine German woman with baubles chewing "Nicht Wahr" with her friend at table—haggling over prices with the Priest while her blond thin son in leather Jacket behind desk whistles thru his teeth "Is too little, is too little"—the waitresses have French flourishes and serve single little potatoes with awkward manipulations of spoon & fork—the husband in sportjacket & sportshirt without tie in the swank dining room—half the customers in business suits drest for supper, other half in ski sweaters (the young girls in white wool ski sweaters too hot for the warm diningroom)—husband serving dishes himself rumpled next to waitresses—and if you order plain water no wine, they give you water specially prepared to make the shits—Aqua fresco filtered thru peasant baby shit—then the odor & color removed by Chemicals—guaranteed to attach 24 hours after leaving the hotel— preferably on crowded Argentinean bus going across Andes

Feb 25
   Woke Dreaming of Explanation at table or soda fountain bar—talking to some widow—"and so please explain once for all how your husband died?"

Concepcion Feb 27, 1960
   Left Barriloche—to St Martin, spent nite there, & A.M. Bus to Villarica past Lacar Volcano down Andes Jagg—crags—on wrong side of bus, couldn't see Vast Deep from there, angry—Past Villarica to Town of Villariaca—then train to Temuco, spent nite in R R Station Hotel $1.50, then 6 AM train to Concepcion, lunch with Edw. Eyde, then as

Argentina

now waiting in airlines Terminal for plane to Santiago again after fast walk around Concepcion—and never went up Sierra Caracol.

Feb 27

Supper in Santiago Café El Borro—Avenida O'Higgins—fried chicken livers & potatos a heap, Belz sweet drink, & coffee—

Alone reading Peter's letter of a month ago from N.Y., the muzak radio letting fall gold snowflakes of Chopin piano—"all the old feelings come back"—Love—"I'm always chasing rainbows"—a little sweet pain around my heart that Huncke[20] screwed Peter. The music above and apart from the man across from me eating "Choclos"—and now, aethereal—Schubert simple piano sad music—pure love—Farewell, in Death —ending on a strange faraway up note, that the world will always be there, the Love will always continue, the music fades away, endless— though our ears vanish, or the human piano gets tired.

And I will go on by big rough iron smoking train up the Andes to Bolivia and will take formal cocaine with the Indians.

"Ah sweet mystery of life."

Later, sitting against wall with glasses off, dressed in black, feeling my cranium—the skull is already dead.

11 PM

Went Hotel, Changed Clothes, as before—went to Bier Hall, Club de Jazz (closed) & several turns back to Bosco til invited to a free Coke w/

---

20. Herbert Huncke (1915–1996), Times Square hustler, drug addict, and model for Beat writings, was a natural storyteller and author.

Argentina

group at table who discussed that & that Chilean poet—"Es Marve-llosa"—"Es preciosa"

Feb 28

8:30 Mon Eve

Eisenhower to pass in Nite in front of El Bosco Café Santiago—White Jacketed police w/ high belts & revolvers—after a wait, the Alameda is cleared, in the darkness, traffic stopped for miles along the way—then squadron of mobile vehicles speeding down the vast street with red lites blinking on and off—Jeeps, followed by a flying wedge of motorcycles followed by a dozen limousines riding rapidly with motor noise—the crowd silent waiting for the appearance—then, suddenly, a black limou-sine in the center with white figures discoursing inside—the light so bright on their white jackets—Eisenhower's ruddy face inside the bril-liant fishbowl riding forward, one hand up, one on knee, telling a story, at ease, ignoring the outer night & the crowd which whistles and ap-plauds a little but there's no time, the black cars speed by almost in the blink of an eye—the crowd almost gasps with surprise—I'm amazed by the floodlights inside the car as if the president were on display in a store window—an expensive bejeweled store window—it's night the Tiffanys of Men, Undersea in their own world telling an affable tale—Million-aires and Powers with all the world gathered round to watch the crowd say ooh, and then disappear down the block—I don't know what to say or think—it's gone by so fast—more than I expected that speed & the lights inside as they go on about their talk business inside the car Looking rich and strange—Amazed suddenly that all his Power—Eisen-hower's—is real, can order a million cops to guard the city—order mur-ders in the night—a sudden explosion outside the Café where I'm wait-ing and I gape in Surprise I'm afraid of them, presidents with vast armies, industries, airplanes, diplomats, countries at their disposal.

Argentina

Mar. 1960

Back at the Santiago Zoo

The Anteater is looking for an ant—he's mad for ants—pacing back and forth along the concrete wall, sniffing—suddenly rises up on two legs to investigate a crack higher on the wall—leans his front paws and sniffs rapidly—then down

His front paws: Tough strong shoulders with a streamlined zephyr stripe rising from his breast and scimitar on his mid back—huge round nails and the paws turn in walks wobbly on these powerful front legs— Boxing gloves I can see they're used for scraping thru the hard clay into anthills underground. Long fine hairs on his tail—brushwork, like iron brushes—a— delicate fan of rather stiff hairs. And his face—so long a foot long from the forehead to the wet black nose tip—always sniffing as if had a Cold—

Goes over to this food tray by his little house—in which there is some mashed red meat—puree of meat?—substitute for ants—goes back to sniff the wall.

Little small Ears—what does he hear, the chirp racket of ants?— hardly disturb the arch of his back from nose to tail.

From the Zoo hill,

　　　Sunset, sad and tired over the day.

　　　The large white madbirds with long yellow beaks raise back their heads and begin a long rattling epileptic tattoo one half-beak against the other—archetype sound—Siempre folklorico in their cages which can't see the sun—

　　　And the oso Hormiguero paces up & down after his ants.

　　　And the black lambs enter their crude house.

　　　The sun turns orange red and bends behind the coastal hill.

　　　And the Parrots all scream goodnight

Argentina

The Australian White Cucutoo Chicos wave their wings & caw
The golen pheasant sets & sees,
The African grey Loro whistles

[...]

Riding in bus at dusk—a street organ harmonica—Suddenly saw Santiago 1960 March 1 at Dusk, riding alone in a bus—the nostalgia of time —music streaming thru time

One eyed turk—Rembrandt in Bellas Artes Santiago

[...]

Walking down Grand Avenida, Turned on Blanco Villa to hit Dr C. Ramos' house—walked two blocks hitting my head under low trees on pavement—suddenly, the mummy of a cat—dry brown paper mummy with eyeholes and broken thin bones setting on the dry earth in the powered dust of sidestreet.

March 3, 1960
Sunday Afternoon at Nicanor Parra's
Catherine, daughter with Guagua (baby) is visiting, sitting on front porch, Violetta Parra is touching the guitar & singing, old song to Catherine, Nicanor relaxing with eyes closed, on sun chair, in the shade, the kitten stretching under her foot, Violetta's nose is eaten by worms and wrinkled, singing—the boy of 12 half naked in bathingsuit with smooth brown skin, twists around the porch post & listens, I in easychair inside the open door, relax and watch with morphine. The wind is rustling thru the trees in Chile.

Argentina

Off in the distance below the slope of La Reina, Santiago in the misty
blue air, and beyond that can see the coastal range. A fly buzzes round
the empty chair under the tree.

♥

Buenos Dias
    Communistas
Hello, Communists

♥

Morphine Dream:

$\frac{1}{N}$ = Mirror image
      self repeated

At end of a long corridor of mirrors, the Buddha Seated—I approach
his and of the vista & find it is a mirror: So the Buddha figure must
be I

♥

March 8—Poetry is an accident.

♥

[...]

March 12, 1960

Moon goes eclipse
here come the poets

Argentina

my left eyelid
begins to tremble

A branch of the olive
    Tree moves
dog gnaws a
     bone
De Rokha & Neruda
     see the moon
thru one eye

♥

Parra spits
     eclipse,
he sneezes
the family argues
in the back
     room
about a red spot
     in the
     penumbra

♥

the sound of
     flute
my ear—people
dancing in taverns
in the valley

Argentina

    Not enuf lite
to see my
   notebook
my handwriting
gets bigger—
"Braulic Arenes
must be looking
w/ one eye &
sleeping w/ the
other one"—

[. . .]

La Reina—Santiago
    Chile, March 15 1960—the fading page—lamp-light, an old picture of
the virgin on the wall—easychair—an antique phonograph playing Chi-
lean Tangos recorded 25 years ago—the ancient violins now crumbled
to dust, the voices cracked, or mute—butterfly soprano waltzing to the
staccato—Parra, sad in his Professor's suit, remembering a melody his
father touched on the violin nearly thirty years ago—

    Hymn of Love
           To Peter Orlovsky

And listening to the broken
phonograph over scratched

Argentina

discs, all that I remember
in the sweetness we missed
in time

Huilca or Vuilca—narcotic snuff of aborigines produced visions—Bing-
ham Vilcabamba (Valley)
(huica-pampa) Seeds powdered, called Cohoba
Inhaled thru nostrils by means of a bifurcated tube

Dream March 20, 1960

Fragmentary—Approaching Oxford again, in an ancient high 1920
Ford very roomy inside, I am a peasant father, short stocky & depend-
able, with my little son and his tiny black cat.

I feel nostalgic to re-enter Oxford, revisit my old school—is it my old
school? I tell my son don't worry I know the way—After all I did spend
2 weeks there—or was it two weeks—when, in what lifetime—oops need
to turn the car around—The road is the Central one with a big Hall &
statue near the Ashmolean Museum—

(as sad as all the old plaster Greek statues in the first floor basement
of the Ashmolean)—I get the car turned around as on a dime—but as I
reach the other side of the road, it seems it's all iced over a foot thick,
and the ice ends in wheel-made ruts—which I successfully navigate the
car down thru—Meanwhile time to get out & enter the portals of Cor-
pus Christi—I am afraid the cat has not left the car but I see he has
slipped—small black cat like drunken Chilean poet Stella's—who
slipped thru the window at her house—thru & is on the road too, with
the little child.

—Unfolding some old clean clothes—I need new clothes, I think,
when I wake up—a pair of shorts, very fine & thin, and a top, both green

Argentina

grey—and a green grey shorts, thicker, like German leather pants, to match—very nice.

When I am old and grey wandering thru Oxford I shall need simple clean clothes & not hideous handmedowns like what I got now like Pablo de Rokha. I think when I wake up—my white hair at Oxford— better be a clean old man & have some dignity. Walking with students, the butt of their juvenile idealistic jokes.

In front of my eyes,
six different kinds of trees,

In front of my eyes
Pine, weeping willow, black
    berry, grass,

& yellow stalk of hay,
resting in the low branches
    of a green bush.

Dream—entering into a thin tunnel, seeing real forms turn around thin & Disappear.

Me enter into the mute of life.

Dream of how dreamy-thin people are in existence so that they change & disappear like phantasms in a circus crazyhouse.

The Latin American Republics—D. F. Munro (Appleton NY 1950)

"Once in power the new President (Malgarejo) showed a complete

contempt for legal restraints and private rights, cruelly suppressing every evidence of discontent and using the public funds for the gratification of his vices and the enrichment of his friends. During his frequent periods of drunkenness he was capable of atrocities that terrified even his unprincipled associates." p. 330

Latue—"Alakaloid extracted from Latua Venenosa h, is the same atropine which before this was encountered in Atroopo Beooadona O, Datura Stramonium L. (Chamico), Hyoscianus Niger L (Beleno) . ." p. 9. Editudio Chemico del Latus by B. A Becher Univ de Chile 1918 gathered at Maullin

[. . .]

Flashes of Last Days

The [?] on the bus to Punto Alto—"I see the sun running with gold, gold streaking in the sun, the moon is full of silver, full of plata, potos"— Louder & louder till he lets up, his young son stops him by the arm, they are eating tropical fruits, the pits all over back floor of the bus—all the ladies in the bus get scared and descend, bahar-like driver comes and orders him off—he's clinging to the seat-handles.

Walking around Punto Alto looking in store windows for cheap colored clothes & overalls.

Old cars in Santiago streets.

Arguing with Parra last nite and many times before over Marxism— he saying Chink Marx is the only possible responsible mature position Made me feel bad—

Argentina

Raquel Signoret, white dress & breasts at lunch yesterday—with George Tellier.

Enrico Lihn shy at San Pablo—the day before with Theophilo Ced and

Tellier & La Raka—(Rachel)—Cid's grey eyes—

Braulio Arenas—playing chess in back of the Café, same table every day—

Chico Molina rubbing his forehead "Es Espantosa" describing some new causa horroroso—his mapuche lover—

The last nite, Inez Del Rio looking like Mme Sosotris at the Card Table.

Efrain Barquero, Arabic in black suit, acting sincere at supper—his neurasthenia over Telephones—

Oxley the blind psychiatrist bumping into my nose when he goes to embrace me—

Aloft 7:15 Sunrise Aril 1, 1960

Over Valley Central of Chile Aconcagua a jagged cut out on the horizon, the sun yellow & blinding over the grey sierra profile, raying over the mist that covers the distant town below, can see only below straight down thru the light, the brown hills beginning to creep north toward the Atacama Desert.

After an hour, see many hills, dry, with valleys dotted with trees & by streets, rivers watering them from snow-gleeks above to the Andes—peaks gleaming with a little water mirror—and flashing in thin brightness midst the hills nearer the coast—to run almost dry underneath the airplane—

Until the Mountains level out to high sheeplike backs of hills—a big lane—with long dry curvy runnels of flat bottom sand—waterless—all dry—here begins the Desert.

Argentina

The railroad snakes thru it all very thin & fragile from above—a long line around hill peaks and along the side of dry rivers.

Suddenly in the spread of clouds covering vast patches ahead—low misty clouds not powerful high fliers in heaven—blanket thin summerblanket clouds.

De Rokha—genio del pueblo—the genba, folk, people—but more, a Pantagruelesque Patchen—with communicatical sophistication, paranoiac, and huge belly—wandering over Chile like a fool selling his books.

Now the high Desert Continuing—Atacama?—the soft hilly land hardrock red, with spots of white I thot were salt—pure sand—lakes of sand—and then roads of White.

Little pools of sand along the riverbank

After, a huge flat Central brown desert, scratched with dry roads, dry scratches, spider-webbing the brown tundric.

A few poblaciones—also dry & brown the earth nearby pockmarked with cottony white dots, specks of digging—

In the midst of the amorphic flat, shape of Arp, wrinkles making small hillies—their sides serrated like myriad ribs with gullies of no water, maplike.

And the streaks of black ugliness, nomanslandish developments of erosion or rock—farther along the place, a shelf of cloud—and all the way on the edge of the world, the Andes—Cordillers blacken—with further Cordillers of clouds on the other side (in Argentina, how do I know?)

Argentina

Finally miles & miles ahead perfectly flat—inland—in the valley—the other side of the plane, rugged hills toward the—blue immense misty Pacific falling off like into space from the coast lands. Might be pure blue void, or air.

♥

Nothing Devours—is the stable element which devours us—my vision 2 nites ago of cancer of the asshole slowly eating away life—the worm in the nite—

♥

The Andes nothing more from this height than a long range of wrinkles on the earth's skin—with silver caps some, ageless in starlite (How should I know) or sunlight now.
    "Nil, none a dream,
    A Bubble pop, a foam suit,
    in the immensity of the sea
    at midnite in the dark"—   J. K.

And the world is a sea of Change.
All these women laboring in the
sea, working over dishes in
        Monterey like Sheila
alone, without company, without
understanding, solitary, loveless, lone,
While the secret of the Alma Grande
hides hidden in a basket of hair.

Bueno, an arroyo now, deep cleft in the desert where an old river winds its dry head toward fate.

Argentina

And now the molesting sun is above my airplane window head.

Window hair, eat my window hair.

And now, Mark Van Doren,[21] tengo mucho sentimento por los communistas—I am riding high over the earth gazing down at the desert of South America—astretch to the Andes, above the roof of consciousness, gazing at the world, philosopher higher than the great globe itself.

A dolls head hanging down from the suitcase rack, gazing at the passengers in the seat below, fixedly.

The Communists want to change the world and give everybody eat?

The desert is now absolutely dry without roads, including soft hillies and sand softened rounded ex-watercourses.

Suddenly immediately beneath me a huge sloping cliff dropping down from the flatlock of desert—to the sea—Impossible roadless cliff-slopes—

Until a great old rivervalley cracks the plain—dry canyon.

The earthcliffs, very red—and some hills on edge of sea slope green.

Antofogasta had been in one of these great "Quebradas."

The plane flying lower—a sudden sickening dip—over the ocean, half a mile out—almost on level w/ the huge cliffs—to approach Arica—

The Morro—a huge outcropping of naked rock emerging peninsular from the clay cake on the shoreline and under its Protection as ugly din City, flatroofed, faraway with boats in harbor—and one large launch approaching Southward as we fly low—

And in on a desert—where with oil tanks a black outmoded fighter plane w/ guns, a passenger station w/ bamboo & serrated tin roof—outside a blast of blue sky, and the wing of the plane writing, seen thru the

21. A poet and critic, Mark Van Doren (1894–1972) taught Allen Ginsberg at Columbia University.

Argentina

door, baggage rocks and red baggage dolly truck sitting on the desert as in a Miro or Chagall—Tanguy, Dali, nostalgia of the infinite—Waves of heat flowing over the concrete runway.

Was about 4–5 hours.

To La Paz—The ship revving up—seatbelts fastened.

Death is being eaten by a metallic monster.
Death is being fucked by a robot.
Death is losing control & being dragged into the sea by red airplanes
Death is submission to the black hole of Cancer
Death is losing feet, hands, teeth, hair, eyes, tongue, stomach
Death is flying into the black cloud and never coming out forever
Death is Eternity, forever, nothing more, or else—
Death is a big long tunnel full of wolves
Death is a mouth of iron ore,
Death is impossible to see without
Death is being eaten by the man in the ocean,
Death is being eaten alive,
Death is being invaded by electricity
Death is a noise too loud to bear,
Death is lights entering the brain,
Death is burning alive,
Death is the worst thing that can happen
Death is lying in bed knowing you're going to submit to the disease that's eating away at your asshole.
Death is another matter (come true)
Death comes true
Death is turning around in the wrong direction
Death is what you knew all along

Argentina

Death is what you were afraid of—
Death is a Cannibal headhunter.
Death is a flying machine
Death is a stupid Lion
Death is high on marijuana
Death is—am I ready?
Death is screaming at the executioners
Death is no Oxygen
Death is The One,
Death eats hands
Death is a big mouth,
Death is being eaten by a wildmouth skeleton horse.

Plane turning round on ocean for height to gain, swerving inward for 45 minute flight to the Andes and over. This is the first time I'm flying over the Andes!

Way high over the cliffs over the Morro of Arica now miniature as before we came in at level of the sea cliffs to the first airdrome.

The Valley of Arica, with some trees & farms in the back wash valley floor—boats underneath in the sea like white zizzflies over melon. And nothing but fans of high desert beyond that little strip surrounding the triangle.

Pure, very Pure, desert flattened rolling into the wrinkled [?] toward center Andes—plane lifts—high snowpeaks in blue air, bright as clouds.

Plane marching along, I hear the locomotive of the air Raptre of the height attacking me.

The Volcanos are under the cloud roof.

The first range of the Andes past, the plane jigging along in the air—a vista of peaks to the left, North—solitary & linked

Argentina

A fly washing its hands on the windowpane overlooking the altiplano that leads off the volcanos—like a mad rowboat in the air, obsessed by winds.

The Desert now dotted with dry greens

    . . .

Inland the sky mistier, then earth a little wetter, lakes, some dingy green overspread in the many hollows—patterns of agriculture dividing the land's surface thinly—rivers in flate to Bolivia—forked lightning of erosion to the small hills. Clay enclosures far below—coming down lower—soary flights—

More green & deep brown, wet wrinkles—and mist—

The edge of a vast plane—the airport. Bus down—La Paz white & red in the huge hollow valley—descending on the bus—Bolivian women sitting with hands over their noses.

[. . .]

April 4, 1960

Bolivia is like Paterson with revolvers—Café Gally full of Politicians with thick eyeglasses, mustaches, little pins in lapel, dark skin and black hair—all like Eyen Zinel—Cab Calloway politician with long fingers—getting soup from tables ^ shaking hands with all. I order Mate de Coca.

Dream March 6—

Arriving at the top station street of Paterson at high as Calle Max Peredes in La Paz, I miss out something is happening below. Nebulous

Bolivia

horror takes place in Universe—buddhist or Tibetan revelations—L.[22] saying denying me the night on the floor of his kitchen—"stripping me bare" he thought—as Parra the same on politics—I am in love with a dying thing. Loveless, in bed in Bolivia, my life seems sterile.

Dream: Around the supper table in Paterson, with strange family— my own family, but a young stepfather—like Eugene's[23] brother-in law— with L. for supper. There is to be a dance in Paterson—L. is at my house alone with me—at a loss for life, what to do. But there is the dance to go to—I am embarrassed to ask for the car—it is the first time I have asked for it. My stepfather has little money, but since I ask he fishes up $5.00 for the nite, like Harold asking Louis for loot—an awkwardness between us—but my stepfather wants to do his duty right and I think that by asking him it is a subtle form of flattery anyway—Considering he is responsible for me—in front of my friend. And ask also to borrow the car. He says, reluctant but glad I asked, & wanting to be fair, OK— but "Can your friend drive"—"Sure we were in Mexico together"—besides I realize, worst comes to worst, I can always drive the car myself— I've driven it easily home at night in Paterson before & have a memory of that—in case L gets drunk. We go.

We get to the parking lot in front of the tavern—it is a dance in Paterson—Miles Frost is there with the dancers, preparing for the dance— All the men are dressed in Spanish—black silk thigh pants, white open ruffled shirt, and huge red sash wrapped around the waist—others there, too—as the parties in NY the girls give (Barbara, Dodie, Francessca)— L is reluctant but suddenly I realize it's been dreamed—I draw close to him & say "Imagine, do you realize we are here as in my dream—I

22. Lucien Carr.
23. Eugene Brooks, Allen's older brother.

Bolivia

dreamt that we would come down from the mountains to a dance hall here in Paterson together, to my stepfather's borrowed car, and would find a big Paterson dance with all your male friends from N.Y." and I draw my head next to him to hold him close to tell him about the dream—but he is reluctant to accept much attention—wanders off—

We are trying to get home—up an escalator from a deep street—up a high fire escape as in another ancient dream of a Valley City—ascending I see an old huge man like Auden in priestly clothes—it's Father Ford, aged & white haired with white clay dust over his features—huge temples & white hair—great old woman face—I salute him, introduce myself—L. follows, listening listlessly.

"Ah," says Ford, "Yes, I've heard that you've reformed your work & eliminated all the intentional obscenity"—He hasn't read me, he just says so from what's he's heard—"Rumors of my obscenity are much exaggerated" I try to say wittily without arguing with him but we are descending now down to the street—he offers to see us home—to get a taxi, which we would, anyway. I drag L along for the Free Ride—"Don't you remember him?" "No, I don't & what's more I don't see why I should remember an old fuck like him after a lifetime"—

"Well," I say, "I'm curious & besides he's been kind to Huncke, gave him some money" trying to explain my friendliness to Ford—and dismayed by L.'s refusal to live in the past or acknowledge the old crimes.

L. starts out in the street—some strange Bolivian agricultural machines with huge collapsible street—paving backs—he drives one in a circle till it topples over backward—I help lift it up—he gets in another & almost wrecks it driving it in a circle—as if he's drunk & in despair.

I am in love with a dying thing, I think when I wake.

Bolivia

To Frank O'Hara[24] & John Ashbery[25] & Kenneth Koch[26]

How real is Bolivia

With its snowy Andes lifting over the modern city

Now that one is in La Paz

Which means the Peace in Spanish

Tho the natives speak their native tongue

Especially the women in brown bowler hats

Sitting in the mud with their hands over their noses

Selling black potatoes and blue onions

In the marketplace which covers the hillside

Over which one can see electrical towers

and airplanes landing from Santiago and Lima Caracas

It is strange how real Bolivia is

Its Capital cupped in a valley in the Altiplano

Two miles up in the sky

So that I have a headache and continually take aspirin

Which is relatively expensive tho the taxis are 10c

and the poverty seems especially created to make me seem a Prince

with my beard and black hat and dungarees

Strolling thru the market buying silver flies, spiders & butterflies

And green and purple shawls the ladies use

24. Frank O'Hara (1926–1966) was a poet and art critic.

25. Poet and Ginsberg friend, John Ashbery (1927–2017) won the 1976 Pulitzer Prize for *Self Portrait in a Convex Mirror*.

26. First draft of "To Frank O'Hara & John Ashbery & Kenneth Koch," published in *Wait Till I'm Dead: Unpublished Poems*, ed. Bill Morgan (New York: Grove Press, 2016), 31–32.

To carry babies and garbage in
while I watch them over rich green pig stews
in the Rembrandtian restaurant filled with waiting bearded prophets ·
dressed in rags and ancient grey hats over their white brows
All the same I feel a little out of place in Bolivia
Which was a beautiful name in my geography book
Lazing alone in my hotel room with two extra empty beds
Tho I have seen various unhoused Indian boys
I'd gladly share my solitude with, not knowing their names—
and the coca leaf does not really get me high as I expected
So that I masturbated 3 times this week
and wrote postcards to all my friends
in NY, Paris, Florence & Kyoto
—I think I'll take a trip to Machu Pichu
Which is a famous Inca ruined city in Peru.

Ride to & from Sirota cemetery, saw Illampu's hide glistening under
the snow

Bolivian Horrors
I shuddered in Bolivia
Hanging round Bolivia

April 9, 1960—WAR manifestos all day, beginning at dawn with pop-
ping of rifles in the hills and a hysterical band screaming in the blue
emptiness of Plaza Murillo. They rode down Calle Soobaya under my
hotel balcony in a truck with mustached leader shouting in voice already

Bolivia

hoarse, "Viva La Paz" and "Viva La Revolucion"—and passed, the music operating again in front of City Hall down the block—the only one in the street being a drunken cripple staggering up the hill.

The bands hung around downtown all day—Crowds coming in trucks to the huge Buenos Aeres—

Later around 2 PM huge crowds of marchers with Banners—Martyres de la Victoria—Syndicato de Mineros—Bolivian flag a block long—crowds perched on statues & trees

Smell of Coca breath—nauseated me after a few days chewing—sides of lips green.

Dream: in Sorata—in the AM I wake up late to catch 6 AM Truck back home to La Paz—I go to put on my socks and they are rotten—I can't get out of the hotel in time to catch the bus because the dumb brown middleaged Indian pimp hotel owner didn't wake me in time—

I wake up in First Reality—it's true, he hasn't woken me, it's 5 AM & the trucks have all gone—but one little yellow one that I catch to Huranai—walk from there near Lake Titicaca—then collective (bus) to La Paz.

Dream in La Paz—the night of the Mass March on Plaza Murrillo to see Paz-Estenesoro & Allende orate weeping in a dream for the Beauty of Russian Socialism—Naomi[27] should have gone back—the whole family should have gone back to Russia to live after the Revolution—Naomi's tragedy was that she missed the worker's state and was

27. Naomi Ginsberg, Allen's mother.

left deculturated in America screaming at the Capitalist system—I realized in dream that the whole family belonged in a small apartment in Moscow—working as accountants & teachers.

Dream—Kerouac & I in Mexico—living in Bill's house—his mother kicks us out (Bill's) for living together—someone I slept with—Harold or Joel—He had a wan on earlobe, I suggested he take it off—the neighbors see us & drive us out of underground room we had fixed up—nice French bed there & furniture, we were living like Capitalists underground (this another Communist dream)—so we have to leave, I put on my sweater like pants, upside down while walking street—we hit a hot-dog taco stand—I go away to outside to change in a dark lot—I see by the paper our case has been transferred from old Folks Department—to more efficient police action bureau—we are wanted for murder—Kerouac's sure (as usual) we will not be caught—I full of anxiety that *someone* knows & will gossip—wonder if we can stay where we are or be extradited, what country is safe to flee to. Will they notice we are leaving to another country?

To Caranavi Jungle, parrots, the bed with the silent harvest hand in same room, shat on side of roads & rose covered with garrapatas, my feet hurt, blisters from week old work—shoes, changing to heavy sox, walked next day from 10 AM on road back to Coroico—couldn't get truck till late afternoon—slept at Yolosa (you lose) junction on Pallet for 1,000 pesos 10c—dreamt I was getting off bus—But I left my coat behind, I yell at driver as it is pulling away—someone in bus tells him, he doesn't stop, I can't get back on bus to get my coat (full of medicine & sweaters & maps bulging from torn pockets)—same sense of frustration as when driver of Camions who wouldn't pick me up on the highway.

Bolivia

Tonite in Coroico room high up—owner old man with stiff leg—met
& talked to the priests: Coffee in the small appley refectory, Franciscans,

Chulumani Valley—so large you could hear an ant whistle
   I close my eyes in bright sunlight—see red eternity—I am looking at
myself, as exploring Bolivia I am visiting an area of myself
         "High on the peak tops, Bats—
         Down in the Valley the Lambs"

                       Hymn to the Resurrected Christ
                       Easter Sunday 1960   La Paz Bolivia

Friday Dusk against the neon halo of Calle Commercico
The yellow effigy moved march step
                   Military band funebra wailing amid
                          Mountains
Tragic, flayed, bleeding Christ, eyes upturned over Colonial
                            rooftops,
Undulating toward the Cathedral
                   The silent Crowd of Indians,
Politicians with dark glasses, hats off—
                   O Christ of Horns,
Christ of Brasses, Christ of
               Mary and Disciple, hands lifted
   pleading with the Invisible
a Jew, 33, with a beard, naked
       It is true—

Saturday in Palca, refuge under the mountains, Ayamara
   drunken Indians with brilliant flags of light

And drums and bright batons
   waving flagpoles dangerously at the mountain
       heads
a row of women in Colored sheets selling onions against the wall of
     the Plaza—

The rooster crows in the valley
the clouds raise over the mount
a car crawls on the ant road
The locusts whistle in the air
Woodsmoke drifts on the hill
Hitler issues epistles
But the Bolivian Army marches on.

Fri nite saw Via Crucis Parade downtown Bolivia—martyred, passionate, flayed Christ carried in slow undulating march step in Funereal Band music around Plaza Murillo to Mercado Luiza.

Sat—to Palca in the rain, drunken Indians with brilliant squared flags beating drums & waving huge white wood flagpoles at each other's heads—The rutty mud road, scared—then back to La Paz—Tea in Sakyaru coffee shop on Calle Commercio—two intellectuals talking at next table reading each other papers on politics—another table a man who looks like Eugene, sunk under the weight of tragedy—receding hair, wounded look, glasses.

Bar Cena sign "Hay comida"—but comeda no hay

In the Church, a Cracked and dusty mural of the triple
     Christ once seen in Mexico.

And Death the Skeleton triumphant standing over the Priests hats
staffs and

Landowners and Saves—Crude skull, Crude skill—

Death the Skeleton Triumphant over Bolivian politics.
The La Paz crate from the Presidential
Balcony

Soldiers, Priests, Doctors, Syndicates, schoolchildren, old Indian ladies
incapable of goose step and correct V finger sharp salute, fumbling
with packages of Babe aback—The army marching amateur with
hauteur and white gloves—

Last nite 2 ragged men with rifles
and long overcoats
barred my way on Calle Potosi—"Coorduration del Estado"—
and I read the newspaper today,
the blacks advancing on America.
Christ
Creaking Sunday in the silent movie downtown, picture old as me
Scenes from the Life the Passion and the death N.S.J.C.
The million signs were given in old long haired Jewish Bethlehem
Triple cock crew, Pilate with a bowl, Mary sitting on a rock—
Visages of Michael and Gabriel and the Choir of heaven
I am here down on earth below in Bolivia waiting
hiding my money in a long black beard
Christ
on the Cross, in the old time movie in
everybody's mind—the exact same image of my death

Bolivia

or His who sits with black hat in the Restaurant

                               eating meat again—

Inside me, the Image of the Savior—crucified, lost,

      rejected with the leper, lunatic & cripple

rejected with the whore, rejected with the beggar, rejected with the

      cigarette vendor, the Indian lady in the doorway

—Rejected with the fat old lady in bright shawl & brown bowler hat

      waddling up Calle Commercio

in the opposite direction of Christ

      with a huge pack of white Andean flowers on

          her back in a brilliant shawl

—Does nothing worse than sell her flowers, good lady—

Sunk in our sufferings, awaiting death, and unresurrected yet—

8 million ignorant Bolivian Christs, 80% Indians speaking Ayamara

      and stooped over a wooden rake on a dizzy green hill, attacking &

      plucking at the earth for a handful of black potato or artichoke—

Christus Resurrectus Est today, somewhere, the Images are on the

  Streets

      All mankind knows, but don't I know where, I don't know sitting

      in a restaurant drinking tea to keep warm another 10 minutes—

      Where is Christ but resurrected for a minute in my soul

after seeing His Creaking Movie in His Bolivian oblivion where

      6 million Indians believe

Magic

    is not/is the answer.

                    End my doubt.

Christ, said manure, said the dirty fingers of the market, mid the moans

      of military bands, the crying priests in streets, the silence of the

      Whiting Crowd, my own soul still as water in the dusk—

Bolivia

Be resurrected as before, Be resurrected and second to Heaven
      as of today—
Step with invisible feet over the human stairway, life
Thy lightness to the Platform of the City Eye, Sit
Triumphant in my soul and all Souls watching earth
To see the Flayed and broken man below enduring nails and blood
A cup of bitter wine and black teeth and broken shins and rage
eating and dying here below ignorant under the clouds of the Andes
Lifting up millions of Crosses of Death to thy high Transcendency.

April 20—To Calle Buenos Aires & Tumusla, La Paz, to pick up bus for Peru at 5 AM after restless half awake night. Passed Tiahuanaco Sun-gate, changed my mind and didn't stop, continued over hills and Alti-plano to Desaguardero border between Bolivia & Peru on marsh-farm shore of Titicaca Lake. 9:30 AM now and sound of 20 buses gathered in field in sunlight just opening forth—before an iron rusty gate on a bridge between countries. Against walls of the adobe houses all Indian ladies in bowler hats selling coffee & sheep meat roast & donuts. Passed by church on Bolivian side—old ruin with 2 delicate towers, on top of the falling red tile roof, a strange screaming-dog in statue red terra cotta perched some old antiquity joke. Back of church a ruined graveyard—all numberless stones so that when I saw one name I was moved. Passed shepherd against wall playing with rocks while sheep ate. The pig screeched & grunted trapped in a big oven igloo. He'd been put in for the night, rocks piled before the door. Everybody piling out of the trucks, 10 minutes to 10 waiting for the rusty gate to Peru to open—car-rying light knapsack & a cylindrical package of Chinese green cubist mountains, the scroll. The hill rocks here streaked to the bedrock with erosion, rather pretty dell of marsh & adobe houses with dirt and tin

Bolivia

roofs only 7 feet high, held down by rocks. And crowds of minute flies on a soggy brown piece of cardboard in the mud—as in the air passing thru the graveyard—whose wooden closed gate was useless as the adobe wall had collapsed as had several of the adobe coffingraves—and many shaggy Altiplano dogs.

Bolivia

Ginsberg in Peru

Peru

Ginsberg was glad to reach Peru, which, he felt, held more promise than the early portion of his South American sojourn. He missed Peter Orlovsky and wrote often to offer his love for his lifelong companion, as well as to deliver news of his activities; he was homesick, and traveling alone did nothing to ease it. His lack of sexual activity, coupled with the slower pace in the South American cities that he visited, only served to remind Ginsberg how far he was from home.

Peru offered promise. The splendor of Machu Picchu and the prospects of finding and using ayahuasca excited him. He knew enough Spanish to muddle by, and his curiosity about native cultures and food rejuvenated him as he entered still another unfamiliar country.

April 25—The Peruvian firelight—kerosene lamp in bridge-side inn, Pisac—waiting for firefoot lady on dirt floor to cook me Asado & eggs & rice—white dog sniffing at my feet—the rough owner—blackhair & hanging nose going over his books—at his side his babe, she with chicken leg in right hand and the jawbone of a sheep in the other, toying with them on the table.

April 25—Machu Picchu

Express train roar down green below the movement of white Vilca-nota water amongst the tracks & footpaths.

Constant cricket chirp, the loudest from a near mount side.

A flock of lambs running away from its owner over the green steps and down a field, a white puppy barkyipe, can't follow fast enough.

Lovers picking each other's noses—an amber black & white spot tropic butterfly on the brown soil under the sun's hitching post on which I sit.

April 26—I put my black hat over Machu Picchu—Climbed up to Gatepost then walked down from heights Machu Picchu to the R R track & along track with basket & cane & black hat into Peruvian R.R. tunnel—looking back apprehensively—to the Pension—Alojiemento 2 km. down the track—huge wood room whitewashed with tree-pole center, 4 big tables with worn red linoleum fruit-pattern covers, old dusty calendars showing red girls in the fields of Calif. showing their legs—at one table a captain in green, police, two widows in black, one a dwarf, eating pasta and boiled beef, tastes slightly rotten—a baby boy standing on chair to sip his little plate—

At other table an Indian couple, he in brown leather jacket, finishing with coffee—ducks waddling around the floor, a black cat, and a dog with an injured paw.

The radio is too loud, and wobbles in and out of synchronization with the bare transparent blinding electric light that seems only to disturb the eye and sheds a pale irritating light against the red linoleum.

Moths have been wavering and gyring around it and slowly climbing with tremulous wing against the centerpost only to fall off and gyre again around the incandescence.

One fell whirling below the level of the table finally to the floor, exhausted. A nearby duck extended its neck, waddled over quickly and snapped it up from the floor, gobbling rapidly with its flat beak.

The dog yipes for food at the side of the policeman The widow girls are laughing "ahhh-bueno."

The young couple pass from the table to the outside darkness—"Buen provecho" at the side of my ear as I write.

Peru

Three vast Calla lilies in the shadow of the counterpole, including a juajua baby in dress, standing on chair with a spoon in the darkness, staring at me.

Thru the door, a great dark smoky black kitchen with pots on charcoal fires—a boy barefoot torn sleeves in baggy pants, serves coffee & carries off the plates. The geese flock on the kitchen floor, one adventures into the eating room.

My hat has a bright yellow daisy set against its blackness. There are four different calendars against the wall, with picture of another in addition, and a filthy green Cuzquena Beer sign.

A tin can with sausage label, holding a bunch of wilted small flowers, over the lintel of the door to the street-railroad track. Glass missing from several sections of the windows, a big pink table against the opposite wall, in front of a large pink rack holding several dozen bottles of Coke, Pilsner Beer, and Naranjada. And in a glass case, a few pieces of bread, a bowl of large yellow eggs, cups, and cheese.

A voice, crooning like that of Pablo Neruda, "Da me saus manos," breaks off and over a whistle of static 3 men warble in cadence with accordions. A tin roof.

Later, by shadow & candle-light.

In bed, upstairs by candle breakdown hate to write what I have to write.

Dream: a spread in *Life* with Robert Duncan[1] & Jess Collins, their

1. Robert Duncan (1919–1988) was a highly influential poet and member of the San Francisco literary establishment when Ginsberg lived in the city in the 1950s. Duncan, an open homosexual long before "coming out" was acceptable, had a thirty-seven-year public relationship with artist Jess Collins that lasted until Duncan's death.

Peru

domestic life together, nicely treated, with photos at breakfast, the poet in his study, the painter at his walls, the garden, the hand-made books. Duncan transcribing his Medieval pensées under the statue of the Virgin. Nicely treated by Rosalind Constable. I muse in dream—see picture of *The Field* by City Lights—think, well, now Duncan and Spicer[2] can't complain about being neglected, 10 million Americans exposed to their propaganda—for what—for Art's sake—and for all the publicity I had what good did it do—as I had nothing to say or Announce—not even an Art of Medieval Illumination—as Duncan—

Realizing before sleep, the Inti Pampa—is field of Gold—*The Field*—filled with golden marvels, "grasshoppers & bees"—thus the *Field* hits *Life* mag while I sleep in shadow of Machu Picchu late reading about the Incas before blowing out candle—my feet hurt, from descent from ruins—the visit here a complaining nightmare, subjected to same primitive molestations for Economic reasons as the lowly or middle class Indian Peruvian—tho I'd ignored Communist political complaints, when it touches me, the foot-suffering and inconvenience of Peruvian poverty, all I do is complain verbally to my own—as must the conscious Indian—instead of being inspired by Machu Picchu to some noble transcendency. 1/3 my thought ascending to the pass to Cuzco by Inca road was annoyance at hotel prices & personnel—the stay here a horrible footsore fiasco only to be alleviated by con or money.

So I dreamed, told Duncan saw his Field, Inti Pampa—he asks "Ah, what poem is that [. . .] of mine that you read in the Field?" No, yes, I say, the complaint a la Pound about "Have you gold for Adornment on your house?" etc. I remember from Anthology—he seems not to remem-

2. Jack Spicer (1925–1965) was a Ginsberg contemporary and poet during the San Francisco Poetry Renaissance. His volume of collected poems, *My Vocabulary Did This to Me*, was awarded the American Book Award in 2009.

ber exactly where he saw it—is sexy—we are in a cab—I change cab drivers, take cab with David Amram[3]—to Duncan's boudoir—Duncan & I go to bed together, he kisses me with big nose, I am a little embarrassed but feel hot, am all feet, he goes down to blow me, but I can't exactly come—I feel ashamed—some treason to Peter?—and his huge corpulent body (last night a pig reminded me of Ansen)[4]—(a pig scratching its ass wriggling against a post)—wake & hate the dream.

[. . .]

April 28 Woke—on my lips, "the sweepings of the moon," being ruins, lives & earth chips.

Slept in Guardian Julian Peredas hut—chili his. Hot coffee in morn with his sweet-bread-cake.

Last night watched sunset from Intiwatana stone—the dusk fell, darkness with 5 rays of light over the mountain Collpan from the hidden sun—started walking back down terraces to the hut—The city in early dusklight had been a green mossy grey stone, but now with obscurity, sudden darkness over the dead city, as if it were fading into darkness, a blink of the eye of history—The new pink & red hotel set up of transient boards & tin roofs of workers—"Darkness falls on the dead city—the last tourist bus drives down the mountain." Saw all history vanishing in the general dusk.

3. David Amram (born 1930) is a jazz instrumentalist, composer, and conductor who befriended Ginsberg, Jack Kerouac, and other Beat Generation figures in the 1950s.

4. Alan Ansen (1922–2006), a poet and playwright, was a friend of many Beat Generation writers, including Allen Ginsberg, Jack Kerouac, and William Burroughs. He helped organize Burroughs's *Naked Lunch*.

Peru

Now on top of Huyna Picchu—looking down on the city, mid-afternoon—had set out in back hat & cashmere coat & dungarees & feet hurting in Bolivian workshoes—Inca cigarettes, yellow round bread & carrot in my pocket—and chose a stick to keep me company. So high up over the green plazas a man in white coat moves, a speck of white. Had prayed against rain. Divigated twice before settling on a stone on the peaktop. There's the little white dog that barks too much, in the hectare the workmen are clearing under Picchu Chico.

Lay back on top rock and gazing at the sun took down my pants & looked at my naked belly and began handling my cock, till I came staring with half-closed lids over the smoky peaks and over the dark clouds to a strip of blue wherein the sun appeared with the same gold Heat and Name as the heat in my loins as I was to come——————

Then descending, an area of terraces below a ruined empty gate, thru which I see the blue clouds—burst into a Millennium chant & song, Resurrection—seeing the colossal high terraces in total ruin, the colossal jungle overgrown, and cleaned away again to reveal the dirt striven rocks of the terrace walls, steep down in a crevice open on the top of the sky—Total ruin—Thought of what music I might hear in a dream seeing the ruins of New York after a millennium.

Descending, a small sunny rain starting, to wet my hat and feet again, but very light—Came to the sadde between Machu Picchu (Chico) and Huynu Picchu—a vast 180° rainbow from across the canyon and center of Pitumachi over the R.R. tracks—to the foot of the ancient village filling the valley—same as yesterday. Must have had always many rainbows when the city was new.

Peru

Intiwatana, crescent moon, city strictly in the clouds,—now alone at night—living in a hovel drinking cold coffee—the last priest.

Up there in the cave it's very dark

The bodies are even gone from the tombs

More stones for the locusts, Pompeii, Rome, Herculaneum, Cuma, Chichen Itza, Uxmal, Palenque, Machu Picchu—have lived in all these dead cities.

A rabbit and a lizard, and a white dog that barks too much and the southern cross.

Black centipedes over the stairways

The prow of the mountain like a ship in the night, this city.

Standing on platform looking into the obscure forum by the dim light of crescent, the house shapes and terraces half invisible—addressed to them—where are you now? What are you dreaming of—what war?

The half-mad scholar bending over his notebook in the darkness 2000 years hence—questioning the inhabitants—This I did with my beard, resting book on balcony and peering at it to write, then looking sideways scared into the fields below.

If I had summoned a ghost to talk to me, which I did not because of fear—in that vast obscurity—and

What language would we have spoken?

The ghostly solitude—I am the king of the dead, on their ancient throne—sitting 1000 years later lording over these ghosts, questioning in the later moonlight, from the height of the sacrificial stone.

And the stars over the dead city, so far away—suddenly in the presence of the Universe itself.

Tonite on the hard bed in the caretaker's house, sleeping with 3 blankets, he gone to Cuzco to collect his 300 soles—12 dollars monthly wage.

Peru

Tin roof, noise of hotel generator down the high road, my hat on a nail, newspapers on wall to hold out the draft thru cracks of wood white-washed, ate 2 bananas, 1 egg & onion sandwich, one anchovy salad with cabbage, one anchovy sand., one cup of cold coffee, & pieces candy & water.

April 29—After a hearty breakfast I sallied forth in a cheerful mood to climb Machu Picchu proper—am toward the top of the first peak now, set against a rock wall cliff on a bench of rock to gaze down in the bright sunlight at the toy houses of the dead. With a strange orange and violet flower in my hat—colors which are at the opposite ends of the Arco Iris band—orange-green-violet.

Two huge, extra-turkey size brown condors at the point tip peak of Machu Picchu—one circling around sailing on the air currents as I mounted the stone steps toward the top—now as I came up to the last platform, saw this huge brown heavy bird—all brown, with very clean soft smooth feathers, nearly bald but furry & not ugly neck, & dark brown eyes & beak—cleaning its breast feathers with trembling birdlike delicacy, & plucking a crude red blossomflower weed out of rocky studden earth by its roots—eyed me, and did not move. I didn't move—stood silent, protected by cane—and slowly began activity, turning round to look at view, down on Picchu city fanlike way down below, north, and the classical terraces on the peak of Hyuna—They are now standing 10 feet from me facing into the wind which ruffles their righthand wing-feathers.

Heads can turn 180 or 360 degrees & see all thru beady eyes, but I am sitting on a rock a few feet above them—they don't move much (the second circled around the scene for a few minutes before joining us)— the air is clear, blue and hardly any haze—Looking at the birds I also with the same eyes look down now (I am seated on the crumbling highest wall) on the city under the shadows of a noon sun directly overhead in the blue space of heaven. A white flash that gives blinding weight to the eye when glanced upon, up in.

The city from this bright calm height hath its condors—miniature fanlike terraces & walls very proper & symmetric tho there are jagged lines, Capriccioso, the paths of the terraces changed, in origin or by time. It is settled far below, near the earth on a small height. I am perhaps twice or thrice as high as the city—perhaps twice as high as Pintumachi or Huyna Picchu.

"Are you guarding something? Eggs? Nothing to be afraid of—I'm only another butterfly—albeit I am the King of the Dead. I feed you," and more conversation with the condors, who lead very philosophic, airy, panoramic lives.

"Is it on account of the flower in my hat you're so still?"

The train whistle far below—and the trains no more than the long black centipedes—and just as slow.

"What shall we do with this city? What's your opinion of the Dead?

"You eat the dead, I hear. How does it taste? Does it make you vomit? What thoughts when you pluck out the eyes? And when the train whistles what distances do you think? While you're feasting? Don't you ever lust after butterflies? How long have you lived near Machu Picchu? Ah the things that are here are before your time.

"Would you like some more bread?"—.

Suddenly with a great shocking fap of wings the first buzzard took off into the air, & circled for 10 minutes around the height of Machu Picchu, steadying its path thru the air currents with the movement of its tailfan. At times above me—so that I raised my stick in case of need defense—at times below, running huge distances till small toward the next mountain.

Peru

ILLUSTRATION OF CITY

Coming back down, slowly, sun setting behind first clouds—saw a Vibora in the woodsy part of the trail; and a walking stick insect; and hummingbirds that clicked & swooped like fish; and yesterday a rabbit in the prison area, & prehistoric little lizards on top of Huyna Picchu—as well as numerous centipedes—one which had its head cut off (which was gasped like a fish with horny mouth) whose body also wriggled feebly blind.

Dusk—from the terraces in back above—the mount takes on a brownish-greenish-mist with greywhite stone hue—dusk emerald for the laying field, oval in the center.

May 1—Coming back from the "Moon Temple" in the bosky glen path, sat down & drank beer—coke with the sad check-shirt chauffeur on his way down as I was returning. My feet hurt now an hour later, sitting on a nondescript Incan mountain-step—contemplating the little archetype ridge edged with steps, that joins Chico Picchu & Huyna Picchu, a little thin wall of rock.joining the mountains, thru the curve of which I saw a rainbow 2 days ago and today for the last time look at Machu Picchu City ruins.

In the Center Field, in the grass—all around motionless masses of rock balanced as for centuries & a complete silence except for the high whistles of crickets, a feel not unlike the ball court at Chichen Itza. Have stripped the bark off my staff in the afternoon's walk. 2 p.m. The craggy grey pinnacles—now a grey day—clouds hanging over the nearby peaks, my hat off, a sense of blank white space over me, slight wind. The grass here is vivid green, and a few red tall stalks of flower grow on the terraces.

What demons & what Neals have shouted & murdered on these terraces, what Bills sunk in reverie sniffing Huica, what Peters playing ball on the steps, what Allens hunched forward in the dusk musing past Incan housewives grounding maize, scheming how to get into the upper temple & work miracles, with new hip Inca career—despite the authorities that ordered the stones cut for Inner Authority Sanctions. The Sun emerging for an instant with a golden glow, and birds warble on the mount. And what Inca ladies shocked at my sex life—and what difference did it make, now that the City's bare of men & little flies move around my hand.

Leaving having seen this wonder I dreamed of as a kid, I am dying also—one phantom seeing the trails and bones of an earlier phantom of earlier eternal days. Dusk.

Nightmarish walk down Machu Picchu to R.R. station at nightfall, with heavy clouds over the evening, twisted my knee, with bedclothes wrapped round my shoulders as I've seen Indians carrying their bundles, finally dark fell as I got halfway down & had to take the auto road roundabout way instead of human shortcut: a beast rustled in the grass & my toe burned in the dark. Many fireflies hundreds of feet up in the bush, and on the road, crawling express train light-bugs-worms, as if seen from airplane; finally made it down to the Uilcanota Bridge which rusted & leaned over the locomotive sound of the white flood below—And along the R.R track two kilometers to the station—last look back as I turned the curve, the hotel light & campemento corporation light burning way high up on the peak, in the dark mount, high as a Dantean peak in Inferno, a single star-like light revived the impression of utter high remoteness I first had seeing the Ruins from the trail on arriving—way up there in the sky, a city, dead, like an ancient idea of heaven.

Now back at Hotel after coffee, by the R.R. tracks, the mad dog still chained to the back porch with 3 feet of rusty iron, barking hysterically with rabid inhalation of growl everytime I stumble on the rocks of the front porch & step up the rickety wet stairway in the blackness—in the café downstairs they are all getting drunk for May day, poetic youths that make 40c a day working clearing the ruins or cleaning the R.R. track—all up the single street barefoot women following barefoot after the drunk men—and the radio blares from Puno, Mexican music too loud to stand, so that I have to shout to ask "How much?" for my coffee & Inca cigarettes. The drum throb below from the whorehouses—cantina next door, the dog still barking, and myself lain back in bed with two candles at my head burning like funeral tapers in this wooden room papered with last year's newspapers filled with stories about the white smoke announcing a new Pope and the Einsteinean significance of the Flying Saucers with photos in Spanish.

In the Railroad tunnel darkness, with sack on back, I tapped my cane against the rails to find my way thru Death.

* * *

Chessman[5] dead, the United States has a dirty asshole, the Governor is a coward, what would Lincoln have done—The people are full of shit. "Therefore I prophecy the fall of America"—all night in rage on the puno of Peru between Cuzco and Nazca—couldn't sleep, finally dreamt I was caught with pot by the F.B.I in Ester Mate's drawing room in Hell—enraged there too, arrested, & after the noise & formalities taken

5. Caryl Chessman, a convicted robber, rapist, and kidnapper, was executed on May 2, 1960, after an extended period of trial, appeals, and stays of execution. The case became a focal point in the national debate over capital punishment.

Peru

to office or home of the High Eye official, a sort of ratty already elderly faggot with white hair and threadbare suit, who lectured us on Social Behavior, till I burst out in rage denunciation of him, the Eye, the USA, J. Edgar Hoover is an evil fairy—mounting to rage on the Bridge—& plucked or threatened to pluck on the great broken Harp of Iron strings and stone, a huge ruin like Machu Picchu—strains of Tchaikovsky thru Hart Crane's skull.

A Long Dream
The Moth in the Dark

Machu Picchu May 1, 1960

Parts: (1) The Sick Junkie & the Maid (Hall, door, window, 5,000 rooms, the Positions of body)

(2) The nurse (Spilling the tray)—the story, her comment (analyst)

(3) The Tammany visit—the secretaries talking

(4) Work in the Canyon

(5) The Fat Salesman & the check-Eating chocolate buddha

(6) The Bank call

(7) "I don't hurt anyone but the babe"

(8) The twisted soupspoon of Naomi

(9) The visits to the Restaurants

(10) "Deep as Picchu"—& the Moth

(11) The foetal position & the Junkie

I start out working for a living in the series of canyons, but I'm not worried about money.

I direct the huge derrick at the tops of mountains laying down vast sheaves of rock on the valley floor, I live & work on that rock—The rock slabs are my pay, my own land to farm & own.

But I've been working so long I forget what valley I'm in and what pay I've collected & what I've traded away for cash in the bank or other goods & services, like, a Chinese scroll I bought somewhere back, which is worth the whole lifetime of effort in the deep Andean Canyons.

Someone asks me for an accounting, I am confused, I see the latest valley floor, slabbed with me & derrick working, half finished—huge red rock bottom—It's mine now but unusable, wanted to convert it to something portable so I can travel free again.

We had been talking (Jack & Bill & I) and they were telling me about a visit to the Political headquarters—guys who control the building of the canyons are the union leaders who hang out there & have offices— We go to visit, a big school-like building—I see what they mean—all the Syndicate heads are there clasping hands, like when you carry someone with four hands—but they are 3 or 5 people. "See, we put our hands together," they say, grinning violent & evil, "and we give them a shove— like this"—and all their hands Buddhalike together give a shove—I see them in action & am dismayed & annoyed by their indifference to their victims.

But we have to carry the visit thru, so we ask for the Chap this Sophisticated Boss "our Friend" whose handsome secretary says he's not in. Nothing to do. We—or Jack or Peter—starts talking to the Secretaries. One is a Negress, he tried to get her, with her fine dress, silence, & glasses & white school-teacherish ruffle, to talk to us, depending on her innate hipness, and she does suddenly respond & begin jiving us with a long hip complaint about the boss in Parable of description of her abortion, of abortions, & how they treat the young. "See, mister, I always was told & I do believe maybe it's true, but I don't know": "Yes"— "It don't hurt nobody but the Babe.

Peru

5

guys who control the building of the Canyons
are the union leaders who hang out there
& have offices. We go to visit, a big
school-like building - & see what they
mean - all the Syndicate heads are there
Clasping hands, like when you carry someone
with four hands - but they are 3 or 5 people
"See we put our hands together" they say
grinning, violent & evil" and we give them
a shove - "that sets the jack (money) out
of them" - " we put our arms together &
we give a good sexy filthy evil violent
shove - like this" - and all their hands
Buddhalike together give a shove - & see them
in action & am dismayed & annoyed
by their indifference to their victims.

    But we have to carry the visit thru,
so we ask for the cheap then Sophisticated Boss
"our friend" whose handsome secretary says
he's not in. Nothing to do. we - or Jack or
Peter - starts talking - are Secretaries. One is
a negress, he tries to get her, with her fine
dress, silence, & glasses & with school-
teacherish ruffle of talk to us, depending
on her innate hipness, and she does suddenly

"I mean, you cut the life out of a creature and maybe he suffers and maybe he doesn't, but you don't know and nobody know and only one that know is the Creature and he can't talk he's all alone in his universe of life, a whole universe maybe but nobody in control or contact in that womb but the creature and he just don't say when you kill him, whether he like it or not—so they cut the life out of my womb like all the others and nobody say nothin but just think of that poor babe down there in the bottom of his creation and what do he know except here come that gleaming knife my scalpel—and the same for all God's creatures them poor thing—nobody suffer but the when they die and that's the end of that" I weep, Naomi,[6] Joan.[7]

There is a subway rush and I am weeping and hysterical in it.

I think to myself, "Joan, nobody suffered that one death but Joan but that's ok because she chose it, it wasn't forced on her, she sat there and accepted it but just the same at least she had the final choice—tho at the last minute what does it matter, the whole universe take over & suffer inside her maybe it changes things even if superficially nobody suffer but she—somebody's got to pay for the destruction—she paid & suffered & so did the great Unconscious God where we all are. And Naomi suffered when I put her away, I thought nobody's suffer but her poor Babe but she too at the end was a whole suffering universe that knew its death."

Running away & weeping, I'm in the Hospital at closing time with

6. Naomi Ginsberg, Allen's mother, suffered from paranoid schizophrenia and spent much of her adult life in mental institutions.

7. Joan Vollmer, friend of the Beat Generation members, died when William S. Burroughs, her common-law husband, shot her when the two were playing a drunken game of William Tell.

the nurses preparing a tray of surgical knives, I'm in the room with the Scalpel tray alone, balanced on a table, it falls off the table & the nurse comes back in upset, I tell her it wasn't my fault I might upset one knife, or be upset, but the tray fell on its own. She starts picking it up—all the knives like wood carving sheath instrument machetes—and I start weeping, I tell her the whole story of the politics visit & the Negress's story & the Babe & Naomi & the Subway rush confusion & end it all explaining why I'm so agitated. She says—"That's all very interesting but as you know it certainly doesn't explain the *deep* source of your emotion, your incidents only serve to catalyze on the surface the effects of some deeper earlier worse unconscious trauma which analysis in depth would undoubtedly as you know uncover."

I think, quietly, "she doesn't accept as beautiful & meaningful this story about sterility & isolation of mine she looks deeper & I thought it was already deep—I must be lost & trying to make a good cover story to impress her. But she isn't impressed."

And I certainly do remember the real sad sterile lost thing I found, when I was looking for a restaurant—I went to one but I don't remember what was wrong, like Wimpy, I wound up in another and there it was a diner where they had ok food I was going to eat it when I suddenly saw the soupspoon, the big silver soup ladle, all tousled up, the ladle art bent over double from the handle & flattened out, old thing, I remember it—it's worn & old & the design is all half rubbed off it but it's still Naomi's old soup ladle that I've given away like my pebble (cork)—it looks mashed—as if it was bent under great pressure after I gave it away—I recognize it's of old, a beautiful and familiar useless object that I no longer own—but should I have tried to keep it, collected like other objects, like all that I lend, this a million other remembrances & tokens & symbols—so I give away Naomi's silver set early & young & there's no way of getting it back now, that soup ladle, except by fraud & trickery from the restaurant that now owns & uses it, second hand object that it is, like all the poverty stricken second hand spoons in the cabins with tin roofs in the realm of Peru where the Caretaker lives.

It's just like the first scene dream land reform problem—here I am caught at the end of my service but where are my accumulations & goods & money & land, what have I done & remembered of my work—here's the last slab—and someone comes up to me to ask where's all my land, & I don't know except that I've traded it in for something else, like one valley slab floor here for money, or food, or goods—like I have a scroll somewhere that's worth remembering the whole world of valleys—so I really haven't neglected or lost the Value of the property I used to own— that scroll is way back somewhere in the dream, in the bank of the office—I go to find the Bank.

It's the office of the Trader, the fat young politician like Towncoller, Inc. baby Brat Richman executive—he has an office. I ask him if he's cashed my check yet, he says he didn't think it was good, but I say, "O No, that Scroll here is mine, I'll bring the others, you have my check for a half year, you can cash it—I want the scroll."

"I hardly didn't believe you, dear sir, or son," he says, "but if it's good sure, the deal's on"—

"Well, let's finish off the doubt, phone the bank," I add I want to make sure the check don't bounce after all this time, it was good when I gave it to you but now a year later maybe, who knows, but I'll call"—

"Here's the phone," he says, giving me a white phone, "what bank is it?"

"I don't exactly remember, the phone, I remember where it is—I'll get it on information."

I call & try for information but they don't know. I keep reminding them at information it's the bank on 5th Avenue and 43 or 53 on the Northwest or *southeast* corner, on the block on 5th and 43—there—I go to get information from the fat trader—where is that, what's the name of that there Bank?—

He hands me his own phone which turns out to be some fake interesting expensive Chinese box, a toy not a phone, useless to continue the call that way, but the money's in the bank. Passing out of his door upstairs to the door of my apartment, near his shop door a tray full of Chocolate Buddhas, look like wood Ho-Tee's I grab one & eat it. He maybe sees me but it's minor compared to the check & scroll & I know the check is good, so I own my scroll & all the lifetime work is accounted for.

So I even have my apartment, I'm in it, with a maid to serve me, a French maid who's out the glass door (that can see in my bedroom) in the hall—

I'm inside, in bed, a knock, it's a young thin Norman Schnall or Huncke—come for help.

"I'm junk sick I can't stay alone I need your help a place a bed"—

"No, man," I say "I've had enough of that old police-death-guilt Just had a riot at the Politicos office, Joan is dead, the place is hot, I'm too hot."

"But man it's real only I suffer but I need you to lay down next to"—

So I change my mind when he grabs & embraces me, I see that I can sleep with him sexy & maybe from him when I get him junk naked in my bed he crawls into—

But the French maid has seen him grab me in bed & is knocking on the door I get up & let her in, she's shocked (like all women) but really doesn't understand or believe & she says, "I'll just come in & supervise you two, I'll sleep in your room."

Peru

"No," I say, "definitely not he's sick & needs rest I've got to take care of him in the other room & this is my room so scram & stay out."

"O.K." she says, mollified "If he's so sick."

"And maybe," I add the truth & bold & malicious "since he's sick & naked I'll fuck him too".

"What!" she says, confused!

"All right, get out," I say "You heard me"—tho I had a slight fear she'll call the police—which I didn't want. Heavy fear sooner or later the police will catch up with Joan's death & find me responsible.

I lay down next to Norman—(Norman boy)—my scroll is safe, he & his body are in my hands, my work & early life is justified—all I got to do is lay down with my back to the Needer, the Boy—and let him try and make *me*, the situation in reverse from what it used to be—they have to make me sexy, now, I play hard to get—I've got my scroll, & he's sick & he needs me—

At which I begin to awake or be conscious that I am alone in foetal position in a bed with nobody there even to make love to me & it's all dream & illusion and that I've gained naught, there is *no* love here tonite in bed with me as eternally perhaps in the end result of all the illusion, as when Death comes, I shall be loveless & alone with no progeny & son, just an imaginary sick Junky lover dependent.

When I wake the dream unravels in my mind with Lacunae & gaps as what was the cause of my grief? The thing Dying, the Babe? comes late—is deep as the Canyons of Machu Picchu—and lighting the candle to write, there is a moth fluttering, small moth on the wood footstool, one wing caught in the wax, dying alone in the universe. I free him roughly from the wax, but his wing's been destroyed & he flops and flaps in candlelight to the floor to die.

Peru

Meeting Brando

1. Burroughs-K. letter—Train
2. In theater—the seats—package left
3. Intermission
4. To the Movie
5. Conversation in Elevator a/Mason

          The Party

6. Return to theater
7. Brando's At
8. Conversation, Burroughs

    1. Kerouac

    2. Responsibility

    3. Magnif. Ambersons

    4. "Indians"

   The wrestlers

9. The party Costumes, folks, teacups
10. Go to my house
11. Return home

"Let's not run this thing down, Surprise me later"
Wrestlers climbing over balconies

In theater, a theater party to watch a rehearsal with various society folk, theatrical—I reading a letter from Burroughs at Vesuvios—at the mount—an enigmatic paranoiac & proud letter advising me that I was missing out on the great psychic mystery—secret of the Incas due to my sociological preoccupation with the workers there—letter including some very detailed delicate Kleelike sketches of the mountain—Pompeii —but with grotesque delicate thin lines & a meaning, on the margin of the letter, and some kind of date mark—1 AKIN KATUN 1. As if it were Mayan.

I show the letter to my neighbor, Elia Kazan, the Brando director—asking him if I should take it seriously—he shrugs Burroughs advice away—"He's an intelligent & corrupt Lunatic"—I think, yes, Burroughs is turning into another shroud like Cameron—in fact they're the same person—best to enjoy & ignore his force—

. Then, long delicate conversation with Kazan—"Take the first Brando Rushes Rehearsal you've seen?" "Yes" I say & explain earlier dream & intuitions & premonitions about meeting Brando—The Movie Begins.

It's a scene shot from the back of Brando's behind, he's squatting in tight pants, very laconic & hip & handsome, physically very active—he's riding a motorcycle forward on the road—except it's done in mimicry without the motorcycle & his control and subtlety pantomiming the foot activity of a bike rider moving forward is very apt, marvelous—suddenly the scene breaks, he turns & faces the camera—now the scene is over—talking directly to the director, but with consciousness of a whole theater company & half the world watching him—and he changes—he's stopped formal acting & is now egomaniacally just having a cozy chat.

"It's these toes," he says, illustrating his bare feet & showing Kazan his toes—"I have to keep the toesies straight"—He puts his big toe forward & his second toe is a little strained, he with finger gesture pulls up second toe to lie above (it's reddish & dirty like mine) the big toe, not, below it.

"If I keep my toe in line, straight, like I can make that Motorcycle activity but it's too much to put-put-put forward realistically if my toes hurt, it all depends on your toes, the whole genius of the Bike."

The audience is swooning with bliss at this lecture, but that ends the rehearsal, Brando goes upstairs to his apartment for the day and we all file out of the theater for Intermission—

Peru

At least I had assumed it was the only intermission—I left a book or a camera on the next sect—Kingsland[8] also in the audience—and some lady cultural attaches that I know—

 I'm still charming Kazan, we are now headed to another Movie or Play (earlier vast dream wandering around huge moviehouse looking for seats, I'm alone in Life's Balcony of Darkness)—Kazan suggests I go back & talk to Brando—

I go and knock upstairs in his rich apartment—he's home & is open—I walk in and pace the livingroom around the couch, talking with him—he's courteous to me—we neither of us explain, our names & fame is enough to make a reason for rapport—except he keeps reminding me how good he is—we're talking about old movies—

"Now, the Magnificent Ambersons," he says.

"Yes," I say, wanting to criticize him but refraining, so doing it indirectly by praise of that quality in Magnificent Ambersons which in Brando's later films he lacks—

"Yes, I saw that, it's a very passionate tragic picture."

"I did the commentary," he boasts, I am a little shocked at his needing to remind me what I already know, he's trying to make me praise him—and in dream his voice I get confused with Orson Welles, thinking they're the same.

I explain the price of fame & its disadvantages "Well" and I launch into my old lecture "once the sense of responsibility closes in it's the end of a sense of liberty & naïve honesty and Beauty."

He agrees tho what I say is obvious I expatiate & am trying to impress him with this covert reference to my own famous problems.

Kerouac. What does he think of Kerouac? Well he may have had con-

8. John Kingsland, a Columbia friend of Ginsberg.

Peru

versation too precipitously down unsympathetic channel but try to save it by (old) speech praising Kerouac. Brando suddenly does an imitation of Kerouac drunk, stumbling over nonsense phrases in center of party—"No genius would dry up & flop in that situation—a real Creator wd. invent some magnificent obscenity—or some great psychic music surprise having seized the limelight—but he doesn't make it, he just doesn't sing internally at that moment, if that's your Kerouac."

I defend Kerouac's genius, pointing to the writing & the sadness of that.

Just then there is an interruption, a knock on the door, which opens and in walks Huncke, hip to the fact that I've contacted Brando, to dig the scene & make out too, followed by Peter & Lafcadio[9]—which is great —sort of—I'll introduce them & Brando will dig them—Huncke coming in looking secretive & with his shoulders askew, as if to ask why he wasn't invited to the movie in the first place, Peter and Laf silent—Elia and Kingland come in, then her friends and a whole bunch of other people, in fact a huge party of 160 people all at once have come up past the downstairs door & are filing in laughing & making noise to party to take the cake & share my time with Marlon, I am desperate, they are ruining the scene—Brando is amazed & tolerant, but he's seen it all before—realize now the whole night is lost, he'll never get a chance to dig individually anyone, esp. Laf & Peter—

"Let's all move over to my house," I say—as after Bob Merins party— to evade & avoid their trick, they are taking advantage of the scene purposely fucking me up almost—I grab the initiative and (to show Brando I'm not responsible for this invasion of his house & privacy & nerves) take the burden of the party, lead it, downstairs toward my house.

9. Lafcadio Orlovsky, Peter's brother.

We all file down—I see two guys with naked chests, acrobats or mus-
clemen, on the stairway—his prop men or studio Messeurs—

Downstairs everybody grabs at the delicate chinaware on the lobby
table—It's a masquerade ball surprise party for me—some giants on leg-
stilts—one removes his mask it's LeRoi Jones.[10] I can hardly be offended
—Irving too without costume, neurasthenic—they're all there, balling,
and by the elevator I start back to Brando's flat, feeling the scene has
degenerated but maybe now pick up again & invite him to my house or
maybe continue talking to him—

I put the Chinaware, about 12 pieces cups & saucers balanced deli-
cately on my fingers, fanwise all the saucers, on the mahogany table by
the elevator, all safe, the house man, the lobby Supt, an old thin white-
haired fellow, comes over to sniff & observe (I notice one dish is broken
or cracked maybe he hasn't noticed & won't see this till I leave when he
examines & replaces the pile in neat order)—

I go upstairs—Brando sitting on the second flight in his underwear
tops, sort of relaxed, waiting, I can see he's already changed his atten-
tion & has forgotten his interest in me—

The two Masseurs now with huge hairless muscular chests are crawl-
ing acrobat & panther like up the stairway, as if by appointment, stalk-
ing Brando in his apt—it's some prearranged sexual ritual, they stalk &
overpower or fight & rape him or he rapes them, god knows what paid
obscenity & delight—

"Would you like to come to the Party?" I ask, for he said earlier he'd
be along.

"Let's not run this thing down now," he says, "let's not run things

10. LeRoi Jones (Amiri Baraka) (1934–2014), poet, writer, playwright, activist,
teacher, editor, and critic, was a friend of Ginsberg and other Beat Generation writ-
ers.

Peru

down so soon" he says sardonically—eyeing the ritualistic musclemen & disinterested—telling me in effect not to bore him or bother him now with demands that he dig this my anarchic party scene. He caps it by saying, as a kiss off, but open—"Surprise me later." The wrestlers are climbing at him over the balconies I realize I won't compete with his extravagant game & activities & perversions & indulgences as the sex men apes he has in tow & won't really have another chance at him. Wake up in Machu Picchu station, light candle & write.

Afterwards—Continue of Dream—In theater again—in upper balcony, with Francesca & L.[11] & Brando, L drunkenly hits Brando, or challenges him. B. is much bigger but scared by L's drunken intensity—They disappear together, fighting Francesca and I follow as a crowd has gathered, we rush thru crowd down back theater stairway to another balcony—at the bottom of which L. & Brando are battling latched to each other, neither giving up.

May 3, 1960—Dream in Cuzco

The Life of Ginsberg
by
John Hollander[12]

Documentary Movie

11. Lucien Carr.
12. John Hollander (1929–2013) was a poet, critic, and teacher.

I meet John Hollander in street and learn he's making a scholarly documentation of my early life as he knows it. I am surprised & flattered & confused but as he requires no cooperation on my part it is not up to me to yes or no or choose but to avoid the subject—which he wishes me to do as he is doing it on his own as an homage as if I were dead anyway. There is a sort of scholarly festive weird air to the campus, Columbia, as preparations for the surprise centennial or celebration are being made in secret without cooperation of academic authorities as well.

Preparations are being made in a Yale Lions Den or Bookstore Basement with Anne & his friends, scholarly queer librarians—Shakespeare majors, participating & preparing for a big party People going in and out of the Ivy League basement carrying posters, lettered signs, bunting, coffee & cake, old photographs, letters, newspaper clippings, volumes in translation.

I have a conversation with a bald poet, Richard Howard maybe Howard Moss or Hart of Schulman or Sackler—(is Kerouac left out of the Academic Festival?) or John—am I invited to the opening? No, I better not go as it is not my proper business. Anyhow, If I go I'd be suspected to make a dada negative demonstration & interrupt & negate the scene, end it, smash the camera or pour water on John & myself, so it would be best if I stayed away.

I go anyway on the afternoon of the opening, it's like the opening of an art show—people filing into the basement—or it's a pre-opening party to which I *am* invited. Everybody filing into the little camera observed room to see the surprise document.

I'm taken to the side room, the Periodical Room of Library, where I am shown a collection of stills supposedly documenting my life.

It begins to my surprise before my time, Depression or WWI, with a sort of confusion between me and Benjamin Paul Cohen, a sharp Jewish NYU philosopher—as representing the last of liberal USA thought—

Peru

a series of still photos or movies of the U.S.A. & statements drawn from letters—mostly Cohen's—with mine at times thrown in anonymously—misquotes from conversations or excerpts from letters—

> . . . Friday
> is the time of American Food
> That is to say blood
> running in Times Square
> where I sat in the Cafeteria

or

> "What I wonder about is where are
> you all going with your suits
> to Mexico or China or Bowery
> and will I die alone in tears still
> True to the Proletariat or no?"

etc. almost meaningless but with slight pessimistic religious fervor. Then there is a movie of the Ceremonies rededicating the Statue of Liberty & putting it back on its pedestal to which I also am not invited. Begins with Photo very phuzzy of John & friend and/or some Hollander standing in a stone stairwell gossiping at the ceremonies. Then the President, J. E. Hoover, making a microphone speech to a crowd—Then a quote from an irrational early rhymed apocalyptic personal poem—having nothing to do with the status—then a shot of Peter Orlovsky entering on a stone Incaic Platform.

I shudder in audience wondering what they'll do to Peter in film & how he'll behave. He passes in front of Camera descends step to tomb, then hesitates, looks at Camera half smirk, but saves the scene by suddenly eyeing the edge of the stone (the artwork line) strangely examining it, twice, before entering the obscurity below & disappearing.

Peru

The point is that we are subterraneans at the public festivity, present to represent the mystic, democratic spirit, but not officially there, just sneaking around the background on the stones.

Then a shot of me—in new black leather jacket—slightly ill fitting and very affected, smirking & camping, and in addition I've got on shiny new black leather pants—since I look uncomfortably silly & middle aged bourgeois almost it looks weird like some Lawrence Lipton[13] hipster outfit—

Dream breaks 4:30 AM I'm worried about waking in time to catch bus to Lima at 8 AM.

Lima Hotel Peruro

Welcome

Welcome me
Welcome, Universe, this new moment
Welcome, my thoughts dying with closed eyes in bed.
The blue dawn light entering the hotel window in Peru
Welcome this poem which comes to the table like a red lobster brought
    by a waiter in a Chinese restaurant, filled with arsenic vasoline
Welcome Death
Welcome this two sided mystery
Welcome the King on his squared couch, leaning on his elbow, misery
    again
Welcome my soul's indifference, for I am dying

13. Journalist and poet Lawrence Lipton (1898–1975) wrote *The Holy Barbarians*, an early study of the Beat Generation writers and their literature.

I haven't slept with anyone for four months and don't care
Whether it's human or not
Welcome the dead city of Machu Picchu
alone at night by man's hitching post
in the darkened center of the city
afraid to call the ghosts up
"I am the king of the Dead" I said
Welcome Ghosts
Welcome my white bare room near the central market
Welcome the Chinese Indian with the old beard
Sleeping in the street with his ass exposed
Welcome the red meat truck slowly moving in the darkness
Thru the wholesale flower sellers sweat night street
With 10 skinned goat carcasses flat on wet boards
Welcome the enormous majesty of the Pyramids
Welcome the tourists' guidebook that helps me appreciate
Welcome that I'm willing to admit
Welcome here & not here, whether I have overexposed myself
Welcome the unreal—a glass aptyrix
Welcome a new volume of writings by Corso[14]
Welcome the publication of many secret documents
full of what men really think, exposed, explained invented on, free
Welcome my ignorance of Poverty
and my knowledge of how badly off the Indians are in South America
How hard they work, and how little they get in return
but desperate footcramps in the rain on overcrowded buses on the Puno
Traveling all night to Cuzco to sell their sack of potatoes for 8oc

14. Poet Gregory Corso (1930–2001) was one of the core members of the Beat Generation.

Peru

Welcome selfish American people with too much to eat

Welcome, Caryl Chessman to poetry, you deserve it

Welcome the United States has a dirty asshole

Welcome therefore the abolition of Capital Punishment

And Clean water and Clean hands to that asshole

which must be considered everytime we take a national shit like that

Welcome revision of my opinions on the Korean war and new found
   sympathy for the Communist Camp

Welcome my war with the Communists for the future,

for the U S has failed me and I must fight the alone

for the preservation of poetry that is to say beauty

That is to say the Communists will soon get tired of improving the world

and take up the problem of States of Consciousness

By prohibiting what can only be found in the dark

which is to say, Death, which is to say

They cannot deal with the Impossible

which is to say that I can

which is to claim a great deal

Welcome Great Claim! that will murder me

But I will find out the answer and transmit it before I die

I am awaiting the proper state of Consciousness

when I can both receive the Light of Death and write it in fords

For I guess it is ready to come forth

I cannot force it, it will emerge when it will

It is alive and knows the answer it's true

and will manifest itself by accident to us but

according to Divine plan & Universal Fortune

Welcome the Unknown, unthinkable, Miraculous Being

about whom I constantly think and almost can't write

for fear of selling short with a few rapid vague words generalization

Peru

But whose Presence I have felt often enough
more than twice
to make me trust
that I will not be disappointed
in placing all my eggs in the one Basket which can't exist
like an obsessional monomaniac
to the point of interrupting the proceedings with my stupid enthusiasm
for calling attention to what is Mysterious by its own nature
and is perhaps hindered in its manifestation by my clamoring conscious-
     ness
Clamoring for relief and aid
to make a poem, or a life,
Based purely, in its final structure as will be revealed—
I will reveal it on my deathbed
to myself if to no other
Tho god grant I find some last minute way of expressing
what by the nature of this illusionary world
Cannot be admitted into the Illusion
lest the universe crack apart
and we all disappear
and my subjectivity & paranoia take over completely
and all doubt disappears from my eyes
That I was the being
that now what you say "Dies"
i.e. the houses disappear, all of you—
and that this trick may be accomplished by anyone
to the exclusion of his wife his neighbors and his dearest friend
including the four religions and the seven dead cities that have survived
     thru his lifetime
Up to that final explosive & disillusioning moment

"beside which the atom bomb is a noisy toy"

For which reason I will never run for president

Leaving it up to them who wish to remain in this world

to improve it, with all its suffering

tho the main suffer is really old Death Inimprovable

Perfect in its part, making perfect the uncomfortable for the moment

Who has happened what passes for real and can be really painful

Tho it is erased.

            Therefore Welcome,

this Confession that I am ready and not ready

to admit to four months of total solitude in irrational travels

Digging Bolivian Politics and Indian workwear

mummies & pattern weaves of decaying baskets in black museums

and emotionless musings on my own strange situation

of alien solitude and indifference to any greater cause than

Waiting to welcome

            Thee, stranger visitor

temporarily here from another world,

                to welcome me.

This is the first poem I have written in a month

since worrying about death in the airplane over the Chilean Cliff on the
    Pampas

raising up to clear the Andes & fly down on Bolivia

But I must wake at nine to talk to a reporter from a Peruvian news-
    paper

who accosted me without a tie

whom I must explain what I am thinking next

Who will think I am kidding or worse.

In the sense it's a dog's life a poet

working with Indecipherable materials

Peru

Easier to be a Communist prophet at least you can get angry at the suf-
ferings of the workers
While I admit I do get angry at my own
They pass & at better moments I think of something else, like Death
That has more limited tho probably more crucial significance
than any temporary aid I could give to the World Revelations
Which I do believe is a good thing for the masses
To leave them time to think of their coffins & trusts
and not have to stay up the night selling flowers in the streets
Including children who suck in penny candy
and can hardly wash their underwear.
Welcome Death & Death's Children.
Let us prepare for the Market
If you sell your vegetables, I'll sell my meat,
Week be both nuts
when we finally get paid equal
by the Great Capitalist of Darkness
and his foreign exchange of total eclipse instead of just dead chickens
incurable cancer with 6 mouths to feed.

Codeinetta—May 14, 1960—Hotel Commercio
5 PM—Lima, Peru

I'm full of yellow water which I discharge from time to time
like a locomotive or a cow, bull, turkey, elephant
The human machine, that shits and dies.
I have some interests—my crap's yellow and gurgles in my belly in the
street
They use newspapers here to wipe that part of the body—
oily rags for locomotives

Peru

Alone in hotel across the street from Presidential palace.

Pizarro's bones, I glimpsed in a glass coffin one block away,

500 years before me here.

My mother's bones in America too

How many bones in the ground—and more get born to that old trick—

and never suspect till the time comes—I had cramps for six blocks, run-
ning home

to take codeine and relax in bed with a bright bird on an Indian blan-
ket—wool.

God in Pain for our fault—consciousness.

Like a lover rejected.

Alone, here in bed in Peru, with a beard—the hotel clerk knows my se-
cret, he read it in the papers—he thinks I'm crazy and what does that
mean in my solitude when all I want is—no boy comes up to me out of
a dark street and looks me in the eyes and takes my hand, and lets me
kiss him in the—Soul, or body—where is it in a dark street full of beggars
with their bones that die at 32—too early—and I would be tender, if I
could tell the truth to one—but my beard's too long and black, and my
head hair's beginning to go away, like life—my Craziness is only a lot on
death, so be a spy—tell all my secrets fast to the streets—in poetry or
newspapers, open my mouth to Someone, even the abstract Ghost of
Everybody in the World—Lacking one, in the night, in the dark streets
in Lima, near the market, when my feet hurt, and I am afraid to lift my
head from the pavement, and look in all the eyes long time—men with
racks on back, newsboys, girl flower sellers, looking for eyes like mine,
that might give Hope, a wink and a long hand full of soul, and that secret
liberty that comes to two men fucking in a bed anonymous and new like
a cock rising on the belly, making a sign older than Peru, or Spain, or
the first king of the Incas—that any handsome boy might make, if he

Peru

had secrecy and trust—get back to God's original nakedness—or man's—where we are friends—have met before, will always meet in any city, a street in every age—O street of Life—and now more dusk again I walked last night all thru the Shoemaker's pavilion in the used clothes market, took a bus downtown, and ate alone in a Chinese restaurant, waiting for Sign—ate a poor dead delicious fish rotten red tomatoes—enjoyed that Sensuality—slowly the year's passing—and I've watched 33 & that's the half—losing hope—only the memory of a Light that might be More—requiring some dreamlike change, some kind of death of me—without which, incompletion, love ache, mental trickery, and boredom till one Day of Fright—and I don't know any more. Where's Redemption! Not in this world! Not even a little love, that'll last—a minute in the Vast—Hourglass—that's my eternity—all in one instant and begone from here—where I might have been—if I had remembered.

Because yesterday morning when I woke coughing from Inca cigars, life was thin—almost disappearing to my consciousness like an apparition—a phantom killed by its own cough—felt that on my deathbed I would know what mistake I made that killed me, made me disappear, wasted my life to that thin disappearing Phantom smoked too much—some fatal flaw, without which, is eternal life—which by my bad habit, Karma smoke—I had run down and wasted, lost, neglected—all's unusual, waking from one dream.

And when my time comes it'll be too fast, like the end of an unconscious cigarette. Like when I smoke too much, and suddenly see I'm down to the butt—and it's time to put the cigarette out—or burn my finger at the end—but the spark'll die pretty soon, there's no hope here.

And the other day visiting the Catacombs of St. Francis (Lima)—all those anonymous bones—that went nowhere—these people & careers—nobody left in the basement of that Church, but their dry bones, mum-

Peru

mies, shells, & empty thankless skulls with holes for eyes and empty space where a brain once palpitated and thought and schemed more Cathedrals. It's amazing once they were real as me.

and how many Indians on the street see death every day and take their Cancer for breakfast in silence, knowing they're lost—all the enormous bones.

Nasca, Paracas, Chancay, Ica, Tiahuanaco, Purkara, Mochica, mort. Left some pots behind, they're beautiful effigies. That pot's dead like a skull, and lasts a long time—some thousands of years. I have one with a living fish painted inside it.

Tinkle of guitar from adjacent hotel room, in the warm foggy dusk, down the wooden hall, 1960, always return to one note.

an old Frenchman, with silver rim spectacles & white mustache—my eyes closed—sits down on the bench next to me with his arm over the back of my chair—

This room is where I'll take the Ayahuasca.

—a shiver of fear. A real magic mirror.

> Banjo, harmonica
> in the hall, suddenly
> the heavy cathedral bells.

Lying in bed knowing death in advance, twinkle of genitals, hearing guitar.

The headhunters don't care, thru this transience. They enter a black universe, where each head is magic. "Peace" down the hall

The illusion takes place in the void, because there's nothing to stop it. Anything can happen—even headhunters

Peru

Civilization not far from the headhunters—army majors & barefoot longhair visionaries in the jungle. O the poor starving and straining to the Lima streets.

"Circa allegira"—Happy Wax—and the colored carved velas (Candles) they sell in Churches here.

7 o'clock church bells in Lima—this Century and all day the winter warm fogs come down the street of Time here.

Ah in Paris how I used to lie back in Git le-coeur[15] with the white smoke of H. in my head & my nostrils full of its death sweet smell.

The great sadness of death in mankind.

Oh, Neal, you too in my dreams tonite—as often in solitude traveling—and Gregory, the joy of his black hair, and Peter's long nose & Jack's ruddy belly, and Bill's long thin skeleton—and the dead Joan. To Peter Orlovsky in all his radiance. And dear Al Sublette,[16] half paralyzed with explanatory wine.

All that time in San Francisco's gone away—but could come back if we all collected there again—and Neal's just out of jail[17]—next month.

All our sincerity is lost except to each other, in the great wave of poverty and war.

I do not wish to lose the key how to open the door to the secret other world—once it's lost men may not be able to enter again—it's hermetic—and there are many universes? This road—or the other? and all may go one way, or lose track in Time of the other. The formula for Ayahuasca.

15. The "Beat Hotel" in Paris, where many Beat Generation figures, including Ginsberg, lived in the 1950s.

16. Al Sublette was a friend and influence to Jack Kerouac.

17. Cassady served two years in San Quentin after being convicted of selling a small amount of marijuana to an undercover cop.

Peru

My beard my beard my hanging Beard my innocent wisdom my curse in the streets my magic hair my Mask of Death my ode to Anarchy & Transcendence my face disfigured and hidden behind olden habit my Hebrew Sign of False Face, my Destiny that can be wiped off—lying back in bed, eyes closed, glasses off, I rub my eyes & wonder why it is there, how strange of one to be beardy.

"I am in Pain, Colors are pain and we are Pain." Imaginary Yage postcard to Bill: "Who knows more"—I have seen this before?

Still fighting with Self, but I am almost ready to give up my soul to the future unknown—take the Drug.

My Command—to tie up the mystery in a knot—of words—forever—it is a mystery to understand the nature of consciousness.

Function of consciousness is to examine nature of being.

Being hath consciousness, which is built in to being. Strange the tong of the ball tongue of the bell reminds me of the small (Great) Illusion (Universe)

Being. O Being of many Beings! Of King of being (kink of Beings)

Codean's [*sic*—codeine?] thickness of mind—passed already 2 hours away.

Dr Johnson struck the pavement with his cane, and shouted, "I exist"—Poor skull. The block was real, but only for a minute. The dimension he should have measured was not space but time. Forget that, he did. And now his proof's undone—the cane and street are gone, or nearly gone, and he's poked a hole thru the universe, personally. Time proved Berkeley right, the solipsistic thesis kills—the dimension proof's in Einstein's "Space gets warped?" by too many winters. How many summers has his skull? How many summers hid his skull—

Ice in the United States? Helados in Los Estados Unidos? See in the United States.

Peru

Dream—

Walking in Street, old New York, trying to cross a bridge past a truck—small bridge over stream the water is almost curved & a swift rising & falling current that I enter (wake thinking of Mochica) (clearcut human pottery figures)—& enter the stream & can't get out till I struggle thru the well defined current of water to the other side— arrive—after a whole bus is lifted across a bridge, washed in the current backwards—I get to the steps of the dry side—to the dry steps, thinking ... these are the "Magic steps of Poe"—dry magic steps of Poe, old houses with burnt crossbeams, dry, on one side of the Dutch water— Corso, received letter from him today, too.

To Martin Adan[18]

Because we met at dusk
Under the shadow of the railroad Station
Clock
By my hotel Commercio by Accident
while my shade was visiting Lima
and your ghost was dying in Lima
old face needing a shave
and my young beard sprouted
        magnificent as the dead hair
                in the sands of Chancay

18. First draft of "To an Old Poet in Peru," *Collected Poems, 1947–1997* (New York: HarperCollins, 2006), 247–49. All citations from this book will hereafter be abbreviated *CP*. Martin Adan (1908–1985) was a Peruvian metaphysical poet.

Because you saluted my eyes
     with your anisette voice
and I saluted your 6o year old feet
     which smell of the death
         of spiders on the Pavement
and I mistakenly thought you were
         melancholy,
and you mistakenly thought I was genial
         for a youth
(my rock and roll is the motion of an
         angel flying in a modern city
your obscure shuffle is the motion
         of a seraphim that has lost
            its wings
I kiss you on your fat cheek
Three times once more tomorrow
     at nine o'clock
Under the stupendous Desguadros Clock)
before I go to my death in North America
     many years from now
and you go to your heart attack on an indifferent street
     in South America
(Both surrounded by screaming
     Communists with flowers
     in their ass)
much sooner than I
     That much nearer the great Black Door
and a long nite alone in a dark room
     or in the old hotel of the world

Peru

   watching a black door
—where a stranger enters the door
   And in his hand a mirror
Concentrated shifting brightness of the void
   Blinds me in my bed
Surrounded by scraps of paper . . .

      *

   Die greatly in thy Solitude
old man
   and prophecy Reward
Vaster than the sands of Pachacamac
Brighter than a mask of hammered gold
More swift than time passed
   between old Nasoa night
    and New Lima
     in the Dusk
Sweeter than the joy of armies naked fucking on the
   battlefield
more strange than that we
   meet
as strangers by the Presidential
   Palace in an old Café
ghosts of an old illusion, ghosts
   of an indifferent love—

The Dazzling Intelligence

  Migrates from Death

To make a sign of Life again
             to you

Fierce and beautiful as a car crash
             in the Plaza de Armas

I swear that I have seen that Light
& will not fail to kiss thy hideous cheek
        when your Coffin is Closed
and the human mourners
        go back to their old tired
             Dream.

And you wake in the Eye of the
        (Time—) Dictator of the Universe.

Another Stupid Miracle! We
        are all mistaken!

your indifference! my enthusiasm!

        I insist! You Cough!

Lost in the wave of gold that
        flows thru the Cosmos.

Agh I'm tired of insisting! Goodbye,

        I'm going to Pacallpa
to have Visions.

Peru

    Your clean sonnets?
I want to read your dirtiest
    Secret scribblings,

          your Hope,
in His most obscene Magnificence. My God!

             May 14, 1960

          Chancay

on one side of the road roses and corn
    irrigated green fields by the Sea
on the other the desert up to the hills
    Sand Crotches in the rocky precipices
And vast plains of dust, scattered
    with little golgothas,
        skulls brown as rain
  or parchment-black, with long red hair
    wound with rope turbans
thigh bones, jugs, fragments of clay\
      animals
    whistles and baskets in the sand
a thousand holes where the graverobbers
    poke their metal wands at night
and I took a Crap in an open grave
    my shit and blood and
      white toilet paper
fluttering limped in the sand
    under the foggy sky

next to a polished skull, white as the sun,
and fragments of Chancay Pottery
with abstract designs.

May 20, '60

Poem of the Phantasm

As the fantasm Beyond
Big white sheet two holes for eyes
inside black mystery
like the inside of a skeleton's head in the dark
behind the Catacombs
Here in broad daylight
I appear with a hollow voice
in front of the church in the street
on top of an automobile
Proclaiming the Reign of my Kingdom
Beyond where man can't go
But with millions of entrances to my Mystery
Death, Drugs, dreams, suicide, fantasy
theater, music, hunger ecstasy of the sex
nausea of the air, moments of absence of the mind
instances of the black camera of hallucination
each one a million windows to my skull: Come in.

 I will now proclaim what you cannot know
What's impossible, what's behind the big white
sheet of the mind, behind the Illusion of that universe

I phantasm am the prophet
I phantasm am the sex fiend of the Infinite
I phantasm am the voice of God
I am the great white elephant of Eternity
Wherein the little larks sing on the summer trees
All these thousand of my years—
I am the million leaves that fall all the time
Like leaves falling in a globe of water slowly—
I have as many kingdoms as you have your minds
as many heroes of suffering and dying to every one
which is real, and endless deaths to offer Beings
from every quarter of the Universe, all transcending their poor flesh or
    rock or filmy substance as they're made
to join me behind my sheet and laugh
at the tigers stalking the fawns
in the jungle of Existence

Die! human beings: suffer and rot and die
and know my kingdom and the filmy loss of yours
and all of yours, phantasms! with the same one mind
behind waiting for the entrance of All Souls
garbled in ecstatic deliverance
To my one Bland Crack

And sweeter Joy
    than naked armies fucking
        on the battlefield

God is so beautiful
that it doesn't make any difference

Peru

whether he

exists or not.

Mercado Mayorista

Lima, 20 May 1960

Or that is to say, God is so beautiful it doesn't make any difference whether we see him or not.

Or, there is an X resolution of the paradox of existence that is so perfectly sublime that it makes no difference whether we know it or not.

Which seems to leave us out, as human level from importance, but as I warned you the resolution is so sublime it makes no difference that it includes us in an inconceivably beautiful way.

In Chinese restaurant on Avenida Arion Lima sitting at midnite with notebook after good bite of badly fried shrimps, over cup of coffee, scribbling—I must look crazy to the waiters—strange wildhair debonair self-assured prophet—in Chink restaurant of the World-Night (Lima 1 a.m.)—and above all scribbling the final definition of God. While Peruvian hepcats, girls with long red hair, pour beer at next table under fluorescent lite.

This is the understanding perfected in nearly mathematical form in words. Now to the next stage which is to incorporate it in my body so that it makes no difference whether I live or not to this Consciousness which is called Allen Ginsberg & clings to that energetically, afraid of blood.

Beauty or truth is so perfect it makes no difference whether the universe exists or not.

This reconciles the Void of Laughing Gas with the Transcendent Dancing Spirit of Lysergic Acid.

Peru

Tomorrow to take Ayahuasca. All this thinking excited by preparation & several doses of thoughtful codeine this week.

Opio makes you think & dream

Pot makes you perceive

Peyote makes you doubt thought & perception

LSD makes you transcend thot & perception

Laughing gas obliterates the whole process

Nature makes you know.

I.e. with opio, I conceive of the transience of Universe with pot I see the archetypes dreaming with peyote I see thru the solidity of the dream of archetypes with Laugh Gas my senses and the universe are annihilated with LSD I transcend my senses to see the Ideal and Eternal and in moments of Natural Illumination I see the Eternal in the archetypes of Transience.

Cocaine, Snow, makes the archetypes seem more brilliant.

Suppression of these drugs is intentional suppression of an available Western technique for developing the consciousness.

Suppression of drugs is suppression of consciousness of the secrets of Nature, i.e. the substitution of a limited soul consciousness, geared to mechanical social suppression for infinite divine consciousness.

All the above, Mercado Mayorists night notes.

"all straw"—

That means I will have to be destroyed.

Peru

Ayahuasca—

I have come home, I am the God, and I demand admittance thru the Door.

I have suffered enough ignorance in chaos which is Creation—May 21, 1960

[...]

Last nite drank till 6 AM with half fairies
   Mean boys of Lima that wanted to talk
   to my money
and staggering home in the morning presented
   100 Sole bills to old lady grabbing
   in the paper rubbish by a bank.

Death being a blind crack in the universe is evidently a great strange joke on existence.

The Universe is nothing but a lot of accumulated (comic) consciousness that will drift away—after men die, the rocks & trees will perish then the worlds & suns decompose then matter itself will return to its immaterial origin, then we will have some peace. Meanwhile we have all these problems of maintaining an unstable & disintegrating universe. Because it rests on the Void, Being is transient, because it will be forgotten, illusory. There's nothing to know or remember.

Therefore to be ready to release consciousness is the universal dangerous final thing—Mystic, Death.

Peru

A Glass of Ayahuasca

in my hotel from overlooking Desamperados' Clanging Clock,
with the French balcony doors closed, and luminescent fixture out
"my room took on a near eastern aspect" that is I was reminded of
    Burroughs
with heart beating—and the blue wall of Polynesian Whorehouse, and
mirror framed in black as if in Black Bamboo—and wooden slated
    floor
and I in my bed, waiting, and slowly drifting away
but still thinking in my body till my body turned to passive wood
and my soul rocked back & forth preparing to slide out on eternal
    journey
backwards from my head in the dark
An hour, realizing the possible change in consciousness
that the soul is independent of the body and its death
and that the Soul is not Mek it is the wholly other "whisper of con-
    sciousness" from Above, Beyond, Afuera—
till I realize it existed in all its splendor in the Ideal or Imaginary
Toward which the me will travel when the body goes to the sands of
    Chancay
And at last, laying in bed covered my body with a splendid robe of In-
    dian manycolors wool,
and yelled in my mind "Open up, for I am the Prince of eternity
come back to myself after a long journey in chaos
open the Door of Heaven, My Soul, for I have come back to claim my
    Ancient House
Let the Servants come forth to Welcome me and let Silent Harp
    make music

Peru

and bring my apparel of Rainbow and Star show me my shoes of
    Light and my Pants of the Universe
Spread forth my meal of myriad lives, My Soul, and Show up thy Face
    of Welcome
For I am the one who has dwelled in the secret Temple before, and I
    have been man too long
And now I want to Hear Music of Joy beyond Death,
and now I am he who has waited to Welcome myself back Home
The great Stranger is Home in his House of Joy."

or words or thoughts or sensations images to that effect.

This for an instant the Sensation of this Eternal House passed thru
    my hair
tho I couldn't liberate my body from the bed to float away—
tho did glimpse the foot of the thought of the gate of Heaven—

Then opened my eyes and saw the blast of light of the real universe
when I opened the window and looked at the clock on the RR Station
with its halfnaked man & woman with cubs, creators of time and
    chaos,
and down on the street where pastry vendors sold their poor sugar
symbolic of Eternity, to Passerby—and great fat clanking beast of
    Trolley
with its dumb animal look and croaking screech on the tracks
Powered by electric life, turned a corner of the Presidential Palace
where Bolivar 200 years ago in time planted a secret everlasting Fig-
    tree
and a fog from another life crept thru its own dimension

Peru

Past the cornice of the hotel and traveled downward in the street

To seek the river—had a bridge with little humans crossing, faraway

—and up in the hills the silver gleam of sunlight on the horizon thru
thick fog

—and the Cerro San Christobal—with a cross stop and Casbah of
poor consciousness ratted on its hip—

and overall the vast blue flash & blast of open space

the Sky of Time, empty as a big blue dream

and as everlasting as the many eyes that lived to see it—

Time is the God, is the Face of the God,

As in the monstrous image of the Ramondi Chavin Sculptured Stone
Monument

A cat head many eyed sharp toothed god face long as Time,

with different eyes some upside down and 16 sets of faces

all have fangs—the structure of one consciousness

that waits upstairs to Devour man and all his universes

—turn the picture upside down—the top eyes see more than the hu-
man Bottom rows

Indifferent, dopey, smiling, horrible, with shakes and fangs—

The huge gentle creature of the Cosmic Joke

that takes whatever form it can to Signify that it is the one that has
come to its Home

where all are invited to Enter in Secret eternally

After they have been killed by the illusion of Impossible Death.

Then to Bebe Montoya's house, a taxiride thru Lima in 1960 after-
noon to the waiting suburbs.

Lay in the dark & heard the Clang and Trumpets of Mahler's mes-
sage of unearthly

Peru

Resurrection and read poor pious heartfelt Bruno Walther's

testimony over His Secret Friend and Translation of Mahler's

Poem—"I am

    reborn, Life after life"—And the great rainbow of sound making

    Affirmation in Chorale and Tchaikovsky's 5th Symphony final

from his consciousness raying over the Sea of Music.

"The universe is my family" said Philip Whalen[19]

Message: Improve your consciousness & you will improve

The material conditions of the universe.

Otherwise, Create nothing by more chaos.

This, a selfconscious message to the Communists

as for the Bourgeois and the reactionaries, they have Created Hell

But it does not Matter. Find Heaven!

It is a big secret of the Mind.

 Read the message of the Ancient Pottery. Art is a Catalyst.

There is no answer! in what is thinkable Only Miracles are true.

The Desaguaderos Station Clock Struck 15 minutes before 2

May 24, 1960—Lima, Peru—red glow in the sky

    a huge dog barks a block away

        cough rattle of old cars

        Creaking fast on the street—

    a locust singing on my balcony,

19. Philip Whalen (1923–2002), poet associated with the San Francisco Poetry Renaissance, was one of the readers at the Six Gallery poetry reading during which Ginsberg publicly read "Howl" for the first time. Whalen, a devout Buddhist, assisted Ginsberg in his own Buddhist studies.

Peru

half heard by my

        Consciousness—

                              on a white bed

    A cot for love, lay down next to Neal—the vultures as I write settling down a dozen black on the RR Station Cornice—both of us naked under a white sheet—his body hard as skull or steel under the soft flesh—both of us not having come for such a long time, both of us not having made love—I put my arms round his thighs and with my elbow feel he has a delicate hard phallus, so touch it gently with my fingers & close my hand around it & pull my whole body next to his touching skin to skin my upper belly against his hip & side. He puts his arm around my neck & holds me close, and I start to go down on him to put his cock against my lips & kiss, then he twists down in abandon with part of the sheets aside so that his ass is on the bed & cock sticks up, and his body relaxes off the side of the cot with his head on the floor, luxurious, watching me, but I want to hold him and blow him I start to pull him up, his cock touches my asshole—I have hemorrhoids—I shake free say no—and lift him—he is huge and hard, his whole body—back on the bed to lay all the way alongside him to blow him completely—the sheet covers his belly and face but his cock is exposed—I lean down to take his cock in my mouth— a moment elapses, I can't in the dream—then I get there and touch lips to take it all the way in my mouth, holding on to his back—he has a large & very stiff stick, rock, pale, total boy waiting—exchange of desire between us is beautiful—I wake with harder hardon at 7 AM in Lima than had in 4 months.

                                   May 25, 1960

Later in the morning—all over town, the weird begins, wires reverse, trolleys run backward, time goes upside down—you start to call the police and find yourself in jail, you demand to see the judge & the cops are chasing a fire, you set out for home and find yourself downtown. The gods or the controllers have put a hex on the world. I'm with a paternal friend, i.e. a protector—who is also helpless—a large dark man, Neal or Brando but Jewish—An Armor is over everything—we are trapped in a room with doors locked, or we lock ourselves in with several other people, schoolgirls & boys—Unable to reach any control hq. or make sense out of the situation—and the houses are covered with a coat of petrified mud that blurs their contours—(like a peruvian huaco covered with hard stony dirt).

I offer myself up for experiment with electricity—to take a huge shock treatment & see if I can reverse the reverse—"Shock for America"—That is we are in a state of amnesiac control and if by shock I can break the spell perhaps can reverse the blackout—

"You might die."

"That means god is behind the action so I'll go up & complain so that's OK too."

I get up on a table & they wind the wires around me from shoulder to foot lengthwise round my body—

My friend lies down next to me & holds me to prevent me from falling or being flipped off when I receive the shock.

For an instant I suspect him of being the malevolent genius behind the World-Reversal.

"You'll get the shock, too," I warn him.

"Never mind, you might fall off the table," he says comforting me—wants to protect.

The only worry is that the reversal has affected the electricity—that somehow it may short circuit or have effect opposite planned. But it seems the only way to resolve the enigma of the rehearsal (for Death).

They turn on the power—nothing happens because the thin black wires snap. I wake up, waiting for them to fix the wires, worried, but resolved to go thru with the attempt.

I wonder why I was so brave, audacious in the dream—knew the electricity would fail perhaps.

May 26

Yesterday I was writing in heaven[20] or of heaven or the day before yesterday and this morning back where I started from dreaming of Neal—And

Went to a Turkish bath

And wrapped my Belly in a white towel

and set selfconscious in the

dry steam clear hot room

staring at my knees

Then under a shower soaped my balls and ass

Then went and lay down in the small dark dormitory

with a white cloth over my genitals and put

my arms behind my head

and relaxed—a hand crept up my leg

and a mouth came down on my cock

and a warm slurp greeted my mysticism

with the lights out

but an old German with white hair and glasses sneaked in and took over

20. First draft of untitled poem published in *Wait Till I'm Dead: Unpublished Poems*, ed. Bill Morgan (New York: Grove Press, 2016), 33–34.

Peru

from the younger Peruvian and after saluting my knees and belly with
kisses

and further slurps

flopped down to suck, and I thought not after
    4 months OK I'll come—
but he got impatient and the Peruvian
       watching hissing in Spanish
     heche te bastante de saliva
     make a lot of saliva
The old German lifted his wings
   and sat down with his ass over my prick
     like a tomb
ground down with his pelvis on my pubic hair unside down
and began sucking away with his asshole
       till I thought I would come
       but he quit—and went

     and sucked off the Peruvian
     and I lay back with open eyes in the Dark
in Lima
And enjoyed my nudity and the Creepy sex of the World
    Waiting for some white skinned angel to come
        Finish off the job.

27 May '60
   I spent the day with Walter young Peruvian hip boy taking Paracod-
ina[21] in afternoon and in morning left Hotel Commercio with him to

---

21. Paracodina is a powerful cough suppressant.

walk by Rimac to El Monton Mountain, The Mountain of Garbage, a mile wide and ten stories high, with a huge road big as Jiron Union entering it in the middle and ascending majestic as the hiway Stairs to Paradise of the movies—herds of pigs with shepherds with rubber whips, horses chasing each other trailing ropes on the mesa of rotten anchovy smelling smoky garbage—land—a boy sitting on the soft vegetable ground eating a mirror—Garbage trucks drove up & the people with their sacks & baskets all rush up fighting for first place to grab tin cans, woodsticks, bottles, urine-stained stockings, rotten lettuce leaves, crazy tomatoes, vomited potatoes, bandages—all the leftovers & filth & throwaway shit of Lima for a generation piled up in a mountain with streets, corners, alleyways, barriers, even a banana vendor's cart & soda stand atop the monstrosity—the asshole of Lima—and a sexy acrid smell overall, pigs screaming & mounting each other, mules fucking in broad daylight on the garbage, whole families relaxing in their corners waiting for favorite trucks to arrive, boys resting their wheelbarrows of broken chairs, and several blocks of specialty shops—wood, cans, broken chairs, bottles & glass—lining the alley to the ruins.

Aether in Peru—(Chloraethoyl Merz)

5:45 Notes—

(1) Therefore there are two certain repeated determinate indefinite referential points of understanding in a limited by definitely (whistle) (bloody) apocalyptic universe—Fini—This is the revelation of laughing Gas Also the effect of all other repeated states of consciousness.

(2) The Universe is an illusion.

(3) At moments there is a sensation of repetition of mathematically preformulated states of being.

(4) I hear all the other universes (in operation)

(5) Somebody's got to pay—if the bottle ever drops or explodes (an-

other universe, which will (I sense it) occur—all conditions occurred. Concurrently.

After Aether (9PM) (May 27)

That is, *someone* (me) has to *experience* & *suffer* thru as *real*, all the imagined situations in all the imagined worlds.

The sense I get was that these situations (horror scenes, dropping bottle, situations the reverse (mirror image reverse) of what actually seem to happen *do* happen *have already* in fact happened, and are going to happen again. Each to be repeated an infinite number of times till infinity is all played out—but that there *is* an end, an escape from the wheel of ignorant repetition of Being.

In another world, Walter who liked me when we sniffed, will not like me, will reject me, or we will have horrifying heart attacks & drop dead on each other—Ugh, what a spirit has to put up with! All the Maya-real horrors of all the real worlds. As long as they are real.

11:15 PM Same Day—another try-—

4 sniffs & I'm high—
Underwear in bed,
    white Cotton in Left Hand,
  Archtype degenerate
      bloody old taste in my mouth
         of Dentist's Chair
     remembrance of sound
         of clockbells & Airplane Buzz
    and music, and Loud Farts of Eternity—
(use that word all the time)—
An owl with eyeglasses scribbling in the   cold darkness—

Peru

Black hat on a mirror,
    Mirror thin mirror against the blue
and the sound of cricket chirps, wall—
    against my ears in the
        instant before unconsciousness
            before,
the teardrop in my eye to come—
the Fear of the Unknown—

 All the time the sound in my eardrums
    of the trolleycars below
and the itch in my ass of hemorrhoids,
    —No, not my "human" ass!

The ringing sound in all the senses
    of everything that has ever been created,
    All the combinations recurring over and

One does not yet know whether Christ was
        God or the Devil—
Buddha is more reassuring.

Yet the experiments must continue!

Every possible Comgination of Being—all
    the old ones all the old Hindu,
        Sabahadbabadie-pluralic   universes

        Ringing in Grandeloquent
            Bearded Juxtaposition,

Peru

with all their Minarets and moonlit
          towers enlaced with iron
              or porcelain embroidery,
all have existed—
          and the Sages with
white hair who sat Crosslegged on
              a female couch—
harkening to whatever music came
          from out the wood or street,

whatever bird that whistled in the
          Marketplace,

Whatever note the clock Struck to Say
          Time—
whatever drug, or airs, they breathed
       to make them think so deep
        or hear as simply what
          had passed
Like a Car passing in the 1960 street
       Beside the Governmental Palace
          in Peru, this Lima,
in the year I write.
        Kerouac! I salute thy
wordy beards. Sad prophet!
      Salutations and low bows from
bagged Pants and turbaned mind and horned feet,
      My own! The Devil's—that which
must exist—that *all* exist, with all

Peru

Its horns & arched eyebrows and Jewish Smiles,
All! All! All! All! Including that which
  will break its back & suffer on the
    Mountain
of garbage where I went 2 days ago to see
   the goats & pigs, mules, copulate,
   One Single specimen of Eternity—each
of us poets.
Break the Rhythm! (too much pentameter)

   I should write K. a letter—I owe him one, full of everything . . .
i.e. Confession. Afraid to write because of his mother.
Kerouac whom I love most.
 Who tries me most—
 Who makes me devil most,
    Kerouac who's true,
    Kerouac who's hypocrite,
    Kerouac who lets the chain fall down,
Who heard the whoosh of car wheels in the rain—

My god what solitude are you in Kerouac
 Now, and *why*?
And Every ball went off on Time,
And Everything that was Created
Rang especially in view of the Creation
For
This is the end of the creation,
This is the redemption spoken of
This is the view of the created (those Created)
 By all the Drs, nurses, etc. of

creation;

i.e.—

*I just nodded because of the secondary
negation*

The unspeakable passed over my head for
    the second time
        and still can't say it:

i.e. we are what is *left over* from
    the elimination of perfection
    left over from the irrational—
The universe man old mistake
I've understood a million times before and always come back to the
same point—

The

Sooner or later all Consciousness will

    be eliminated
        because Consciousness is
A by-product of—
        (Cotton & N2O)

Drawing Saliva back from the tongue is
    concomitant symptom
        (always experience)
With breasts—

(This) *Consciousness is Relative* to this
      Existence which is *not*
        Absolute—

     So what's the Good of it all.
Christ! you struggle to understand
   one Consciousness
  & get confronted with myriads—
after a billion years
    with the same old ringing in the ears,
     and smile of accidental creation,
and known it *all* before.
    A Buddha as of old, with the stress of
Whatever machinery making ringing noises in
      The street.
And a triple light reflected in the RR Station
     front façade window in a
       dinky port in Backwash
   of the murky old forgotten
      fabulous whatever
      civilization of
       eternity—
with the RR Sta Clock ring midnight,
   as of now,
      a waiting for the 6th
      you write your
       word,
and end on the last Chime—and remember

   This *one* twelve was struck
     before,

and *never again*; both It's every Case
at once, and all satisfied

Everything ratified to the third fourth fifth
Germanic, part.—this excludes 6th, 7th, etc.—

        All the others left out in the dark—
The other Creates its *own*

        The universe is Ether has horrible
meaning (See W. James)[22]—
    That madness of germannesses looking forward
        in the dark
I am one of the experiments on the way to my own
        Consciousness
& side result,

      Horrors!
I have feeling Walter will come in any minute—
and that every incident in the universe is a
        wave (of the different possibilities
   & eliminations) (a click in the light)
another recollection all tied in a flick in the electric current
and I turn back alone, & sad, & sentimental
     from the balcony where I stand looking
        at the cross (afraid) and the
        Stars above—
in Lima, thinking of you, Jack, as you think or have

22. William James (1842–1910), labeled the "Father of American Psychology," was a psychologist, philosopher, teacher, and the author of *The Varieties of Religious Experience*, which had a profound influence on Ginsberg.

Peru

thought or will think & now do

think again of me—

old lover in the night.

The universe is created in every

language—including German—

in every *other* than my one, own

speech, Mind

I would continue, but won't—get away the

cotton & the scientific tube of

mystic scent & sleep,

with all my disappointments & regrets—

Hopeful of whatever void—

─────

W has got to come, this is one consciousness he

can't avoid—

Including the last light out in all the worlds

"God's last "put out the light" was spoken"

Old Frost & Louis too, & all the rejected Fathers, will

be justified, all will be justified

in their own time.

including the moment I stood on the balcony

waiting for an explosion—

in *this* life, of this real mind, of Total

Consciousness of the All—

with or without dependent accidental conditions

Like being Ginsberg sniffing ether in Lima

Peru

The same old struggle of Mind, repeated over
  and over again, to understand itself.
And failing everytime,
   and repeating the experiment in the void,
not reaching the Thing,
  which eliminates all experiment
    and all mistake and dubiety
  and ends the process with an X
   which comprehends
     All that came before
  and will come after
and is unexplainable to each, except in
  a secret recollective hidden
   half-hand unrecorded
    way. . .
as the old Sages in Asia, or the white beards in Persia,
  Scribbled on the margins of their Scrolls
   in delicate ink
remembering with tears the Ancient Clockbells of their
     Cities
and the Cities that had been—
  as visiting Machu Picchu
I thought of the Wisdom & Secrecy of the
   Priests
buried, in beautiful clothes—Cat gods
  of many colors, a repeated pattern
   with changes of color,
  back to the original
   a funeral Shroud
    for a museum—

Peru

or lost in the sands of Paracas—
none remember their wisdom
but all return to the same thought before
they die
or many times before they die—
and in Streets of Machu Picchu—what sad old
knowledge, as my own
or yours—and what finality,
as my own or yours
which we repeat again,
only to be lost
in the Sands of Consciousness, or wrapped in a mystic shroud
of Poesy
and found by some lad in a thousand years
inspire dreadful thoughts of his own?
It's a horrible, lonely experience. And
Gregory's letter & Peter's letters. And unwritten letters to
Jack. Thanks God I wrote Bill. And Louis—and Gene—and Irving &
Huncke
& everyone I love.

♥

May 28, 1960
7:30 PM
. . . In the Dregs of Circumstance.
"Male & Female He created them."
with mustaches.

There *are* certain *repeated* (pistol shot) reliable points of reference
which the insane (pistol-shot repeated outside the window—madman
writes—the Pistol Shot outside—the *repeated* situation the experience

Peru

of return to the same place in Universal Creation time—and everytime we return we recognize again that we have been here & that is The Key to Creation—the same pistol shot—<u>bending over (the madman) his book with his mustache,</u>

9 PM Useless to seek a "meaning" because the "meaning" has no meaning in this existence, and only makes sense in another Spherelessness where our Brain & existence don't exist & operate.

—bending over (the madman) his book of Unintelligible Marvels with his mustache

What I experience in Depth, is unintelligible to me. Unintelligible realities.

That pistol shot—didn't I hear it also in the dentist's office[23] a year ago?—

Madness is intelligible reactions to
    Unintelligible Phenomena
        Boy—what a marvelous bottle
the magic bottle,
            a clear glass sphere of transparent
            liquid Ether—

23. Ginsberg's cousin, a dentist, administered nitrous oxide to Ginsberg to help him with his consciousness experiments. See "Laughing Gas," *CP*, 197–207.

Sniffed[24]

1111   High at 4

But pickup snuffle—a Crack of iron whips incyde the silinders. Whistle & smell of brakes. Laughter & pistol echoing at all walls.

I know I am a poet—in this universe—but what good does that do— when in another, without these mechanical aids, I might be doomed to be a poor Disneyan Shoe Store clerk—

That this night occur only in *one*
Of the possible universes that do

    happily exist

    strangely, *really*, with crossed eyes—

            exist

One of those that exist with $N2O$ or

    any gas—this is only *one*

of the myriad miracles—
This accident of Consciousness of
Ether—is an accident of the Ether
World, one of the Ether-possible
worlds, not the Final World—

Humbled & more knowledgeable acknowledge
the Vast mystery of our Creation—
without giving any sign that
   we have heard from the

       GREAT CREATOR

       WHOSE NAME I NOW

       PRONOUNCE

24. First draft of "Aether," *CP*, 250–62.

Great Creator of the universe, if
    thy wisdom accord it
and if this not be too
    much to ask
May I publish your Name?
    I ask in the Lima
        Night
    Fearfully waiting
      Answer,
 hearing the buses out on
the street hissing,
Knowing the Terror
    of the World afar—
I have been playing with Jokes
and His is too mighty to hold
      in the hand like a pen
And His is the Pistol Shot Answer
     that brings Blood to the Brain,
and Bells & Tears in the eyes
      Screams & Locusts and
All that which jumps in the Cricket
To inspire the Voice of
    The Myriad rushers of the
     Brainpan
And—
What *can* be possible
    in a minor universe
    in which you can see
    God by sniffing the
    gas in a cotton?
The answer to be taken in

reverse & Doubled Math
ematically *both* ways

Am I a sinner
There are hard & easy universes. This
    is neither.

Ferd Monjus—a series of *experiences* just passed thru me which had, once, passed before thru my brain, to the point where I looked up in the air in surprise—with his Columbia fellow student look on my face, & Jim Fitzpatrick—

Then on the couch the last, with *eyes* closed (If I close my eyes will I regain consciousness?)))—That's the Final Question—which we have all heard before—with—all the old churchbells ringing and all the old whispers of responsive demiurgic ecstasy whispering crescendoed in the ears—and when was it Not ever answered in the Affirmative? Saith the Lord?

A magic Question? And a magic answer? That we *get* in a magic Universe—but *magic.*

full of brown shorts & Bolivian Shoes *pure* Magic!

Therefore poetry, which is the key to Magic

Therefore, Laughing Gas
               & Magic Universe

Flies & Crickets & the Sound of buses & my
  Stupid Beard.

And the Mountain of Garbage is pure
  magic.

The Brujos know magic.

I shall study Magic.

The universe is Created by Pure Magic.
But what's magic?
  Voices in a sound truck down
    The street?
Is there sorrow in Magic?
Is magic one of my own boyscout Creations? Am I responsible? I with
my flop? Must I be the repeater of turkey-ass Corso? Ah Silver Gregory!
Lost in Universe! And me condemned to be Repeater? Ah, Justice that
we should both survive and all together singing the same old blood-
cheek swallow tongue throat,
woo, bark, harmony, Carramba, bark,
chain on the street
  what *threat* might
     happen?
Is there any Threat to
    Magic?
Yes just this might be one
  of the universes in which there
  is a threat to magic, by
  writing while high.

Peru

The noise in my ears like a *Crescendo*
     of vibrations
Expecting a bloody nose The sensation in
     my nose.   is.

I have returned to Berthal Hoeniger In this Univ.
I am Walter in this Universe—I am older or younger
     wouldn't want to be either—how sad—wouldn't want to be him—
wouldn't want *not* to be him
     I love Walter, in this Universe. As a strange final statement
to make.
     A universe in which I am condemned to write statements. Too
tired
of that to be Marxist—tho I've *been,* before.

    Dear N. Parra:
     I was a Marxist poet in last lifetime, and tho my present state
of suffering & anxiety is not any better—I don't believe it any more.

     Existential Marxism might be Heaven or Hell.
     Never alter mercy for *Judgment*—that leads to all these mistaken
universes—the bugdda void is right—

Ignorant Discrimination Creates
   worlds—
and this one is joined in
   Indic Union to
Affirm with laughing
     eyes—

Peru

The world is as we see it,
   Male & Female, passing
as it passes thru the years,
   As has before & will, perhaps,
with all its countless Pearls,
   with all its countless Sands
And all the Bloody noses of Eternity,
and all the old mistakes—

Begin anew, and recreate the
  world in thy own image,
    as thou wilst—

and I poor stupid All in G.
am stuck with that old choice

ya, crap, what hymn to seek, & in
   what tongue, if this is the most
    I can requite from consciousness?—

That I can skim & put in words?—
   could skim it faster with
    more juice—

Could skim a crop with Death
       perchance—yet never
       know in this old world.

Could Skim a crop with many blood,
  and one.

Will know in Death?
       And Before?
            Will in
Another know,
        And in Another know—
               and
in Another know,
        And in Another know—
                And
in Another know—
        There is a world in which I continue repeating infi-
nitely
I am afraid to be condemned to that, though I suppose (by my conceiv-
ing
it) it can exist as all the others I've conceived.
   Stop conceiving worlds!
      says Philip Whalen
(My Savior!) (oh what snobbery!)
(as if he cd save anyone)—
   At *least,* he won't understand.
I lift my finger in the air to create
a universe he won't understand, full
   of Sadness. But not more strange
   than any other.
I'm tired of this quasitranscendency.
always the sound of crickets & knocks & locusts
   in my eardrums high & wheeling,
Some scissors dropped downstairs.

Peru

I am *afraid* that in this universe
  the people will enter to enquire
  about the gas (People from Hotel)
            —sensation of being
Ancient London—
            Sensation of the mark on
my finger being 1839 Eng Pirate
Sign—
            Walter & Raquel
  Let them be happily ever
After—as I am doomed
I accept the sacrifice. I have been Raquel. To look up & down,
  shaking the hand in wonder & bewilderment as before, as the
  old Jew.
  What if God Revised his Universe
  Be ye Perfect
  or Jack his books, or me my poems What I do I do. End the
mental quarrels in the world, & that's the answer.
  Jack is the most courageous & most beautiful & I will follow
Example evermore closely
  But have I come another way?
  Not to Revise, lest it complicate thought
  a thought complicated, the universes cross out & reproduce
otherwise, perverted—
  Simplicity.
            I have returned to Jack's
way.
  But his way is not mine?

A gesture of the head, revolving on the neck left, right, thinking, remembering various lives, finally staring straight ahead in surprise & recollection into the mirror of Time in the Hotel Commercio room.

There are 20 million different bisecting
    & interesting universes that I will experience
    & remember,
        my headshake of wonder in
A different   section of the

Scale in each, & I will remember *all*
At once. Ah what

    Disillusions, what
wondrous emotions I felt—being

All—and nothing. But
   a broken page like any other.
Or a skeleton—as that which had
   a broken cheek & some white teeth
   and long red hair bound up & reveled
      in the sand, beside some
        upturned pottery & textile
          weave of no import
in a grave in which I shat in
      old Chancay.
As that skeleton I no longer remember to describe.
      There's always a mirror to reflect a face—
      Time repeats itself. Literally.
      How would I know if I have been here before?
      Am I afraid to find out?
Christ is Right! The thahothelleos? Catholics?
      I proposed a final question, and
heard a series of final answers
      including that series of headshakes
of opposites.

      Drugs exist for those who try them, & don't exist for those who
don't—
      But communication between Beings is important

      6 guys moving down the street—"Cessa la Guerra! La bomba
atomica," they say in matter of fact warning voices (please don't smoke
on the train type) walking up the street in Front of RR Staytion—I look
out my window & Blink my Ears—
      Consciousness in this city—is always Key.

Peru

"Consciousness"—"Existence"—"Universe"—"Being"—"God"—
What is God? forinstance, asks the answer?
And whatever else can the replier reply by reply?
Whatever the nature of the mind, that (not) the nature of both
Question & Answer.
        So Snyder[25] too is alone in his altitude of mind heit (height)
    I don't want that anybody—me—should be lonely, but I condemn all
others to solitude just so that I can have God.
Ah my poor coat, Gary, sagging on the chair,
    left arm down, wrinkles in the lapel
    of sharkskin varicolor like many eyes—
Gary—you right too—each mind is right
        for its own & all other universes—
        since all are visible.
                    As far as
            they intercommunicate & are
                    visible.
one might reject drugs ether since
    it seems to create different
    universes & yet one wants to live
    in a *Single* Universe
                        Does one?

Must it be one?
    Why, as with Jews,

25. Poet and essayist Gary Snyder (1930–), model for Japhy Ryder in Jack Ker-
ouac's *The Dharma Bums* and member of the San Francisco Poetry Renaissance, won
the Pulitzer Prize for *Turtle Island*.

Peru

must the God be one? O what does
the concept one mean?

    It's sad!

God is one!

    Is X

Is meaningless—

        Adonoi—

is a Joke

    The Hebrews are

Wrong—(Christ & Buddha

Attest, also wrongly!)

What is one but Formation

    of mind?

        The insistence on

one certain of Myriad universes & ways—a beginning of mental

standardization & discrimination.

        Monotheism is madness also, pure arbitrary.

        All *conceptions* breed their own.

        As Jack's conception of the Diamond has bred one in me.

        Spreading out in All directions simultaneously

        I forgive both good & ill, & I seek nothing, like a painted savage

        with

spear crossed by orange & black & white bands transversally.

  This savage also knows the laws of Universe & the Jivaro as well

has his own metaphysics which account for his reality.

                And this might

Be exterminated by another reality or Demon.

        Shall we leave the Jivaro alone or not? Or Join him—for a *while*.

        "I joined the Javaro & was entrapped in their universe."

                Then why

communicate with this?

                I'm scribbling

Nothings.

Page upon Page of Profound (est)

    nothing

as scribed the Ancient Hebe, when

    he wrote Adonoi or one—

all to amaze or make money or deceive—

ah what wickedest content!

        And why not

Peru

wickedness, with snicker and a mustache?

be myself? What? Why must wickedness

   Be another?

          Ah that poor other!

It might be me!

        Let wickedness

be me, and this the worse of all

the universe!

          Not the worse! Not Flame!

I can't stand that—yes that's

for Somebody Else!

            yet I accept

O Catfaced God, whatever comes! It's Me!

I am the Flame, etc including you.

O Gawd!

      The same old shit, repeated o'er and o'er

      I'll use the rest up in a wild way

         Crack!

            Circusmaster's whip—mustache—smell of blood—

circumcision—locust whistle—toot of harbor tow—sallow the back of

the nose—

lump of snot if need be but, whatever universe you exchange with—

     I suddenly felt at point of exchange with another universe in

which I was a laborer in cabin D. H. Lawrence writing in Earlier uni-

verse hunger poverty—in other Country—I was *afraid* to enter wall, un-

focus my eyes & be that person.

              (transform universe I forget the

               old me & be trapped in another

                   nescient)

Peru

If I keep trying *I will* be, will work that magic.

    I keep relying on Stability? Why? Might be different. Samenesses.

    Might be millions of exactly the same different repeated possibil-
ities of nothingness not existing—repeated very many times very
many different ways—fogging the focus of the eyes—that male the
Universal

          IMPERFECT—

AND A SOUL IS DAMNED TO HELL!

    And the churchbell rings?

    and there is a melancholy, once again, throughout the realm. And
I am and am not that soul.

    but have thought of it,.

Small as it is.

          It's what doesn't exist that makes the little nut of
consciousness and mirrors the rest in repeated imperfections.

                         And the gas

is out, the bottle's empty 'S no more, 'snot

    And if repeats, has got the same, with many repetitions—

    Have felt same before—

Old Llama

    The miracle of unreality is equally grave in every direction

        (had read Blanca Salta's letter)—

I only create more misconceptions

    & seek to straighten them out

    (creating more) (will)—

    Well an end to this bebida

Blanca made a mystic sign
    courteous & imperfect.
  (to the Bathroom)
I put out the cigarette, in fear
  of entering room & gas exploding
as it has for other consciousness—
   A terrible death
     the death of Drugs
The other machine fuse pulled a hair out of my beard.
   Safe I've used the bottle thru.

Blanca's consciousness also has many
   mirrors.
She who replies to me from the other
  side of the mirror—
has many other mirrors who reply to her—
   in endless succession
like—this very universe is one.
Perfect in repetition. And will evermore.
O Terrible the Death of Consciousness
   and yet! when all is ended
     what regret?
        'shone's left
To remember or forget.
       The rhyme was all.
and's gone into the odd.
    As odd & even were, ever, if.
That were the Last Chance.
  The only thing I fear is the last
chance.

Peru

And that will yet be met—I'll see the Last Chance too, before
I'm done, old mind. I'll see them all, all them old last chances that
you knew before—like going thru rubber glovesuit thru a door to the
opposite, each time thru the Wall of Consciousness to the next door
dreamwall—

      Bill's future city, Yage.
with whatever altitude I hold the cotton to my nose, it's still a secret
joke,

      a minor thing
with pinky akimbo, or with effete queer

    eye in mirror at myself

      or serious brow main,

            and darkened beard,
I'm still the kid of obscure chance awaiting—

      breathing in a foreign

          Chinese Universe
thru the nose like some old Hindu Brahma god.

 and all the possible chances that I miss—that might or might not—like
phoning Blanca now (11:15) and

    she think me an irritant
and I be a mere fool exuberant phoner

   in the Eternal nite and she

     goddess of wisdom—
why should she accept my imperfection?
Looking for an ear to Enter—or before—
tonite I entered Walter's

   Like a little devil with his medieval wings, in miniature—
that Anthony & Francis drove away from their historic minds.

Peru

I've passed a couple fantastical hours thinking & waiting! How many 12, pages—hours, 2 or 3,

And I had prevision to buy a new book earlier today.

"I've come to try your magic" is proper way to address a Shapibo Witch.

O Bell Time, Ring thy midnight for the Billionth Soundy time, I hear again!

I go to walk the street, Thy Same Street,

out to look again.

    Who'll find me in the night, in Lima, in my 33'd year,

    approaching end of that & one more birthday in a week—

Owe a letter to Eugene & Louis, just for that—they saw me come to birth in this world—and I scare them now—*A Babe* of consciousness thought descending the hotel stairs at midnite 3000 miles away from where

they ruminate & muse or sleep or cry, or drink their night-time tea & gossip o'er the cosmos.

God's snake,

Image:

Someone drops a scissors downstairs, cuts in two a dust mote on the floor—our universe ends having been in that dust mote.

Each universe within the universe cut in two by a scissor dropped in the room above us in endless succession repeated, or ends when some-

Peru

one breathes in Ether. Goofy universes like balloons coming from strangest places like Dentist chairs & bottles of Ether. Disappearing back into same.

On Street

   I've been waiting for a soul to answer me in Lima—and heard many answers, but have Answered none—
      As Peter's answers mine.
      The souls of Peter & I answer each other.
      But—and what's a Soul?

   To be a poet's a serious occupation, condemned to that in universe—
   To walk the street ascribbling in a book—
   Just accosted by a drunk—in Plaza de Armas sidestreet
   Under a foggy sky, and sometimes with no moon.

And if a Soldier
stops me—what
to say?
      To make all
Consciousness
be in contact, and
answer each other
on the street too.
   The heavy balcony
hangs over the white
marble of the
Bishop's Palace
next the Cathedral—
The fountain plays

Peru

in Light as e'er—
The buses & the
motorcyclists pass
at midnite, the
carlights shine
the beggar turns
the corner with his
cigarette stub &
cane, the noisers
leave the tavern,
and delay, conversing
in high voice,
Awake, the Grand
Hotel—Museum
lights are on in the
Great Porch,
    Hasta Manana
they all say—
    and somewhere
at the other end of
the line, a telephone
is ringing,
        come again
with unknown news—
a typewriter ribbon
lies on the stone
steps, unwound—
    The night
looms over Lima,
sky black fog—

Peru

and I sit helpless
smoking with a
pencil hand—
    and little book
of death, truth, Fear,
Doubt, wonder &
Delay—Deny—
    the long crack
in the pavement
    or yesterday's
volcano in Chile,
or the day before
The Earthquake
that begat the
World.
    The pack's
not empty, and
the plaza pavement
shines in the electric
light. I wait
    The lonely beard
workman staggers
home to bed from
Death.
      yes but I'm
a little tired of
being alone, ether
has turned my thots
to Peter & Love.
    This young kid

Peru

Macho puts his fists
together in the nite,
preparatory to thought
    The Cardoors
slam, with ancient
creaky sound.
    Keats' Urn—the
instant of realization
of a single consciousness
that hears the chimes
of Time repeated
eternally—endlessly.

All nite, w. Ether, wave
    after wave of Magic,
magic understanding—
the universe is Magic, Sex is magic
huge photo of girl stars over
the public square with tits sweet
& small—the boy at next table
Is now café's magic. And I
know it (Does he know it?)
    Jack writes straight to
stop the Universe—put
a *standard,* a measure, to
the magic confusion. (By
not correcting thought.)
    A disturbance of the
Field of Consciousness, to be
conscious of Magic. Magic

Peru

night, magic stars, magic
men, magic music, magic
tomorrow, magic death, magic
God, magic birth, magic
magic. Magic Magic.
(Title)
    Magic poetry. This
Walt Disney sensation. But
who's on whatsa Magician—God.
Fin Page—God is nothing
but a Magician, a slight
of hand artist. Make
Disappear. That repeats
his tricks.
        Has magic any
rules? Yes, Magic
has all rules. All rules
apply, equally in
Magic.
   Magic is made by
Chance—
   What crude chance
we live in (seeing trolley
like a rude monster
in downtown street
w/ electric diamond
wire antenna to sky, go past
outside under white light (arc)
by Hotel Grand Bolivar.)
The mad potter of

Peru

Mochica made a
pot w/ 6 eyes & 2
mouths & half a nose
& 5 cheeks & no chin
for us to figure out,
Serious side track,
Blind alley universe,
one way street Cosmos.

Back in room (May 27)

The universe is a Surprise surprise on itself
As man is surprised that he exists,
  Universe is surprised that it exists,
    To extent that it is one big
      rolling dragon in the clouds
       & Darkness of a Chinese
     Painting of its consciousness.
It gives itself Birthday. Birth to itself.
 "What creature gives birth to itself?"
     ans: Magic Dragon Surprise
       conscious universe.
How strange to remember anything, even a button,
    much less a universe,
 and the mad smiling dwarf freak statues
     of the past pre-incaic on my desk,
      survival in the Sand of
       All-Forgetfulness,
  unconscient for centuries till I see them.

O Nescience! O Word of yore—15 years of L. C. 1943,
    What'd he know?—but Death?
Universe w/ no rules is magic
       with rules is weirder magic
            either way.
All ways are magic,
   And all magic's mad.
The Universe is Mad, slightly mad,
           or plenty mad, but mad.
And then what's sanity, but a word,
      or a weird concept
         Limiting the madness
To what our bodies/brains can stand, temporarily,
       in this particular form
         we find ourselves
           incarnate in, fleetingly
—the sands of Chancay know.
    And are a madness of dead skulls,
       and skulls with hair, that
          know not nought or n'er,
             nor nor, no more—
The skull is empty! But the air from a
     new universe breathes thru,
and others watch the empty eyes,
      and look thru holes in the bones
        to see the dust,
         and no more Answer than
         symbolic that,
Thru Eyes, we see a million eyes and all one
    eye & many at the once,

Peru

money won't buy that,
but mind.
Tranquility—there's not to do,
and be murderer—if wilt—
thou wilt,
like lettuce, murder worm,
and that's no more than a Shakespearian pun,
—and the two sides wriggle away
in the opposite directions to die
—as the caterpillar hundredfooted that I saw
at Machu Picchu, with its
black head off, and gasping
for air, or consciousness,
The long body curled & feebly wriggling feet in
the blindness—darker than Death.
That suffering, as the illusion slips away—
And the creature feels itself
Destroyed,
At Being,
Feels Being itself dissevered
& fleeing to opposite
Ends of infinity
head and tail of the universe
cut in two
on the grass, green,
magnified to Jungle
in a larger jungle,
in a world,
of many worlds
in a universe

Peru

might be one

of myriad more

that Ends.

I was that caterpillar I will be.

Dead.

And all are conscious—as I often feel on

the street, passing strangers who

I might salute, in the same Being.

Caught, Trapped in the same

Mystery, Magic—

equally doomed & confused,

but nothing to lose,

did I know it,

but knew.

Men with Slick mustaches of mystery have
Pimp horrible climaxes & karmas.

That's me, I fear. "I am the loony one"—
the mad magician that created chaos
in the peaceful void & suave.
With my fucking suave manners & my knowitall
eyes, and mind full of Fantasy
revolving around one me
That I'll have to forget, to die

The me! that horror that keeps me conscious in
this Hall of Birth & Death.
That were in the site, that flies

and sits thru earthquakes,

and survives afar,

Smug worm of Life

"old rockyface look forth"—

"A Cock to Aescalepius"—

Socrates' Sadness leaving this illusion.

34 coming up—I suddenly felt old—sitting w/ Walter & Raquel my measure,
Age of Burroughs (31) when first met

May 31—Almost without thinking, I left Lima this morning at dawn—packed knapsack & walked across street from Hotel at 6:30 AM to take train to Oroya, headed for jungle Pucallpa.

"The soul of Adonais etc"

"A luminous ineffec-

tual angel"—

This one of the most stupid insults in literary history in which a man of broad sentimental experience in a limited materialistic world, absolutely blind to experiences which he cannot have known, had the smugness to dismiss as unreal perceptions of which he was incapable.

When it comes to actual experience of the inhuman I don't mean mere social in human like concentration camps or mountains of capitalist garbage in Peru—it is Shelley's phantastic insight to which I turn—not the human opinionations of dumb Arnold. When it comes to experiential knowledge of the transcendental & sublime—when it comes to the unintelligible—which is our real task. When it comes to the mystery of creation—it is Shelley who knows and who has seen a something beyond his own mind which Arnold, living in a world of houses, never guessed, nor had the insight to shut up about.

A town in Peru with a big ugly sign—SMELTER by name—high up on barren brown Andean puno-plain
Cerro de Pasco—
    dirty but full of Indians, a market blankets, white mantas with orange stripes, I drank Cocoa & had Siroche headache all nite at 14,350 feet. Stayed in Hotel Central—no water in morn.

To Louis—Poet, go home to the king of poets thy Father.

Siroche headache oxygen lack is similar to headache from Ether or H2O after use in a day.

Huanuco—June 1, 1960
    Arrived, day market white blankets w/ orange stripes $2.00—saw movie of Jerry Lewis studying to be a boyscout cop "The Delicate Delinquent"—Ate in Chifa (Chinese) Chicken w/ veg—Pork w/ Tamarand Sauce, Fried Wanton, & Tea Pet—70c.

June 2—Dream in afternoon—I borrow apartment of a friend while his family is absent—huge apartment—and start dreaming—at piano— singing to myself—loud noise—God is Music—the noise of music progress until they suddenly bend into an unintelligible beautiful series of melody—that is it, I hear God—then the family later comes back—I talk to the father, a handsome younger man—but I have to leave the house, & go.

Huamaco—June 2 My birthday—
Beard, in dream, celestial music, unintelligible to the rest of the tune as it snaked its way thru normalcy of music.

In this room in Hotel Argentino, grim cell, really flappy the door doesn't close, yellow stains on the wall near the bed, dry stains of old life—drips running down the whitewashed clay—and the corners of the room stained with old dust—the white water pitcher has a scum-film at the bottom—the clothesrack falls apart—my mochila (knapsack) with mouth open sits on the bed table—I took a nembutal to sleep early & wake for 5 AM bus to Tingo Maria—wrote letters to Gene, Louis, Gregory.

How strange—truly I heard Celestial music in my dream this afternoon of my birthday—and thinking that looked up at this drear room & it seemed even drearer, to die, the universe stain & wear & brokenness of the very door of this room—a double door on the stairway in a quixotic cobble alley back of the hotel, dark, and every old slat of the door ajar, worn holes in it, the grey paint scraped off near the lock for a square foot of pink wood. The old ink wood of former life of trees, in what forest.

What Else? More clock bells, rural rings of 9 PM, from churches in Huamco Square.

My image, beautiful & thin, the bearded, maked in front of huge mirror in room in Lima, masturbating afoot, dancing and wheeling around, glancing in wonder at my figure in the flesh, in the mirror, strange being in Solitude jacking off to himself in Peru, wanderer with no boy or girl friend near, a true bearded freak in the universe, making love to myself, over and over again.

Walking the sidestreets around the Cathedral—drunk at dawn a week or 2 ago—gave lady in Garbage 100 soles—"For dice" I repeated, too bored & drunk, & she offered it back to me, uncomprehending. I didn't remember where my money went till later next day—thinking over and drunkenness of nite before with a bunch of creepy "muata-cheros"—boy whores.

To Pucallpa
in an old creaky
truck covered
with spiderwebs.
June 3, 60

Illumined by
One branch
in the whole forest,
I smiled—it waved
   its arm so strangely

On truck back—
Neal's green
come in dream
in apt.
   Green come drops hardened all over after I blow him, scattered on the clothes & body & sheets.

Rimbaud
had solitude
—& scared
of the "wing"

♥

    All night lay back on truck back covered with sugar—lying on sugar
sacks—tons of sugar flying thru jungle night at 7 MPH—began staring
at individual trees—"Everything is alive"—and noticed one wave its arm
crookedly—and another spray up out of the ground—and another view
all leafy like a king—and another sprig from the crotch of a plant, un-
natural sexy union—on the road bank—and another a huge wave of
grown fans, with brothers all up the road—hung many with orange or-
chids which when cracked open reveal a long white tooth or cock or
sprig of pollen secretly protected by inner golden sheath—

    Then the stars, and a half moon for my birthday—"Joe May, Man Ray,
Hal Chase, & Henry Miller"—began praying for Joe May, lost soul
somewhere back 1943—and our conversation 1949 about Souls that had
known the Void "you wouldn't like them" he said, knowing some, he af-
firmed.

    The Stars—and Catullus voice—remembering his latin—sensation of
a shrunk & wrinkled cock, the feeling of old time sadness, realization
omnia vita brevis est nox est una perpetus dormienda—perfect drone-
through-time statement of brevity 2000 years ago—and he died, can't
even find Catullus' skull—yet his sentiment & longing did premancer—
Perfect sweet understanding of that we die—so he knew, so I know or
knew riding in starstruck thru 34th year.

    Then Joe May, & various others I knew coming into memory again,
as if I were to die soon—cancer of the Asshole—remembering everyone
with longing—my father—and his autumn leaf "freighted with loss"—
and I said Jack a "hairy loss"—so true—I saw his expression of disdain

& hated him back then—but beyond he insult I'm a hairy loss, all true. (What's he but hairier)—but the solitude that must be, as if I had really left all behind and were now permanent traveler in world with no return to Peter or home—that pure solitude which makes the stars shine sharper, and life even more new strange dream, all universe an old familiar phantasm—recalling Catullus writing it down, same too tonight of poem to Louis, wrote it in mind, rhymed, can't don't remember.

Alone at table in big café near movie in Pacallpa writing now.

Recall Catullus waiting at dawn in Rome by a wooden gate for girl love to come downstairs.

Maybe I just manufacture all this Celestial Music in my brainpan.
Sign of Eternal Imagery
    Immense distance—as far as the
        Star of Bethlehem Buddha or the 10,000th
        World of Buddha Bethlehem

June 6, 1960
Ayahuasca—[26]

Moonlit nite
entered bamboo roof shelter
lay on ground on robe

26. First draft of "[Poem]," published in *Wait Till I'm Dead*, 35.

—entered the Great Being
       again
—we are all one Great Being
   whose presence is familiar
—to be It, need to be
   also the mosquito
          that bites me
—I am also a mosquito
   on the Great Being

June 8—Ayahuasca in Pucallpa—yesterday

First saw a Spectrum of different designs colored somewhat like Chama (Shipibo) pottery & blankets I'd seen all day—then the different beads of color took on organic forms—flies, bees, golden buts, serpents, many serpents, a myriad of miniature serpents making a great sheath of star of visual fabric in front of a great intelligent hole, an empty black speck like the entrance to the great personal nose of God—where I stared in—somewhat like the vision of Krishna in Bhagavad-Gita—and this existed in front of me, at once a little scary, but very little, and mostly very pleasant & personal, intimate, old tune familiar—the mind's entrance into god similar in sentiment to the cock's entrance into cunt—this great creature being bisexual and the lover of all in an extremely secret personal way—he tends the bees and the frogs as well as me.

The mosquito interrupted my contemplation—Kept buzzing and at times settling down on my flesh to bite—finally I came to point of extension of my body throughout universe, that I began to accept the noise as part of the music—locusts, frogs, dogbarks—of the night all crying aloud in communication of the Name of the Great Being of which they were a part—and without moving I allowed several to bite me—until disturbed—tho I created a voice in my soul which said, from Above—"You

Peru

have to be a mosquito too, Allen"—said very dearly. This the condition of entrance complete into the Great Being—Thought of Kerouac on car roof in night across Mexico Border—allowing mosquitos to seep into his body, giving himself up to the Universal activity of the night. What transcendency, then, did he know at that moment? Barely more than pure will power—perhaps he actually gave up his Self for that Great Mess of Creation.

The Voice and the Great Being is that of the Father's Father's Father, a Father way back, lover to each creature—very busy supplying each creature with his proper inevitable Honey Death. So, much like the Great Queen maggot of the African movie saw in N. Y. last year.

Also, that I am a mosquito-type creature in relation to the Universe, that I suck off the divine, who is in long run my one deepest lover—

Realization (over again) that the world is so illusory that what can be communicated, said, writ, in terms of human consciousness bears no relation to the Great Being who is complete in Itself and so perfect that no complaint need to be made—it's all one mess which eats itself—to separate from the process of Death & attempt to preserve the Good of Individual beings in vain, because the Deepest part of each in the Great Deathless Love Beast whose mosquitos and Bacteria have to eat too— each one has his murderous needs in creation, and can't favor us over the mosquitos without murdering & starving mosquitos—So he lets us fight it out outside himself in chaos of Illusion, always retaining the Final Great Black Hole of Love to which we can return after death of Individuality when we have been defeated or become tired of being separate individuals in creation—normal consciousness of the merely human self.

Had laid out for long time several hours in bamboo cookshelter outside Maestro's[27] house (Flaviano?) & Roman had got up, & told me to

27. Ginsberg's curandero.

Peru

wrap myself in his mantle to protect me from mosquitos. A very kind gesture, I felt he realized I too had climbed up thru the Nose of God into Being the Same as Roman—that we were all one, and this was a kindly gesture (wrot from afar by god) to protect me in my as yet delicate individuality—later I went in the house, where they were (4 of them having drunk), sensing a great feeling of communal fraternity & sharing of realization of Infinite Intimacy—one old fellow on a bench, an albanil, moved over & motioned me welcome to join him next to him to sit down. I saw they in Pucallpa had their own secret transcendental nose society, underneath very humane, in huts. And the Indians chamas outside too.

The familiar creepy sexy nosey personal intimate old-known special re-realization of the Joke sweetness of Illusion fading into the Great BlackAsshole of one-Mind one-Love Cat-faced snake-faced dog-faced man-faced Mondalic Universal Newspaper Busybody Gossip God. All mine, all everybody's, all everything's. in what else could He be but He Himself?

The Curandero—Maestro's ceremony—he being ill—was to dip an enamel cup into a tin pot full of green-brown liquor, hold it in front of mouth, smoking cigarette, & whistle a sad tune thru the smoke, following up with humming extension of same tune into the tomb of the cup thru the smoke, then pass it on to me to light a cigarette bow smoke into the surface of the beer, and drink up.

"If the Slayer thinks he is Slain . . ." How did the great being communicate with Emerson & the Transcendentalists? What States of Consciousness & feeling did Emerson know?

Peru

Thus on the human level the method of approach soul to soul on the most intimate level of mutual concern begins to approximate the relation of Soul to God—thus humans as lovers & caretakers & fathers make the Eternal Scene. His intimacy constantly violated by hard hearted madness & politics & business & war.

Thus the saint is the delicate-handed intimate of all—St. Francis and the Birds—recognizing Brotherhood. No morals but Love.

There's no need to communicate the News of God. Those who seek, find. Those who need something else get something else—get trapped in the separate universe of their own making—but are disintegrated and rejoined to the Great Being, surprised, at one time or another, perhaps after Death—which is Death only of separate consciousness. All's taken care of in Perfection.

The police in Pucallpa are beginning to persecute the Ayahuasca drinkers and Curanderos—pressure from local Bureaucracy—Doctors who have no experience of the Mystery of the Beer. A Materialistic consciousness is attempting to preserve itself from Dissolution by restriction & persecution of Experience of the Transcendental. One day perhaps the Earth will be dominated by the Illusion of Separate Consciousness, the Bureaucrats having triumphed in Seizing control of all roads of communication with the Divine, & restricting traffic. But Sleep & Death cannot evade the Great Dream of Being, and the victory of the Bureaucrats of Illusion is only an Illusion of their separate world of consciousness. The suffering caused is only temporary, and makes no difference in the Last Judgment of the Soul when it returns to itself, realizing that the Great Inner Universe always exists in the same person and is Eternal despite the transient vanities of the busy-bodies of Time.

I am only a busybody meddling in human affairs vainly trying to assert the Supremacy of the Soul—which can take care of itself without me & my assumption of the Divine, my presumption that the Eternal needs my assistance to exist & preserve itself in the world. All my worry's as much of a Joke as the equal worry of the police. We are all trapped in the Divine Honey, like flies, struggling in different ways to accommodate ourselves.

The struggle & Pain of Death is only the Soul being forced to recognize its final nature & leave the Separate Individual Self.

Poverty, hunger, suffering also separate the soul from the body, the temporary body, and serve as exercises of the Divine. Tho it is painful—somebody has to suffer, the man or his ox.

The reward annihilates the struggle. God is perfect.

"Vanity of vanities," saith the Preacher. Communists are wrong, Capitalists are wrong. There is something deeper than their Human. Alas, now we all suffer in different worlds, having eaten the apple of Separate Consciousness. And tho this way may be cruel judgment on human goodwill politicians, the meat-bureaucrat is not less cruel. Cows also suffer. How shall we end suffering, by producing & killing more cows, or by teaching man to transcend hunger? Perhaps God knows, or the

Peru

process of creation & illusion is endless, to give each Self a chance to Be alone & separate—or perhaps the process of human intimacy will end human suffering (leaving the cows to suffer and be redeemed from the world we have isolated them in, as now we isolate the Poor). (The mass of mankind is still Poor.)

But the suffering, a world in itself, is Nothing, compared to the redemption, which is all worlds at once.

Meanwhile are we called to make this world livable, and organize Farms—or let things take their Bloody Course & rely on Death?

Human suffering annihilates awareness of God's Brotherhood & makes man brutish in their materialism like longwinded communists, crying for human brotherhood to combat suffering—but what can you do? I'd feel different if I were poor—but poor see God too.

The Mystery goes on above my mind & above my worry & will not be resolved by me, but by Itself.

The original idea of youth—to look in each other's eyes & realize we are the same, as Jack & I did early & unknowing, as poetic instinct.

This prose is vain & getting dull.

[. . .]

My idea to be God, one with Divine, always turns out to be the last refuge of Egotism, or God appears in his Transcendence and the Mystery Deepens beyond my ken, into a huge Suck of Delight. In which my intention is annihilated.

Peru

The feel of the mystery of women & the mystery of God is the same or similar to me—jacking off to a fat woman from my dark hotel window, watching a group of Peruvian provincials leave the Chinese Restaurant, Hong Kong, behind fly scream I came, like babe to her faraway hugeness.

Pacoocha=lower Ucyali River between Contamana & Piccaltapa
 A little below Tirunton
Dr. Binder Recommends them for ayahuasca.

In the Brujos' house at nite—the same scene of surreptitious subreality as in a Turkish Bath—all souls open to the Sex of God—in the darkness, each dreaming the same secret human monstrousness within himself and recognizing it with relief in others too, all guards down & armor folded away for the Séance—Ramon's head on my arm—the albanil dreaming tenderly on the bench against the wall, Flacco folded up in a mantilla on the floor, the sick brujo crooning to himself, applying penicillin to his neck on his bed in the other room, behind a mosquito net The smell of love of a Turkish Bath.

Lying in bed (June 8) all afternoon to escape the sun waiting to go to Ayahuancero at nite—I'm becoming obsessive with preoccupation on this unintelligible, and my drawing is schizophrenic in a universe where magic is real. The universe is made of magic.
    Materialists who don't believe in magic kill, and order capital punishment.

Peru

Had slight headache, wrote Magic Psalm in large Notebook, went out to Brujo—no session tonite, he still sick, so I was defrauded of my exciting-Fear.

All the earth of Chile where I trod 3 months ago has been destroyed by earthquake—Valdivia where I was sick & bored to death is now in ruins.

Maybe I just manufacture all this Celestial Music in my brainpan
Signs of Eternal Imagery
    1) Immense distance as far as the
        Star of Bethlehem Buddha or the 10,000th
        World of Buddha Bethlehem

June 8—yesterday Ayahuasca in Pucallpa
       2. The great squid of Eternity opening & closing its mouth in vast slow motion in the inner phantasmal recesses of imagination during hallucinated state—with undersea fringed labia.
       "Einstein his mythmouth made real on the moonsquid's brain"
       —Corso

    Remembering on bus to Yarmacoche—"The giant Phantom is Ascending"—
A line from mystic poem I wrote in 1948.)

Peru

A great clap of hands—
    And the mosquito—glimpse
        of merciless intelligence.

Hands clapping
a mosquito—glimpse
of murderous intelligence.

"The sound of two hands clapping?"
"I'm not the waiter"—said Martin Adan.
Yo No Soy El Nozo

One hand clapping—a place where our senses don't go,
        Not even a place
     I can't *hear* it.
Fantasy—I tap my skull lightly on top, with my
    Palm—pat my skull—when asked by Gary.

        Magic Psalm[28]
Because this world is on the wing
    and what cometh no man can see
O Phantom that my mind pursues from year to year
    Descend from Heaven to the mass of shaking

28. First draft of "Magic Psalm." See *CP*, 263–64.

Flesh

Transfigure what was thought to pure
                celestial light
Monster rises in my soul with all
        the glory of the peacock's tail
    outspread thru all Aeternity
Catch up my fleeting eye in the vast Ray
                that knows no Bounds
Roar in my heart like the lion of Mythology

    Come home on wet leaves to the palmtree clearing—
Inseparable—Master—giant outside Time
    with all its falling leaves—Genius of
the Universe—Magician in the Nothingness
    where appear red clouds—
Unspeakable King of the Roads that art gone—
    Unintelligible Horse riding out of
            the Graveyard—passer thru the Bones—
Griever, source of all million Tears, Laugh
            with no mouth—
Heart that never had a Flesh to Die—Creator
        of the loves—Limitless Death—Secret—

    Elephant eyes Keeper of Eden and the Hidden Forests where Man
Enters in amaze from year to year

    O Sunset spread over cordillera and insect—gnarl moth—Mother
of Fishes and the Deaths of Myriad teeth—Unrecognizable All Love
Supplier—Jealousy water—champion of the worm, and Indian in
ragged cloth all Visionary—

    Feeder where world has no bread—Promise, that was not Made—
Reliever, whose blood borne is Fountains in a million animals
wounded—

Peru

O Mercy, Destroyer of the World, O Mercy, Creator of Breasted
Illusions, O Mercy, Cacophonous warmouthed doveling, Come

Invade my body with thy Sexual infinite Caress, O Smell of God
choke my nostrils with your infinite corruption, O Sex of God transfig-
ure me into a slimy work of pure sensate transcendency while I am still
alive,

Make my voice croak with Uglier than Reality, a psychic tomato
speaking with thy million mouths—

Myriad tongued, Angel, My Soul, lover that comes to Fuck me
Forever, Asshole of the Universe in which I Disappear, white gown on
the Squid—Sixty raced Sensations—The Whim—O Familiar Wizard
eyeless even in the Jungle.

Ear of the Buildings of N.Y.—Delicate Seer who spoke to Crane—
agglomeration of Fingers in One Hand—Handless Sound Box—

Music that passes beyond the Phonograph of years to another Mil-
lennium—O That

Which I believe, Have seen, Seek endlessly in every leaf & Dog &
Eye—Fault always, lack, Which makes me think—

Desire, which hath Created me, Desire, which I hide in My Body,
desire, which all man know, Desire, which surpasses the Babylonian
Possible World, Desire, O abstract Destroyer of the Heart

That makes me Flesh & makes my flesh

Still shake with orgasm of thy Name which I know not and which
never will never speak,

Speak to Mankind to say the great Bell tolls & golden tone on
Iron Balconies in every Million Universes—

That I am thy prophet come home to this World to Scream thy Name-
less name thru my 3 senses and a Hideous Sixth

That knows thy hand on its invisible Phallus, covered with the
electric bulbs of Death—

Peru

O Peace, Resolver where I Mess Up Illusion, Softmouth Vagina that enters my Brain from Above, Arc-Dove with a bough of Death, that makes me laugh here I weep, and cry in self disgust at my vast worm Worry—

II

Drive me crazy, God I'm ready for Disintegration of my Me Mind

Disgrace me in the Eye of the World. Scandalize my Parents with this Monster raging of mercy, passion, attack my hairy heart with terror,

Disrupt the world in its Madness of Bombs and Murder—Create Roads

of Earthquake-Radiance over the smoggy Sky, Volcanos of Flesh over London, on Paris a rain of eyes, truckloads of Angel Hearts besmearing the Walls of Kremlin—myriad jeweled feet in the Terraces of Peking— veils of electrical gas descending over India—a vast tom tom soaring over the mountains of Africa louder than hydrogen exploding in the sea—

Shovel my Feet under the Andes, Splatter my brains on the Sphinx Drape my beard & hair over the Empire State Building, Splatter my come over the Legislatures of Alaska, Give my Bowels to the Poor of Bolivia to spread out over the mud of the marketplace to feed the Dogs of Money, Give my skull with its cup of light to the President.

Show Death with all its colored cinema vast flights of cranes, Negroes bombarding Atlantis with jazzbombs, Halcyon leaps of the Elephants of Eternity, cities of Bacteria invading the Hypocritical liver, the Soul Escaping into the rubber waving mouth of Paradise like flights of owls into jungle caves—Walt Disney the statistical stalactites of the world with Civilization of Ferns & Fronds

Peru

This is the Great Calle, this is the Toosin of the Eternal War, this is the Golden bell of the church that has never existed, This is the Trumpet of Mind slain in Nebulas, this is the boom of the heart of the Sunbeam, this is the cry of the worm at Death, this is the fanfare of oblivion, this is the Scream of the Lion of the Universe, this the appeal of the alm of Bandless Infinite Castrate that showers the Everlasting Golden Seed of Futurity thru the Quake & Volcano of the World, this is Intelligence weeping the Mosquitos of all Past in the Unintelligible Brain of the Lamb—

Descend, old World Creator and Eater of Mankind, Bomb out My Mind & Fill my Breast with honey inhuman again, I am scared of thy Promise, Make me scream out thy Prayer in Fear assuage my belly with hands of Moss Fill up my Ears with thy Lightning, Blind me with Prophetic Rainbow, that I take the shit of Being at last, that I touch thy genitals in the palmtree, that I smell the Perfume of thy Eternity in every rotten Jewish corpse, that my brain explode in Frightened Skull and the Vast Ray of Creation enter as on the 6th Day once Again, and shower my eternal Senses with the million brilliant drops of Night.

That I drip with prophecy & futurity, that my prayer surpass my understanding and reach thy footseye—that thou change my Karma from its changeless alteration changed to one Flow of Endless Consciousness, that I be Bright, Fire in Homosexual Illumination—Eater of the Last Bright Seed—Selfless as thou—O Invisible Croak of Deathfrog, Leap on me, O Pack of heavy dogs salivating Light—O Monster! Eat my hurt at last! That I may dissolve into thy Love and no more Fear the terror of thy Judgment over Allen of this World! Born in Newark and come into Eternity in New York and Crying again in Peru for the Sight of Ultimate Tongue to psalm the Unspeakable.

That I surpass desire for Transcendency and enter the calm water of the Universe, that I ride out this wave, that I not be destroyed by this

Flood of thy Imagination, that I not be slain thru my own insane magic, that my presumption be justified by thy perfection, that my loud crime of oneway love be punished by thee in the Thunderous Jail of Mercy, that men understand my speech out of their own Turkish Heart, that the Angels aid me with Prayer & Proclamation & Acceptance, that the Seraphim acclaim thy name in me, and that thy Self or myriad selves laugh all at once in one great Quake/Image mouth of kindred Kingdom Universe make meat Reply.

Dream June 8—2PM?
History of the Jewish Socialist Party in America[29]

In meeting hall, a small room or foyer of private house downstairs on street storefront level—we're inside—me, and my friend, a square FBI agent who is arresting us all, but wants more information so doesn't take us in but lets us continue our activity, which is all internal regulation of the party which now has very few members anyway being, as the FBI boy knows to his chagrin, much more concerned with psychic regulation of the idealism of the members than any activity relating to the US Govt—in fact we are completely unconcerned with the US Govt, and far from spying on it we welcome spies in our midst in the hope they be converted and learn something about us—since the internal structure of the party is a mystery still unresolved even to us—a fact which embarrasses the FBI fellow further since he guesses our general crazy goodwill and devotion to more mysterious politics of complete in-

29. First draft of "History of Jewish Socialist Party in America," originally published in *Airplane Dreams* (Toronto: Anansi Press, 1968), reprinted in *Luminous Dreams* (Gran Canaria: Zasterle Press, 1997), 7–12.

tegrity, so extreme that the policy of the party is really dedicated to dis-
covering what the policy is and who the leaders really are—we being
willing to share the info with anyone—even the US Govt—with complete
faith that with such an open policy no harm can befall anyone, even jail
or execution is further opportunity for study, revelation, or martyrdom
in the Mystery of Idealistic Socialism and a further chapter of the Jew-
ish S. Party's profound activity in America—no less profound because
to a small group which pursue the basic study, for the intensity of their
dedication.

Thus we are having a meeting in the foyer—as Aunt Rose's the
smaller 1930—the FBI man, with tie askew & coat over arm, seating in
summer heat, pistol in one hand & other on telephone, is undecided
what to do, so I advise him, after a nervous walk in the plaza, to trust
us & wait awhile till something definite develops. He seems to agree,
nodding his head, tho worried we'll all escape, vanish, and he'll lose his
job & be fired by his intemperate boss a cruel Faggot named J. Edgar
Hoover.

The subject of tonite's meeting was announced by President Berg last
week to be a speech—manifesto of policy—by an old & trusted member,
Dr Hershman—who arrived earlier very disturbed, took over the meet-
ing—and announced—"the Subject of my Announcement will be the
Follows—please take note and understand why I am announcing it so
that anybody who does not wish to be further implicated may leave the
room: *Why I killed President Berg and Member Hoffman.*" This throws
everybody into turmoil—there are only 5 or 6 members & all realize they
will be held as accomplices—but maybe he had a good reason, so why
leave & betray his mad trust?—It's an apocalyptic party full of necessary
mistakes. The FBI man is thrown into a crisis of nerves—He is ready to
telephone to arrest us all, but wants to hear why they killed Berg & Hoff-
man—But also afraid he might be implicated, since he too is (the spy)

a member of this small Socialist Party which long ago agreed to be mu-
tually responsible & share all guilt. If the FBI man waits he might wind
up in jail with all of us, if he don't wait he'll never fulfill his mission to
find out what the Mystery of the Party is and arrest us on basic evidence
of conspiracy—Arrest now for mere murder means little but regular cop
crime to the FBI not a political triumph. I advise him to hold his horses
and stick with us, we all want to find out.

Horowitz is in the chair, talking furiously: "Comrades, Berg was a
traitor to the Party he wanted to end the Party & had legal power to
dissolve it—I realized the danger, so did he, he invited me to address you
on the subject & he also invited me to take the necessary action on the
subject—an action which hadn't occurred before because a similar sit-
uation had not arisen—

"and here is the can of Naphthalene with which I killed him—gagged
him & poisoned his soda water with it, & made him drink and his co-
conspirator Hoffman—I'm going to burn the Evidence—in the Fire-
place right now"—

He opens the (Ether type) Naphthalene can in the floor of fireplace
& lights it—it burns & gives off dull blue flame & great fumes of weird
gas—everybody coughs—I sniff & realize you can get high on it, so I want
to stick around & not call firemen or cops—

"Let it burn," we all yell—the FBI man rushes outside but I rush him
back in—"Smell it & get high maybe we'll all get the Answer that way.
Don't give up the Ship."

The girls are nearly fainting, the can is burning in the fireplace,
fumes dizzy us, one girl faints in chair, her Jewish girlfriend rubs her
hands & fans her, the FBI man is sweating. Horowitz is sniffing furi-
ously—the room is in turmoil—we will be arrested for murder—"Destroy
the Evidence & let's get high" shouts the killer—on this scene of evident
excitement, a new chapter of the history of Jewish socialism nears its
end & the Dream concludes prematurely.

Peru

June 9—

A fly swooping & gyring to the great canyon between my shoulder & knee, as I lean against the wall, sitting in shade on a porch in Yarmacocha, watching girls play footballs with oranges, amid the cheeps of chicks & the clucks of their mothers—a girl threw a tangerine peel at the stray chick in the sunny dust.

Riding bicycle over dusty roads between Lake Yarmacocha & the Linguistic Institute Base of Schweitzer Hospital, sweating in the noonday sun in new brown workshirt, nothing to do, waiting by hospital wall crosslegged in shade of palmtree for vegetarian lunch with Dr. Binder & his family—what will we talk about—am I really welcome to lunch? O Paranoiac—O Sun Hunk—creep—an ant up my elbow—water running down my nose—my pen stuck, butterflies in the grass, my hat's dirty—this single yellow green young palm frond trembles for an instant in the wind, all thirty top light spikes waving together 4 feet from the ground, against the piled up clouds in blue sky—and over on the left's a lake, a strip of blue light down there in the armywall of waiting jungle—as 7 years ago the Jungle was a wall across the potrero in Chiapas—waiting to march against my consciousness—hasn't moved for nearly a decade now.

An ant zigzagging on the concrete, crosses a delicate crack & circles back to my shoe where he came from—traffic going in no particular direction.

8 P.M.—On outskirt of Pucallpa, following road that goes past church & oilfield, passing a row of brown thatchroof houses on stilts, around the back of the iron-silver oilfield fence, up a path thru trees & over a dank stream on a log bridge, to the Curandero's house—bright light in the door and a few dozen men & women sitting on board porch or squat-

ting under nearby trees in full moonlight shade, slapping at mosqui-
tos—the Curandero in his house, on bench, a little distracted—his wife
is giving birth to child in that hour in the next room—one baby toddles
by terrified to the bedroom door—he tells it "Don't be afraid" and
shakes it by shoulder, it calms—meanwhile the patients are waiting out-
side, fellows gossiping "Por la chuchu" at the corner wallbench—the
Babe is born, choked cries from the bedroom—He comes out with a bot-
tle & glass & passes it to the man seated at door at my left—it's water—
comes out again with flashlight—stands in front of house staring in the
darkness—comes in with a cigarette—the ceremony will begin soon I'm
relaxing, sketching by the open door in the light.

June 8?–9? Ayahuasca Session—

Lay back an hour, waiting for something to happen, nothing did, I
just went right on thinking, what was I looking for, anyway, Something
Real about the Universe? And slowly crept up on me that I was in a real
Universe—and had been for many years now in this body—and that this
body was changing, was isolated, but this isolation in the body of Allen
Ginsberg which was my life up to now, would inevitably change—began
to sense a strange Presence in the hut—a Blind Being—or a being I am
blind to habitually—like a science fiction Radiotale—pathy Beast from
another Universe—but from this series of universes in which I do tem-
porarily exist—So temporarily that the presence of the Beast was a
warning of the Future—my body began to shake slightly—I realized pro-
tecting it from mosquitos & sickness was only temporary remedy & un-
consciousness of The Final Proposition of to be or not to be, the Death
which will come to me one day soon, soon enough for me to think of it
was real as this life—and suddenly I felt nausea with life itself, my body
quaking with fear & self disgust at so temporary a Being doomed—I felt

Peru

doomed to Futurity, doomed in Futurity, even if I escape it by poetry queer vanity sex assfucking riding around the world being Loverboy of Boys Allen all my life—sooner or later this lonely farce to be extinguished all this illusion dropped & the skull of Ultimate Reality with its Death rear its head—(O dear Beard in Frisco Angel who taught me, high, *oldage sickness & Death*, Hube the Cube, Seraph, with strange shoulder message of "blessed blessed oblivion.")—I staggered out on the porch and into the garden to vomit, began regurgitating up my sense of Permanence & Security, began vomiting up life—all around the noise of vomit, of the universe vomiting up parts of itself—the snake that eats itself vomiting itself back forth into Being—I was a vomiting snake, that is I vomited with eyes closed and sensed myself a Serpent of Being, or Serpent of Illusion, a serpent of Isolation, the Serpent of Allen, covered with Aureole of spikey snakeheads miniatured radiant & many colored around my hands & throat—my throat bulging like the Beast of Creation, like the Beast of Death—to vomit forth my physical misery to Be—I heaved it out four or five times & remained standing in a trance horrified at my Serpent Self—meanwhile the Curandero was continually crooning to the 30 people dreaming entranced in the Universes all connected telepathically to this one being who expressed one of his aspects thru the tender plaintive Almost motherly Crooning—"Nu nu nu, nu nu, nu, nu nu nu"—I stood in the full moonlight with eyes closed feeling my skull vomiting forth in life knowing the vomit was a little death, only a sign of the frailty of this body, a Sign of What is to Come to the Body—the Great Death which'll envelop it—and communicate itself to the Body, in Time, we can't Escape Trapped, I am trapped in being myself—for tho I cherish myself now & protect me from mosquitos—take tablets to avoid vomit—one day Death will vomit me out of this body— returning to my pallet after a kind word from Seraph Roman, who asked me how I was and if I were "marieado" (drunk enough yet)—I

Peru

saw a man who was sitting against a post with knees drawn up to his breasts—covered with cloth against the mosquitos—like a mummy in Chancay Necropolis' 1000 year old sands—million year old sands—I was his white shrouded face, as if in Xray the hallucination for a moment of seeing thru to the Living Bone that he is, as all men, as I—going to die— and lay down (worried that I might hex him by dwelling on his skull, staring at it too long), I bethought me of my own skull to come & entered such a state of Mortal Misery as I had not ever encountered in conscious life—the realization that we are set here to live and Die, and all man set here set here together in different bodies in a web of realization of the same fate—and I gave myself more up to this mystery— until my head shook back and forth in resignation and defeat, and I gave my fate over back to God who made it—Questioned whether I was yet prepared to Die—The God seemingly discarnate but incarnate in the community of Beings all experiencing the same realization of their Dying Bodies in Strange & unknown spacetime fate—the gentle crooning continuing—I wanted to know if there were some answer, some way out of Fate, some entrance to Perfection which would include both Death & Life, both Allen & Allen's dry indifferent skull—no answer—but saw Christ lifted on the Cross of Death, suffering—I felt Christ—we are all Christ—our Souls are all preparing to be Crucified—for real—"Let this cup pass from me?" but no it will not pass—and I lay there with arms extended for a moment, sighing giving myself up to my defeat, my ignorance of what is and what's to be & who I am & the puny of the game of being poet laying with great Words when the Divine Fire is At Hand, so real, to Be, and to come, and to Die—and the sensation of a presence beyond it all—the void has a billion entrances, a billion deaths—and births—that Billion doored Not Paradise Not Known yet by me only myriad different glimpses of something afar—now Near me—all Creation alive—all beings perhaps the only part we can know—that God

Peru

lives in us, not otherwhere—that *we, here,* are it, the great Presence, *we* are the great Presence of the Universe, our consciousness is the consciousness of the Last Thing—that God himself knows no more than we or I why he was born or where he is going, it is all in us to live or die, to change the Universe of leave it, to be or not to be—and I lay back with my near deadlike body & skull on the mantle and accepted the question there & then—to Escape Being *Now*! And avoided the question—a sudden fear realization that if I chose then to die I might be found by others a corpse in the morn, and news of Allen's death in Drugs reach New York—and scars Peter & grieves Louis—who knows I am sick of Life—but who still thinks I will choose to live—or who still hopes I will come into contact with life again, with women & love creation—I get scared thinking then that I had the power to die then & there—tho I didn't have the power, I was scared of that much power, I shrank back into prayer "In thy Will is my peace" and said "I don't want to die" knowing that if I don't want to die now, when will I ever and yet die I soon must someday & the Great Choice will again confront me—"to reach that Door"—(Hardy)—I began dreaming of all the living whom I knew—Peter afar, who looks on me for Help, for love, for Salvation, for Spiritual Knowledge—and I know nothing—God perhaps knows nothing, it is all up to us, he gives the life to us, his life to us as He, mysterious, without known origin and with unknown end—we are given the Woes of God, we are the God, in existence in the Universe—looking out with open eye at the bright nite sky—clouds a veil of Bethlehem over the Stairs of other Sister or Brother Friend worlds of the same ancient and familiar mystery Universe—like 1000 or one million years ago the problem of the Soul of each Man's existence was the Same, then to him with beast—fur in the jungle under the proud planet stars—but not help.

    Meanwhile the Magic science fiction feeling that all the human souls of the human universe where in now vibrant telepathy contact dreaming

The purpose of life is Death.

of this Problem of Being, what to Be, and what to do, and how to Die—
in realization that the specific secret purpose of life is Death—And even
those like Peter also know not in contact, doomed to be shaken out of
their personal life wombs (such as security with me & My Promise of
Heaven)[30] to come into Terror—Contact with the Real purpose later—
I felt I had been misleading him to trust the merely human fate with
me, to last forever & not die but go hand in hand to Heaven—and this
Skull for him, this crying radio-skull to face him?—

Jack—in what contact was he? With Whom? And how deep?

Lucien & Cessa—Cessa the Angel of Woman, She the Mother—Lu-
cien wisely deciding annihilation of mortal vanity—and to be the Angel
of News—"If Interplanetary news comes I'll be the one to send it out on
the wires"—and hearing more life—Continuing the life of God with his
Babes—

[. . .]

Literally Spiritual Beings Ministering to Me. I see them as seraphs
ministering to my queer isolation—my lack of knowledge, contact with
birth—my fear to be and die—to bear life—They resolved their death by
giving birth first and continuing the race of time—God in this sphere—
in this world—How deep do they know?—or perhaps it is I who am not
deep and know nothing of the Great Radio Truth they all receive and
send—to me, to contact me in time—to help my helpless soul, lost, I am
the lost soul not those I curse and envy and love from afar in my own
lonely way, exiled from Heaven and on Earth.

30. Not long after their initial meeting, Allen Ginsberg and Peter Orlovsky ex-
changed vows in which they promised to help each other reach heaven.

Peru

Naomi, dead, in Madhouse—my mother who I am afraid to (be) return to in sex—all Mother the same—Birth—yet what was she, and what am I that am her product and continue to live in the world of her madness? Is that my curse, which forbids me to live or die, to give birth, but to be neither woman nor man, fucked in the ass, or fucking poor Peter—I resolved to bear Babe, to bear Women, learn women—again—O (Natalie!) Grove Press secretary girl O Elise Cowan[31]—I rejected them—they are my ministering angels—and they believe in me to save them??!!—Horror! They maybe are sent to save me and I not knowing in my ride act Prophet over them and withdraw from their embrace and copulation and vomit of new birth—What will happen to Peter if I leave him, if I change my life, if I die—and *I will* change my life and die—that means he will have to also—I have not let him prepare! I have promised too much and can I deliver?

All souls answered in the séance, with many sighs and thoughts of final deathheads and vomiting in the Jungle night. Experienced a terror that it was all Real, more real than I ever can know, and the great conspiracy has only begun to enter my consciousness—that all know except me—I am alone to die.

Ramon came and told me to vomit where I was if [it] need be—I did again later, serpents in mind and the Little Death the Sign in the vibrations of the nuomenal world I felt as real for the first time

Now I want to sleep—it's all too real—Naomi's death, and Louis to come, Eugene who knows best and marries—Grandma on the verge—careless—

"The Great Pan is Dead" God the Father Dies too, for we are the

31. Elise Cowan, a featured character in Joyce Johnson's award-winning memoir, *Minor Characters*, was a friend of many Beat Generation figures, particularly Ginsberg.

God—and Ezra Pound, why does he hate the Jews? Hate me? Am I that lost, that much the Serpent?

Shit, when I came home, dropping out of my body another reminder of the ghostly state of decomposition and change—

The Height—in the Music of Infinity—my skull rocking back and forth as if settling in the pillow to a final still position, as will be my last movement of head before death—a *NO* sign, in Xray, or realization— No I was all wrong, No I am not ready to die—No, I resign myself to thee, Mystery.

June 10, 1960. Morn next day.

Yes I accept that world of flying bombs is completely disrupted and mad and that God is manifesting himself in some places where there is need and as in the jungle to the simple or thru goodwill to the Indians and psychoanalysts and chemists in the new drugs.

The archetype No yes headshake

Is it real, this terror? What to believe and who to turn to?

Heulsenbeck in New York. Burroughs in Paris?

Peru

My vision is cracked now Right eyeglass has seam, broken maybe last nite.

Thought earlier yesterday all the crazed inklings of the US 19th century Poe-Dickinson-Whitman.

All women are one and all men are one Seraph of Being that knows not its destiny.

In the Universe, the world is mad with flying bombs—something is coming thru from the central control to certain consciousnesses.

Am I going mad? And what's madness in a universe of Death?

That is, while alive, I can evade, I can do what I want, live as if forever in this consciousness—by whatever illusion—read the newspapers or play poet—but sooner or later there is a Reckoning—a "Judgment" that is to say a moment which this consciousness will alter forever—to what? And how to prepare for that "Death"?

My poetry now approaching the place where it is dangerous, where what I say may represent a real spirit talking to Universe in Universe thru Universe—Burroughs' Frontier.

I am afraid to leave this world, this dying consciousness, to enter a permanent spiritual consciousness. And there is no escape from the choice finally. Is there a death, or punishment, or failure? Is there a Hell? Am I the Doomed One?

"What am I guilty of?" screams me, the fat man "All I did was kill a mosquito" and the hand of God comes down smash with redoubled Fury.

Peru

Heal? Says Louis my father? How can I heal my death? Ah Louis I guess you know? You too?

God thinks—thru the telephone—thru all creation—in Us.

I'm going to my madness and don't know why! I'm going to my death and am not prepared! Help! Help! Help!

Aether or this—come back to the Fearful sweetness of "What IS, Is" or "I Am"—and no man knows?

And I can return home, continue my life as before, suspecting a little more—but with creature comforts "And on my head the dews of comfort fell/As ere my woe" (Hardy)—but never escape the Grand Finale, only can avoid consciousness of it awhile more, a short while more.

Buying a pen this morning in broad daylight suddenly the old familiar voice of Nelson Eddy that I used to weep for joy to hear—*Maytime* singing—"Will you love me ever?" and almost cried in the street, another reminder of Death and—what's the sweet answer? And that *Maytime* part of temporary holiday of Creation? And so soon faded, that already Nelson Eddy's voice is old and I am old man looking back to that Early tearful emotional innocence in the Fabian theater where I went to escape life and saw Jeanette MacDonald an old woman—"It is I, the great primadonna" to the reincarnate young girl—and telling the story of her sad destroyed love—

Repeat of my story, of Peter's love, of many loves and early hopeful visionary days.

Peru

Not the last vision I had of Blake was of complete terror—the universe turned inside out to eat me alive—I have still to endure that thru? "Let this cup pass from me?" But it is not possible—and writing this my head my skull shakes back & forth on the pillow in repetition of the last instant of despair I will have before death.

Alone in bed noting my state in hotel room in Pucallpa—green wall on my right, pink wall ahead, huge windows of second story with screens against mosquito & wooden slat-blinds to guard the sun—washed sox & underwear hanging from the blind—a mottled sky, grey light, it had rained this morning—Last night I saw a comet, an aerolith—pass curved & sparkling with red blue center to Earth, near the full moon. I still care for my body, wash my underwear & tend my affairs.

Clung to Joe Peter Jack Bill for family afraid to be alone with Death. All these years, afraid to be alone with no soul to love me, no soul to *sign* to me what is the way of life, no seraph to be my father and protect me—afraid to be born the Lone seraph of Existence—which each man is? The lone & Final seraph of Being? The search that is alone, and dies into the void, not knowing the next transfiguration, if any, to come—leaving a part of Babe Angel behind in human children to guard the garden of Existence?

Many of them Indians, the women many in the dark shelter, humming lone seraphic bee-like tones to themselves in response or continuance or on the same radio beam of celestial telepathy as the communicant seer who was in control, Ayahuascero, Maestro, Curandero. As if from different parts of the void, (as with the vomit sounds erupting separately in different places around the hut but with the same spectral woe) the tunes coming forth—not making a harmony—but many separate voices singing to themselves like lone Seraphs of Being—and being heard by other lone Seraphs of Being—but all disconnected, each born to separate consciousness, separate body, in the same Being—was there some deeper communication I missed?

How Early Christ faced the Finale—That lone Seraph! That poor sufferer, not knowing—giving faith to others?—

Hart Crane—what became of his under the sea? Bartleby "I know where I am" and Melville's cry—

> In dream I thought I saw me Crowned
> Starred Casscopes in a Golden Chair
> & Now awake with maddened eye
> In cell an idiot crowned with straw

We are all waiting for you, Allen, say the others—

> Bland Rhadamanthes beckons him
> But the golden race looks dim
> Salt blood blocks his eyes. . . .

Odilon Redon's Eye—a letter to R Weitzner. With news.

> A consciousness that appears for a moment,
>   like an eye in a balloon in a picture,
>   floating upward to—
> in a picture.

I've seen it several dozen times in this life, Redon's picture of the eye.

It all comes back to me now, "Maytime"—and all the
Choir of Love—

Van Doren, apart from it all?—Weaver's[32] three pictures.
He was a lion,

    roaring in the Void, at me,

   placed there to Instruct,

              a Teacher.

Did I want to go to Heaven *alone*? To be a Saint,

        alone?

We are all equal in Doom & therefore equal

      in knowledge—

All Soul's the same—

The Monk will be poor as my barefoot Indian Curandero
in baseball cap & dirty, vomiting out the sicknesses for
all.

I wanted to be First, so I am last.   (know before Jack,
Bill, Gregory, Peter)—

O Icarus O Icarus!

    To stay in this life, fly not too
near the Sun—and the father grieving—

    Mankind cannot bear very much

        reality

    unredeemable

"If I knew I would tell you"

---

32. Raymond Weaver (1888–1948), comparative literature professor at Columbia
University and author of the first biography of Herman Melville, taught Ginsberg
and encouraged him in his early poetry efforts.

God doesn't know either,
it is up to us to create our universe?
"Thank god I am not God."
All the Ugly ones I rejected my
women & old men & old sweet
farts
Are my saviors—the
Hypnotist in Frisco,
who I didn't trust, so his Magic
didn't take—

I am a Seraph and know not whither
I go in the Void
I am a man and know not whither
I go into Death.

♥

[. . .]

What I saw was worse and more real—a savage spike Cat of Evil.
That awful image as in Blake's watercolor of a man kneeling between
knees of huge fiery smoky devil Seraph—felt myself a primordial hid-
den—in jungle Jivaro warrior vomiting in the grass after a killing of a
soul and the curse on the shrunken head, found myself repeating the
same ritual vomit in the jungle—with snakescales gleaming all over, hat
of feathers and savage grass and a look at skull—Trance on my visage, a
Devil Worshipper. A snarling, savage cat, at bay.

The bands of slowly-moving jeweled snakes rotating slowly on a great
wheel in empty space, making a wheel of which all parts revolve in dif-
ferent directions like an Ezekiel Spirit Wheel.

Peru

All these are "Illusory" but the vision of Death? When there is a death to come? Illusion? Where there is death, where is Illusion?

Sitting in Venezia Coffeeshop, Pucallpa, writing letter, not knowing how to break the news of my death—and not even yet willing to give in to that dream of Death—Not wanting to scare him.

His look to me, near weeping once, on the sidewalk—will I help him? Can he trust me?

With his woes with Julius[33] and his family.

Gregory, is Death man also?

Early movie traumas come back—The Invisible Man, how they hunted him down & he died pitifully transfigured back to visibility in the snow—while his friends weep for his soul.

Dr. Jekyll and Mr. Hyde—His transfiguration to the furry beast (like the vomiter) in the park—I rushed out of the movie of the nightmare of my life to be—into Paterson downtown dark street, age 11 or 10.

♥

Hallucinations are messages from God.

♥

In the Fabian Theater, the floor show, the orchestra, the Negro drummer with the big pumpkin strange round black face and (maybe) eyes

33. Julius Orlovsky, Peter's brother, suffered from a serious mental disorder.

Peru

that looked Death at me from the stage—I am a child in the great theater of the world—terrified of an object Negro on the stage—the Messenger who I'll remember 30 years later & understand at last as my Voodoo Emissary Early—

All life organizing itself around in halo of premonition of the skull to come, the Death.

The Dog & The Convict picture that made me cry age 7 or 6—The police taking the man away to jail forever, and his sad sick dog running vainly after the car, alone—as I am—as Peter will be if I leave him, to die. And the Jail of Darkness forever.

How to send Peter out alone to be born again?

June 11, 1960.

Dream—Peter and I go out to movie hotel, go in early & buy a bed together in the dormitory, undress & get in the bed in a huge bright room off the main Entrance foyer—get under covers, comfortable, like children in a tent—It gets to be 8 o'clock & suddenly thousands of people are coming to the theater & asking for beds—we got the last bed before it was sold out—the house—and we watch from the pillow, leaning on elbows, thru the door to the foyer as the herd of people come thru (from the rain outside)—much activity "How lucky we were to get here a little early—not even knowing the situation—pure accident." Then we see a sweet hunchback woman in green dress, distributing poetry books—setting these up on a shelf, on top of a bureau in the bright dormitory— she's an acquaintance from S. F. of Duncan-Spicer group—gives us new copy of yellow-bound-jacketed poems by Spicer as a gift—And later

someone else comes in with another huge book by Spicer, another gift—
I say we already have his book—but this is a special one to me—I open
the package & it's a glass enclosed collage—it opens like a book but it
is a sort of medicine cabinet (with drugs & aspirin & vasoline & mummy
hair and etc inside) and pasted on the window are cut outs from eco-
nomic & popularity & Gallup statistical reports—graphs—what an in-
sult!—saying all my consciousness is hung on these graphs of Fame—
but it is a sort of weird sweetness the trouble he went to—maybe it is
even true—I wake, forget dream, in huge rain that is coming down roar-
ing outside Pucallpa Hotel window at dawn—later remember Spicer's
face & set of teeth & lips spitting out words as physiognomy similar to
the vomiter.

Earlier dream in the nite of Frank Sinatra & Marlon Brando—

The prick when limp, shrinking back & forth and the scrotum slowly
contracting or loosening, on occasion, an involuntary process So the ac-
tion of the soul opening & closing.

June 10, 1960

Like discovering late in life that you're nothing but a mettaloid mon-
ster—in *that* kind of universe. Doomed to extinction.

The universe is like committing suicide.

The last Blake vision—of such terror where the sky went black on the
campus and the cosmos turned on me to devour my Being in its hungry
maw—I couldn't stand and shut it off, quit, retreated to human con-
sciousness fearful of madness, of being sealed off, fearful as if it were

Peru

true, afraid of that death—the Revelation that the death is real, not merely a happy stage of transformation to more, and pleasurable, bearable, life—that I could not get away with it in that I will be shut out forever.

I am a Seraph and I go I know
    not whither in the Void
I am a man and I go I know not
     whither into Death.

June 11—All day rain and brown gooey mud all over the streets, Pucallpa—stood hiding from water under eaves of police station, looking at the park, an old barefoot guzzler sidled up for a cigarette, "Gringo OK" & wanted to know what my business was. Blindman came along tapping wooden sides of the headquarters—patched blue pants, brown wood stick, old barefoot shuffle, a ragged pouch at his side—following next to the board wall—reached the next man standing 2 yards down continued touching the wall but withdrew his hand just as he reached the lounger—

My accoster after some conversation finally proposed we visit his cunedo, an Ayahuascero. Said thanks, no.

But might start a whole new mad notebook if I went into *that* chance universe, too.

A dream in which I met Mr. Death, and from which I will not wake up. So the choice consciously given is, whether to accept the dream & enter death, or reject the dream as unreal & return to reality.

Can I accept death in a dream, die for real, and *yet* return to reality?

Slept all afternoon, lazy, defeated by rain, heat, floho-ness, but to Yarinacocha unknown when & where to catch—finally got up at 4 and walked out of hotel door like magic the bus passed so I took it, returned medicine for ass & Schultes' monograph on Ayahuasca to Dr Binder.

June 11, 1960. Ayahuasca III in Pucallpa

All day worried, fearing the spectral Calvary of the last drunken-ness—Came later in darkness and mud walking 4 km. from Yarinicochs and then bus, missed meet with Ramon—arriving shining flashlight by sizeable group—10 people waiting—I drank second in the little sidehut, went outside, sat on wood platform bordering the house, then Ramon carried bench out in the moonlight—sat there awhile and then went and lay down, afraid to close my eyes on the stars over my head thru the trees—but subtly felt the marreea or intoxication—stealing over senses —slight motion—something strange coming over me—I put an Aludrox in my mouth to try avoid bad stomach—the instant it touched my mouth I was nauseated and still desperately chewing the superficial Audrox rushed aside to the shrubbery and began vomiting—flash of yellow fire devils like the serpents last time—same beasties—tho much swifter in passage, just an instant of perception like the flash glow of each retch, the Savage Cat Fanged Serpent self vomiting up Death, vomiting out its extinction—not ready for death. Then lay down on bench still per-turbed worried what was to come—and sense of failure already, my body and soul having so (after one-half hour) rejected the potion of Death— a physical cowardice from recollection that made me nearly nauseous— so felt culpable of avoiding the Calvary to come, postponing again then slowly the ayahuasca did take some stronger effect and I found myself back in the same Universe as before, a self condemned to worry about the extinction in the face of—what? Death, yes, the reverse of Life—and

God is Death—thus I who wanted to see God entire balk at the actual moment of realization of the Identity of the Mystery—because realization destroys consciousness & destroys life itself—O Icarus—and Death is no imaginable thing, nor God, tho there are an infinite number of possible visions of the Final Identity because the Final Identity has no Final Identity but is—as the swoop-cry of some nameless Frogbird whoopsing it up under a dark leaf in the jungle with a whistle like a comet that curves from Nothingness for a half God or many Gods does —Yet always the same cry, always same Snell-Nosed familiar whoops of illusion manifesting its presence, reborn a million myriad times in each being—and the Great-to-the-Void of Nothingness where it all emerges from & goes back to—and at the same time as the isolate Whoops in Infinity, the concurrent whistle of a thousand locusts within earshot, radiating outward wherever locusts are to the limits of invisible sound, and the croak of life frogs, the racket of tomtoms in huts by the oil tanks, aggrieved dogbarks and goofy jug-jug grunts from huge toads in the rainmud, the curandero humming na na na in tender tune to all—punctuated by a celestial rifle shot to signal the race of infinity from some civilized bar keep—and my consciousness lying on the beach outside the hut revolving the mirror of its existence on itself and getting no answer—"I see everything except my Eye," said Ramon

Except the presence of the Snell-Void, that is a thing, a Nothing, Distant, near enough to Feel however, with a seemingly Mock-human Presence in my consciousness, a presence *felt*, like, and like I feel the presence of Father, Brother, dead Mother, Family—my immediate family of Being combined in one presence—and so began a long funny conversation.

Naomi-Madness—different real universes—the madman changes from one to the other each real, very confusing to the consciousness of Being—and a flash comes each time the universes shift (schizophre-

Peru

nia)—a flash of—Nothing—or a flash reflected in the Mirror of whatever Being is conscious at the moment—reflected in the way the form of the mirror is built—so that each Incarnation (of Nothing, Zero) is different—even for the same person, each vision of mine is different & contradictory to the previous—except they all involve the indescribable *personal familiar* plastic-sentient (Snell-nosed)—thus how the Hindus make a god with 4 different faces in 4 different directions—many incarnations out of one Discarnate—dog-faced gods, snell-nosed.

As to the Universe—it is out there, here, where I, Allen, am—I opened my eyes & saw the beautiful familiar stars of my present existence, all I ever knew—all I will ever know—glad to still live and share in this Existence that I am so used to—but that later I must depart—Must I?

Well, if you don't want to . . . But I will grow old, hairless, dying

That's the way this existence is—"Do you *want* to live forever?"

No! No! except maybe forever like I am now, young with beard—

Became I conscious then that to live forever in this state of torture too, because always faced with missing out on the great One entrance to the Final—thus always Allen the poet tortured by a goal incapable of reaching—knowledge of truth which is in Death—but afraid of that Truth too—so stuck in this half life—and still with all the old human problems, boys, fear of women, no babies—

I should leave poetry & learn. Mechanics & help out this human existence illusion—it's a permanent illusion—

To be or not to be—Hamlet, I thought for the first time what that meant, really, it's God's question too, of Himself—he's created us out here, like toys, sent us forth from himself in the only way possible, built a whole universe toy apart from his inside Black other self—and made us completely free of him—made us completely—unconscious and inconscient of the Nescience of Death which we are the Free opposite, independent entity, of—i.e. he's given us the only form possible outside of his own, he's actually invented a new form independent of him—probably has invented a billion forms independent—pure creation—just to bear life—but they all (perhaps)—all the separate God entities—all come back to the one same beginning—end in Death—or do they?—why the poor universe is just a baby, beginning to talk—perhaps the Universe will grow up to be a God one day & create its own baby universes—will even turn around and attack God—but by that time, the consciousness necessary to attack God & reach him will be still the same consciousness that God has—so all perhaps a universe can do is to commit suicide— like Buddha—but another Whoops somewhere else will emerge illusionally in Nothing—so the process will endlessly repeat itself—and

I, Allen Ginsberg, in this Universe home here and afraid of dissolution of Me—

But the me is such a trap & figment—there's a million Me's—and it's all one Me—why worry about this universe's Allen's me

And the Xray flash of the Death of me to come.

God doesn't say Me—he just reflects all the different Me's . . . "There is no mirror" 5th Patriarch.

Shakespeare was God's poet—and the Tempest, Illusion—"leave not a rack behind" the final statement—perturbed, him too for his Death— "Thus consciousness does make cowards of us all."

And Carl Solomon?[34] Them 50 shocks gave him a forced taste of the Void—knows too much to stay in this illusion—yet always still, is looking in mirror to Self—has to as we all—so in Void & this world—makes no difference where he is—had trouble thinking of Carl—he's another snell-nosed me—he is me, another me that I'm aware of as another me (all man's another me but I only get the conscious small taste of me in

34. Ginsberg met surrealist writer and poet Carl Solomon (1928–1993) while both were being treated at a psychiatric institute. Ginsberg dedicated "Howl" to him.

Peru

some like Carl). And the sadness of that awareness that we are all the same creative living many different illusions the creative living many different illusions the same creature dying a million deaths & coming back to itself with each one, only to lose that self too in despair knowing another Same-self will be somewhere else born or dying and remember Me, too, at the last familiar snell-nosed wild minute of extinction.

Vomiting, all the drinkers vomiting Death—Death Vine is a taste of Great Death—which the body rejects by vomiting when it gets too near —and the Vomiter sees himself in a flash a living illusion (like a self-serpent) vomiting out knowledge premature knowledge of the Truth, of its own extinction, vomiting away, getting rid of God.

God is to be got rid of to live, if not you die.

We are God's vomit, he vomited our consciousness out of himself into our Being in order to be conscious of himself. If we did not exist there would be no consciousness on this human level, there would only be x-type consciousness which is not consciousness, God knows—perhaps he is aware of his Being thru us—that's the only way he could be aware, in this way of awareness.

Or perhaps he has a million other, infinite other modes of being he was created that he is conscious in.

To be or not to be? Does God want to continue the experiment?

Do you, Allen (asks God). It's all up to the creatures created, if they want to go on or not. They can always come back to me. (God)

Then I should go on & improve this universe?

"Yes, if you want to," says God.

But I want you!

Well, you had me the other day & didn't like it. Besides, in the long run you'll get me alright. Do you want me now?

No! No! Yes! No! I want both I want both life here & life in you. I want *All*.

Peru

Well, I told you what all is, you'll get it.

I want to feel you now

Well, lay back & feel a little & stop asking questions then.

So I lay back & felt a little, just a little, afraid to feel too far. Felt strange, happy, a funny conversation with God—as in a mirror—as with a part of my own mind. Sometimes both.

The Whoop of the frogbirds, the dogbarks muffled near & far, the crooning of the Crooner Curandero—my eyes open—the blue blue biblical sky & veil of holy clouds as in the ancient stagesets of the Prophets —the yellow stars—out there those Unknown presences of Futurity— good to still be alive—what mystery is *this* Creation—and behind it all a Mirror, and behind the Mirror a Great What?

A great What!?

Well, you've always asked me human questions. Ask me something inhuman & you'll get inhuman. I'm you, says God.

Just me?

Right now.

But God being nothing has infinite aspects & he might be someone else next time I get high.

Disillusion of returning to life unchanged, with the same Death problem unsolved—no other way to solve it but die—words words words —"Death Problem," and Sexlove.

What should I do about women?

"Make love to them."

If I drank another cup would I get the horrors? Would I throw up— I didn't try & accepted the mad game of as is for awhile—conscious of the skull afar, afraid to go in again.

The word God unsatisfactory as the Word Die. When dying, forget about the void because the experience is something new & strange— same with God, who is Real, & the word is unreal.

Peru

Not that we are the same creature living a million deaths, a million illusions, but we are all the same Illusion living a million creatures—and the taste of snell-nose in death is the taste of illusion, not the taste of creaturehood.

Or the Illusion is a creature, they are one & the same & at death or Vision taste their non-Identity & the equal non-identity of "God" the void.

The Illusion is a creature. The whoops of the frogbird is a creature, like a whole universe that whoops, one illusory creature myriad times repeated discovering the same old mistake in death.

Laughgas similar.

Lay back on the bench, if I am to live in this way, why not be happy?

Why not? Says God.

So I began smiling—I saw myself smiling over my skull—laughing a little, why not.

I want to be happy.

Well, be happy then. Be anything you want. (Till you die.)

OK, I feel happy.

Well, are you happy being happy?

Not particularly. What kind of game is this?

You're making the rules, says God.

OK, I'll make up life rules. I should give up poetry & mysticism because it's only a word game, and the real thing is Death. That leaves me nothing to do but—work, babies, improve the Universe.

Yes, that's fine for the Universe, says God.

But I'm not satisfied with the Universe.

Well, drink some more Death, then.

Do I have to?

Peru

It's up to you If you want more than your universe you can have it. Painful But you're free to stay here awhile, that's why you were born for—

"Yes, I'm still young only 34 plenty hair left—too young to die."

"It doesn't really make much difference in the long run, does it?" say my mind-God half & half.

"I'm a coward" I think & have failure at the mission I set out.

And the braggart & loudmouth beast of God in my poetry—Magic Psalm is rubbish—tho on a human level it does point the way toward an area of consciousness—tho not the thing itself—that's too real—so the poem "Misses" & is a mess of lies & exaggerations—a deceit in fact— and what's all this external poetry anyway when the real drama's inside, in death where there's no poetry—who am I trying to kid—myself?— that I am an important God representative sent here to tell people something?

Tell them what—to die? They will.

Write a poem tell them how to live?

Why write poems, when the subject is Gone, the Subject is unapproachable in poetry—at least you haven't found the way to approach it with complete experience of the Subject. That being your deepest Feel & Fear—God or Death—which now you, I, am afraid of to the point of refusing second cup of deathvine. Well, there's always later. Maybe you'll be in a more ignorant mood & see worse & deeper.

O.K. I'll give up happy this time & leave the real suffering for later.

That's ok, good. Later, man, says God.

I kiss God goodnight, happy & failed, rather smug, & go in to get blown by the Maestro.

He's in the hut singing a little tune, flashlight in pocket & towel over his head, tune goes on na na na for 5–10 minutes, then he blows huge homemade round cigarette smoke in the back of the neck of the person he's curing. I lean against front wall, sitting, and watch & listen, back in Anthropology. Ramon comes in, shivering, he's been shaking all night, & vomiting, God knows what depth of horror he's seen after 3 years of this—asks for me & reminds Maestro to blow (souffler) me—I sit crosslegged back touching Maestro's knees (he's on chair me on floor) and he hums for 10 minutes—peasant tender little tunes that go nowhere & change, as the universes—then continues, I go into reverie thinking of Voids—finally he finishes & puts hand on back of my skull & blows smoke in my hair there, nice feeling—3 times—says ya'sa, that's it, I wrap towel around my neck, pick up flashlight & cigarettes—another man sitting down to get blown—another man outside had been resting his head near my towel in his own dream. Walk home slowly, listening to drum & panpipe music from shacks by the river, no mosquitos after rain, walking back thru this life, baffled by the Incomprehensible.

The problem is to communicate not these abstractions but the gluck glue glop of God—The poetry problem.

But why do it anyway? To remind people to die? I mean it's a hopeless task to try to maintain this consciousness & still try & treat with Another outside of ourselves This negates all my poetry.

Christ a man like all others, a poor man, arms outstretched, defenseless—the crucifixion is a picture of how.

What I must have experienced last time with skull sort of a miracle.

God has to reject us from himself if we are to have independent existence (or even the illusion of?)

And we have to reject God? To give this universe independent illusion futurity?

Peru

That shudder that passes thru my heart & shoulders when I pee—has it some connection—will I ever see that in a flash, as connected to the Soul's realization of the fragility & weakness of the body, that drops shit & leaks water, and is a skull? Realization of the nature of the body—"What shall I do with this absurdity"—

Bland Radamanthus beckons him—Plotinusis afraid to pass into the Alone, he's too human, salt blood blocks his eyes—he despairs of heaven, the golden race looks dim—in the poem,[35] finally after suffering, his consciousness end[s] & the subject passes over to the "all choir of Love" & Plotinus is no more, drowned & passed on to—the choir? I guess Bland Radamanthus is scary, but *not* the Judge of inferno, he is the Inferno of Death fear—but he's bland & behind him all the choir. No more Plotinus, he's left behind, soul in heaven—But why wasn't Pythegoras' name left behind?

On bench, thinking, in depth—now I understand, now I see why moth goes to flame if Death is God—The flame so clear an incarnation of the Spirit—even Alive, a point of light, wavering, bending, beckoning, a pure brilliant sexy mystery to the moth, like a moving aethereal cockhead—hurts to approach. But the light so bright & uncanny—real—a single example of the Great Same Many—The movement of the light more sinister & significant the longer you stare into it—the realization that it is what you think it is—hypnosis of certainty—candleflame weaving & ascending to Nothing—the fire itself giving itself to die—the noth-

35. Ginsberg added this footnote at the bottom of his journal page: "Yeats' 'Delphic Oracle of Plotinus.'"

Peru

ingness resolution & a sudden plunge into pain—an instant as in human suicide which precipitates total consciousness and the moth buzzing about, unequal to the pain, unwilling to leave God alone, bothering itself, helpless to leave the First light it has approached—

The moth at Machu Picchu which could not enter the lightbulb, dropping to the floor exhausted—suddenly given its wish, gobbled up by Donald Duck.

Hart Crane & Natalie[36] & Joan[37]—what she understood, having had Benny hallucinations & then later "out of the running" & then later to die—Soul Vine or Death Vine is a conscious poison.

If so, why was I "given" Blessed visions of Blake Father & LSD Dancing gayhead?—I couldn't have handled the Black Death of the skull visage so young. The last black Blake glimpse was beginning.

Sweeny Nightingales & Delphic Oracle on Plotinus—both Ellipses & a function of visionary ellipse to present one image of penultimate perception-consciousness, indicate the death of that consciousness by jump to image perception consciousness in another being—i.e.

> The moth enters the bright Being
> I stare picking my nose.

4 Quartets—The complete knowledge is Death—Is the "Love" that moves the shirt of Flame anything recognizable by what I know or feel as love? If not, it is still a mystery.

36. Natalie Jackson, a girlfriend of Neal Cassady, died in what was either a suicide or a terrible accident.

37. Joan Vollmer.

The fear that God, Death, is the Devil, an evil spirit a sensation which when I reach it will turn out to be—some mechanical horror trap—plunge me into another terrible state of threatened being—reborn a fly eaten by spiders—

The Spider & Fly another archetype Mystical Ecstasy. To fly the spider must seem Mystical Death the Father—until the first bite & the Deathmask of consciousness goes, & the fly glimpses the life inside the spider—Indifferent as to which form—

The time before this, the revelation of the purpose a significance of Life as Death—and the bamboo hut filled with suffering Beings, like bees in a hive of consciousness buzzing to each other the tone of sacredness awareness of the great Being Vision they are in the presence of—all the suffering cadavers sitting still listening and staring inside at the hive empty space—humming in praise of the Knowledge—the Deity whose name is Terror & All—whom they cannot reject because he is, no escape—all comforting each other with songs in his presence, and knowledge in Him, and aiding the new born deaths in Him, as we comfort a Babe that cries—the Maestro's babe in arms, red, swathed in flannel or cotton with flower prints, & old thin smiling lady patting it and touching its nose & giving it comfort in its newborn suffering. And I among these presences in the hut just returned to consciousness of my death state to come & afraid to lose myself still, doomed to be Allen, as long as I am Allen.

I never wanted to be born this strange Allen—what a wobblenosed myth that is—a Jewish myth—begun in Naomi's madhair pubis and Louis' trembling cock of Me—a Russian Mythhood, from the old World —yet here I am.

And Eugene did he want to be born that Eugene? He almost cut off his nose in despair at being himself.

Peru

At the cockfight with the Maestro & Ramon—electricity of two heads with beaks, blood red, facing each other tense & moving back & forth in mirror symmetry waiting for break to peck out an Eye.

My fear of seeing, my pain of seeing a cockfite, bullfite, or—ah the Cocks covered with blood &—Christ lifted on the cross the same—a Rastro, slaughterhouse—nothing but fear of my own flesh & blood—reminder of my own—I never want to realize that so avoid seeing death lest I be brought to face my own skull. I run away from accidents on the street.

June 12, Sunday, 1960—

Death Visions—like Ulysses & Sirens—can get near but have to be tied down & protected.

Wax in their ears, the rest.

Do I have to go back with Wax in my ears?

The Incarnation cancels itself out.

A forgotten Memory: II and III Ayahuasca in Pucallpa, particularly early #2—lying back seeking death, feeling my interior skull, my spectre coming up, and recognizing my physical face—twitching—my lips & nostrils twitching like a cornered beast, parts of a snarl—at bay by God—the human face twitching afraid of its own dissolution—as if the cells themselves were asserting their own life, crawling over my face like worms, disgusting the vision of my face & piece of twitching meat, that being me in the face of the Faceless.

This connected to the sensation when vomiting, of being a furry cat-faced wormy savage seraph, evil before God, vomiting up death in the void—my beard outside me, my face covered with worms of twitch, my stomach retching.

To think of in Future (the eye of the Rose)

Blake	Van Gogh
Beethoven	Cezanne
Rembrandt	
Dostoyevsky	
Buddha	

The joyful trumpet at end of Tchaikovsky's 5th—clarion on top of the waves of Death—is that an illusion too? Just another catfaced desire?

Poem using insight of them.

June 13—Crying at nite, 8:45 a.m. now walking round market—Mexican music—everything *familiar* reminds me of death

Samuel Greenberg's *To Dear Daniel*—There was a loud noise of Death where I lay.

Conversation with the Thing this other nite like conversation with a Mirror, as Death or nonbeing or God is the reverse (Mirror) image of life—being—Man.

Peru

(or as the Thing is the reverse of me)—as I moved it moved in symmetrical dimensions.

In Ramon's house—a table with bottle and six arms.
Four arms are afraid of Death. "But not me," said the teacher.
In the middle, Sr. Paternovitz he fears death.
Linares, smiling, not having death fear.
I, Allen Ginsberg, don't know anything—but am afraid—very.

Ayahuasca IV

These conditions
        I am constantly
            putting in front
            of God's hand
        that I die or do not die,
            that he have a
                    form
            thus he be joyful or
                        deathful,
        that he even Be—
O.K.—Unconditional—
                Cease thought—
        that he be beautiful
                or ugly,
        an elephant or a man,
        that he be brought
                into a world or not

that I see him or not.
That I write poetry or
                not—
are irrelevant—
The worst that can
        happen, the event
        most frightful, is
        —most frightful to
        the being concerned—
        to pass from one
        realm of Being to
another Unknown—
in this, Birth &
Death are the Same—
        —weak Ayahuasca.

                    *   *   *   *   *

Thus for God is the Being
        that constantly changes
            his form from one
                birth to another,
                suffering death
                    after death—
It may be the
    heart of God is
        a Crucifix.

Peru

I have been born
  before—
This is the
  lesson,
the old lesson
  of Being—
   My writing is
crosseyed because
I have been born
and will be
reborn endlessly

Before—I felt the approach of a serpent consciousness that intrigued & scared me—scared to give up my own consciousness for another alien consciousness—tho surprised at this appearance, it was a familiar thing it had happened to my consciousness before—and usually—as far as I can remember, my consciousness refused to give itself up to this strange approacher Who could it be? God? or a serpent? Or just another of many, many consciousnesses—I felt plunged—thinking of the moment of my physical Death—into a darkness from which I—so far—have always reappeared in the same person—Allen—tho I feel that I might some day if not now give up what I am so familiar with—to become another Being—Different—and it is a difficult choice to make—tho we are later forced to it. Artemio singing to me in the moonlight. Nice nite—the Cross far off in this weak state—putting his hand out hypnotically like a snake—and I stared at it till realized that it was the very blind living hand of Being in the void.

Peru

Being in a hand
    begging in the
        Night

❤

or God is a hand
    begging in the
        Void
How gentle & innocent

❤

that empty hand &
    what guile can
        it have—
and how did it
    get there—
    Then went in
cabin & drank
    second cup

❤

"The same thing has many different existence[s]."
It is always reborn. Is it possible that it, or I
   —not dying now but waiting to see what the future will bring, old
age, more consciousness—the message seemed to B[e]
   Widen the area of consciousness in the world for that is the only
answer to the question—who are we?—
   To continue where I left off before—Is it possible that I am an old
Allen, reburn, and reborn over again death after death? That is why the
same stars seem familiar existence after existence, I remember them,

Peru

as I am now remembering myself—in the bright light of the friendsy electrical battery operated 2.oo flashlight I bought in Huanuco.

Certainly it is a magically operated little Being-Machine—in a larger Magic Universe—

I only remember myself, with head hung on breast relaxed, thinking Do I remember myself from first this one life—in this exact position in brown jungle-shirt and beard—or do I remember from a life before?

And all I can remember is just asking the question—and the reply is open.

Will I be reborn a pig or a serpent or does it make any difference or can I ascend to a supreme wide total consciousness?

What answer does this question contain?

The end of the book.

—ink run out.

Much thought of Williams—"The Fools"—and have I repeated lives with him?

The bearded stars—or the stars with their beards of cloud—nebulous old beards—

At times I am a strange creature—I found myself a strange creature shitting in the fields, pants down, ass out familiar to the earth, my ass-hole moving in and out voiding the body—moving slowly in and out like a great serpent coiling itself in folds—the *familiar* feel of my known Godly asshole—As all parts of the body is God or as one of the infinite aspects of God which is I guess everything.

It is the Death of Consciousness that stops me—and begins the real mystery of Being—

How close Williams is to that strange event which breaks the human pattern.

Death of Louis.

Poet, go home to the king of Poets, thy Father.

Vultures rise up in anthem to the worlds
Palmtrees and skyscrapers waving in transcendency
One human image in the end remains myriad eyed in eternity

[...]

"Hallucination"—that will be repeated on Deathbed—only then there won't be any "reality" and Life to go back to.

"I want to come back & cook for you," said Naomi, wanting to return to the old life, faced by the Great Change. Yes then was the last reality, same as the transcendent Calvary of Ayahuasca. No illusion. She couldn't face it any more than I can bear to.

Louis on his deathbed turning into the Elephant snell-faced god—or "I'm afraid"—or with burning last eyes "Promise me you will have children, Allen."

Pound on Deathbed "It's the fucking Indian god, the god of Vedas & Snakes & Elephant Noses, the Kali-Shakti sex fiend God with the old familiar [?] of unbelievable rebirth."

Peter's laugh on Peyote made me afraid. I saw the Snell in it, my Death.

"That's the way that is given to keep the Spark of Self alive"—babies— Is it worth keeping alive—Is the experiment of Separate Universes— this—a success?

"That's up to you, Allen," says God. "To be or Not to Be."

"What's the task of the Messiah?

I took on God's work in poetry—now what am I stuck with? To be God & endure many Deaths? Or to be human & avoid death till it comes?

The purpose of Life is Death. I'm afraid to face the significance Now—to feel the purpose of Death in everything at once.

It doesn't seem to mean Blissed Death-in-Life, but complete death, with no reward to self, no Gain, a complete physical give-up-of All.

Peru

The wide spread stars are all old eye the yellow moon over the horizon path is light ½ across Ucyali river, lying on beach listening to the Death Croak of Locusts, content to be back in old reality under the blue sky like ancient Bethlehem—feeling the Elephantskin of Deity in my imagination.

A few times in psychoanalysis—With the Reichian Cott—with Brooks once—got to same depth of "significance" which was hard to bear & drove me off.

I don't want to wake up on my Deathbed having wasted my life—and this is the nightmare I have now.

————————Why was I mad at Louis? What did he ever do? Of the family I knew as a child, Aunt Rose is gone. Uncle Harry is gone. Uncle Sam is gone. Naomi is gone—all gathered away to the Invisible, Aunt Rose the first—Elanor is Gone, with all of New York. And I? And all the rest will go. Ah, Eugene—ah, Eugene! Yes, it's true

O damned Elephant! (What have you created?)—

The Sick Rose is time, which is like the sunflowers, Time—sick because always dying—The invisible worm is God—Death—Eternity—Chaos

God is Chaos!

The bed of crimson joy is the unconscious illusory temporary human self love in Time—the pipsqueak swoop of the frog-bird and his dark secret love?

—[?]

Peru

Doth thy life destroy—

      That's clear

"A sadder but a wiser man." Weeping in Pucallpa hotel room, feeling
the death of my family and the vast Wheel of Time turning Invisibly.
—Invisible wheel of Time—

      "arise from their graves" Blake?

O Blake come help me now
The tears run down the cheek

      that hides my skull

   "Where the youth pined away with desire"
as I have pined away,

    and am no youth anymore—

Peter doesn't realize the deaths will be final yet—and I've
been promising him heaven to get him to have me.

    I can't save anything, not even my poetry

      Death is Emptiness.

Problem is to find language to fit the experience,

    not experiences to fit the language.

      (I've done both)

Early Psalm II[38] is prophetic of what I feel now—

In the darkness, thinking of Peter's Created Soul, his trees bowing
down to him weeping, his poor self, his awkward voice singing "Sweeter

38. See "Psalm II," *CP*, 28.

than a flower," his kindness to me, his aloneness, his tenderness—all the inner Peter of birthday—

And give up *love,* too. That to be sacrificed to the Maw of Emptiness, with no redemption, no return—all to die?.

—"Hence the soul cannot be possessed of Divine Union until it has divested itself of love of all Created things"

But Krishna's Doggie?—
Well there's one for God to resolve.

And all the loves of the world?

Beyond my twitching skull I love, and Peter's voice like a baby Angel in realm of Joy,

and Blake's voice inside my head but imagined

God appears & God is Light
To those who dwell in realms of Night
But doth a human form display
To those who dwell in Realms of Day

and he pronounced it with a young kid's voice, "but doth a *human* full of clear-eyed child-shrewdness on clear eyed child-shrewdness==alto voice almost—as of that were the Resolution of the Scene of Death I've been made—The Radio angelboy voice

Peter's celestial Joy.

And has God also made celestial pain? Yes, I've felt that, too. Peter is my angel who'll save me with celestial Joy?

Peru

June 13, 1960   dream poem
"The snows already told me to be Mephisto & born here"
dream verse first line.

Louis Dark years 324 Hamilton Ave Paterson 1943–50—alone and
rejected by all—I looking for or finding new love in Jack—Gene in
Newark—or Army by then in his own chaos—
To undo all my sins, remember all sufferings before I die—
My vow in ferryboat to Columbia to help the workingclass if I got
accepted in Columbia and could join Paul R.[39]—how does that figure in
now?
Must Messiah-Dyer-Dier—know everyone's sufferings.

Kerouac's skull in Mex City Blues—Death of his Father.

America the first of the new race of industrial giant world trees—
overshadowed now by younger species Russia and Megalocephalical
China—but always will retain the glory of America even when old
cracked & dying—all the old trees of the World, France & the Balkans—
them shrubs.

> To be poet, inspired by life,
> but a prophet, inspired by Death?
> How can poet be priest? as in Whitman?
> How be priest when just playing with His words? Not yet
> dead?

39. A friend in Ginsberg's youth, with whom Ginsberg hoped to strike up a rela-
tionship when both attended Columbia. It never happened.

Christ: in order to get to heaven the whole body thing has to die, Hope Joy & Mercy—to be transfigured into the Miraculous.

Because God is more than the hope of one Man, is the Hope of all—therefore is All including Pain & Frogs & Crickets—Therefore elephant nose, the Inhuman.

Life is a dream in which I die. A dream within a dream—"and what dreams may come. . . must give us pause."

I've heard the Cock Crow three times.

All man like Peter denies Death 3 times before Cock Crow.

Why am I suddenly *afraid* of death—which I thought a sweet thing before?

The situation I've been crying for God all my life, & suddenly discover God is Death. Or seems to be.

The IInd Ayahuasca in Pucallpa—Like a dream sound of the groans of Monk-Creatures gathered together in the Tibetan hive of Creation to feed like bees on the Black Honey of Death which poisons them and is a living thing.

Like the movie *The Thing*. The thing behind creation didn't seem human—& I thot before we were in the Image of the Thing.

The Invisible Thing
The thing which will get me,
the thing which is loose in the world
always has been
always will be

The thing that eats the world
　　thru its Death-Mouth
The thing that exists thru all time.
　old thing that never touches the world.

After 1 AM Ayahuasca IV Pucallpa

The night of the Bearded stars—that is I spent long time, & continually refreshed my vision, by gazing up at the stars—amazed to find myself *back* in the familiar universe—not the everyday one, but the sense of the Universe previous to the everyday one, and at the same time, new as if I were looking for the first time

　　"And this is the first (& last)
　　　　day of the World."

Much on Williams & his sense of what the Universe is—he must see the pigeyed repetition of things—But a sense of Williams as a Soul, a Consciousness aware of the even upcoming disappearance—and what generalization he might make of that to apply to the whole Universe. Saw him enter Non being with huge white feathered angelwings—and his eyes & face—a familiar strange being (Seraph)—familiar & strange as an elephantnose statue with living eyes—human eyes —and homely-godlike feminine chin—and high pitched, also, quavering voice—repeating the Secret Lesson—clear as Death—a consciousness on the verge of disappearance talking to other consciousness— talking in Itself—hiding—confessing—hollow as the universe—another Dream.

The Serpent Sense—Ramon blew smoke over my head to make it go away—like a slowly approaching—"Bolero"—of sensation building up— like a fold of a serpent and a head appearing with closed eyes to enter my brain to approach the verge of consciousness—and then another fold slowly slithering in, coiling around itself, and another coil from a different direction, and then the sensation was of myriad coils of hissing consciousness coming—that might eat and take over my own consciousness—and I would be what?—But Ramon blew & told me it was bad & made it go away—i.e. withdrew or broke my attention to it.

Was this another aspect of God, who seems to appear in an infinite number of different aspects, one each time, sometimes one each thought—

Peter—I have made him my slave. What for? Why do I want a slave? Why does he need to be a Slave—for protection—from life? And I am his slave too, tho perhaps less—I wander off into my consciousness—afraid, too, but I accidentally wander off to Death—or thru life, & change—forced to it—thru alien consciousness.

All this is possible, *is* happening. No?

The impossible is happening. Only thing that could happen in the void is the Impossible—

Thus this Impossible Being—the Impossible Consciousness—which we feel—everyday: wondering how the universe even got here, got started.

Fantasy—why never touched Gene's genitals, nor Louis, nor Edith's, nor the whole families?

Gene must have been sick & embarrassed at me hugging at him, pleading for physical love when we slept together as children way back in the Archetype World of the Past, 1934–1937.

I must have been a sexpest to the whole family, even when sleeping with Louis. Gene was the only one who rebuked me, but without shame or guilt—just elastic rejection of elastic demand.

Elastic beautiful word Title of book ala Gregory. Elastic universe too—Elastic, consciousness is an elastic hand. Sometimes tightens into

Nothing of the Self (skull visions)—sometimes as tonite stretches out the Universe.

I see the image of the Serpent to indicate a nameless slithering alien undulating consciousness that I perceive thru the top of my eyehead approaching my Being.

Ayahuasca is both the same and different everytime—a totally new sense of the Absolute, and yet a sense very familiar from the feel of the stars of the last time around the Cosmos.

Opened my eyes—the fellows all sitting in chairs in the garden in the moonlight enjoying the mystery of Being—like a mystery movie—at the Movies.

The curandero with white towel shrouding his simplehead, smiling & relaxing slumped motionless in chair, listening to Mind.

The others sprawled about in siesta—but at Midnight and not sleeping but Being Aware of things together—in the obscure blue jungle midnight.

Each tree an apparition of Birth, Each tree a God to be dreamed its due for posture & leafage & message from itself.

A few more generalizations—

The Secret All is a consciousness which includes ours but is infinitely wide—we can widen our consciousness but in order to be identically conscious with the All we have to, at the present time, widen it to include the Not-ourselves which is death.

At height of horror & rapture with death, the people in the hut were adoring—as in a book of Revelations—a Consciousness they were aware

Peru

of, beyond their limits, in Death, which they were created to, or had evolved to, the point of becoming aware of needing to enter (it) to become one with (it).

Death is the Lord of the Universe. That's why Christ hangs on the Cross.

That Hole has a billion different doors.

When high, the sound of God, the voice from the depths—aside from all minor batsqueaks & dogbarks—seems to be the cry of vomit erupting from human stomachs, punctuating the total music of all sound with its reversal of being its inside-out meat-groan.

                    —with the meat groan of the universe turning inside-out.

Later today, a pig wallowing in a mud puddle, first I ever saw—and 7 piglets grunting to each other & to mother in the Mud—and she grunted back impersonally, like God. A pig with big teats & her snout covered in mud, black Mother, with Curly tail.

I don't want to Bow before God in fear & Adoration & worship—I want to be Equal, or Be, God—and that is my Cross, of Death, for that is the Death of the conscious soul—which I'm unwilling to face, afraid— yet in Trance I did bow, or hide my eyes & resign my fate fearfully to Him, trembling & vomiting in disgust at myself & my whole life, when I saw *that* Great Being that I'd been playing with hitherto—feeling that I was a snake, to presume to approach Him, who created the Universe, the God of the Whirlwind of Job.

Peru

Rewrite of dream verse:
The snows already told me be Mephisto & born here,
Won't remember manana the old lie—
Golgotha come rainy day forlorn here,
Never wake up in a dream in which I die.

June 14, Morning after—1960
[...]

God's Hand

Consciousness in an elastic hand

As if a big ridiculous elastic ghost suddenly shoved its face in front of
my eye and let out a feral suggestive streetcorner wolf-whistle—like boys
on streetcorner whistling at girls—& disappeared and leave me wonder
what it meant—With the uneasy feeling that someday I would find out.
Disappeared around the corner.
    The whole thing tied up like sex in a big hairy knot.

"All the world's the same," I said to Ramon first time—It's made of the
same stuff. Into subjective relativity or out to objective infinity beyond
the stars the Answer repeats itself.

    Rain in Pucallpa, sitting in the market on a table by the big door,
    the streets running with brown water, it'll be mud—and a man in

the shopdoor across the street—over which sat parrots spreading their wings & squawking and making noise—appeared out of his shop with a big tin bucket of water, and threw that out into the universe into the rain, too.

Poetry is like pouring glasses of water into the ocean.

"No! No! This can't be me," one says as the wound opens—and death nears.

Widen the area of consciousness till it becomes so wide it includes its own death. This is the purpose of life.

At which point it becomes so wide that it grasps its own nothingness—that it is a mechanical thing, an illusion of Being—and it either enters that nothingness—not knowing what is on the other side—probably "rebirth"—the form does not matter—or seeks to extend its present form—but the furthest extension always meets the paradoxical end of including everything conceivable—including an act, and the consciousness of an act, which will make it disappear—it's suicide—

Ayahuasca II seemed to indicate a consciousness that included both being & nothingness—but that was not my present consciousness, I was afraid of the other as if it were an alien monster—or merely another blind alley—consciousness of a frog or imaginary being from another universe. Anything is possible, if "nothing" *has* any form of consciousness.

1 p.m.—passed by the Brujo's house—in the area about the front porch such a collection—people, cats, chickens, a dog lying in the mud, pigs, ants, butterflies, hornets, midges, worms, fleas on the cat—scratching

Peru

plenty—and whatever other unmentionable creatures in earth or air or invisible billion in bacteria.

This is no illusion!

June 16—

Slept late, fatigue lassitude to wake, I was depressed in NY—waking to face Peter & the pile of Beat letters—no vital reality—the old dirty pants of life—I have no fresh clean white Robe. The first cancerous Cigarettes of the morning.

Dream last nite—I was with girl—Tessa or Elise—walking home across superhighway—Cop directing traffic—we sneaking by without looking at him—but see on the traffic Island large pieces of turquoise stone carved—an ayahuasca pipe—in pieces which can be strung together—She picks a few up, I put the others in my pocket too—the cop sees us, comes & asks us how we are doing—"Lots of Ayahuasca pipe around here"—we are afraid we will be discovered as drinkers too—he takes us to his home, for us to give him our address, to register—I give him Gene's address—we are about to go (free) when his son who gets interested wants to know our address so he can visit too—I forget the address & have to start looking thru my papers again, can't find it—but want to get *out* of the cops home. Frustrated, still looking for the address, blaming & asking the girl.

Later Dream before waking—Walking in faraway Housing development in Jungle or Chancay—a modern development like the camp of Institute Linguistics Verano with a main modern street with Eugene

Peru

(or Louis) we pass by some homes—I assure him we will find someone who will know us and welcome us for visit, supper, rest—we pass almost all the houses—then a lady rushes up in car from a mile back—"I didn't see you pass how good you are here—you must remember me"—to Eugene—he doesn't—a nice lady she is, young like Martha Kotch—"We worked together in teaching high school"—she is taking us down the Elevator to her house.

. Welcomed—she knew Eugene, not me, tho I took credit for the prophecy.

I feel relieved that someone *did* pick up on us out here in the wilderness of life, someone who was oriented to the scene.

Bueno June 19, 1960

On board the *Yaguas* 7 p.m going down Ucyali River—Not! At the Captain's table—I am barefooted & hairy & dirty dungarees & sweat-stained khaki workshirt.

Rushed on board ½ minute before pulled off—sweating & out of breath—

Reflections Backward—1. Ayahuasca IV insight, that one existence has many forms, & if it disappears under the surface of Being—which I imagined as a tadpole under a vast pool-sea—it pops up above the surface again, forward or backward in time—similar dark pool of Nothingness to the pool of Laugh Gas. So this sensation repeats itself in both drugs & is constant.

2. God is—none other than Death, is the thing that stays after 5 days from Ayahuasca II.

And where *else* is he in the Book of Revelations?

It is the terrible God of Revelations, searching mind & heart for that Thing that can "Live" after Death, if anything can.

Peru

In Revelations the 7 angels and the White Beards in Chains all fall on their knees and adore and worship and praise Him, His power is so mighty and his Being is so unique and final—and this also was the sensation of Omnipotence & Importance of the Great Being in Death I sensed in Ayahuasca II.

Mark 8:25—The Blind Man of Bethsaida—"I see men; but they look like trees, walking."
"Picaflor Talmenio" is name of sad song I hear in the radio.

Suddenly remembered Blake's drawing of man enwrapped by Serpent in relation to the "invading Consciousness" & sensed and drew the serpent.

Lay in hammock all day worrying what to do with life, half-trapped by irreversible sense of intrusion of new element of death consciousness—then at night lay on top of ship-roof and looked at the Milky Way—then arrived at Contamena, went ashore, bought a Chama pot for 20c, waked up huge Eden-like main street bordering the river, a wide avenue on the river edge, old trees, night and a full open sky full of stars and the Via Lactis clouded over the sky—Now a beer.

They play games, throwing coins into the mouth of a brass frog, everywhere in Peruvian bars.

The taste of beer by the Ucyali River—the West End Bar[40]—all mem-

40. Tavern near Columbia University, frequented by Ginsberg, Jack Kerouac, and their friends during the 1940s.

Peru

ories coming back with the nostalgia of oncoming Death. What is Change of Life for women? The knowledge that the Flower is over, that irreversible change has set in? No more the sweet deceit of twat.

First nite in Lima, the fellow who drove me around big huge breasted boy, with nothing to do, I thot, "Al Capone's chauffeur"—turned on me & wanted prophecy what was wrong with him—I said, "You're not sexy enuf"—and he wanted me to write him up. Never did—but his very request was so strange deserves mention—to whomever I'm mentioning.

Earlier this year, Chile Calbuco, became amazed at all the life I was killing all the billions of bacteria—fish—flesh sometimes I was consuming, every breath, and all the warring sentient corpuscles and germs. The deaths have come home, that I am a mass of protoplasm radiating death and dying too. Meanwhile my ass continues its march toward cancer.

Death makes electronic noises like static, gangster static.

Static of a gangster consciousness.

Kafka's enormous fears of getting married.

Dream, sleeping in hammock all morning on deck, hammock slung from iron holes in passageway next to Captain's room near prow—and when woke, ope'd my eyes on the river and saw the bank laden with green trees and vines, sliding into the river, and the river eating its inch of earth and verdure alike—all one mouth—"It all goes down the same hole," I said to Hal Chase[41] years ago. But the dream was of Neal, whom I was still pursuing, seeking, loving, and Jack—followed them up a

41. Hal Chase, a Denver student at Columbia, introduced Ginsberg and Kerouac to Neal Cassady.

mountain or thru a city to Jack's house—bare hut in the provinces with some black iron inside and a bed and rude stove and no more—and the sadness of losing Neal again in dream

When woke, saw the river eating the bank, thinking Jack & Neal are the same man, who enter my life to warn me, to be (literally) eyes looking at me from the same brain to tell me—what?—"That I too unknowing am part of the same brain—we are *all* the same being, one Life, doomed to suffer death"—in hammock dazed with sleep with vision glimpse of jungle and my boat slowly passing from river to river to the Amazon which'll like Jack, Neal and myself goes out the mouth to Death—to the Sea—

Thus Finnegan's Wake "The keys to"—"Fin, Again" as if lifetime after lifetime the cycle ever repeated the same—(each time I take a new drug it will taste the same)—all going back to the black sea of Death—"Carry me on your back, Daddy, like you used to thru the toy fair," yes, the Nostalgia—"And the near sight of the mere size of him, the moils and moils of it, moaning me seasilt saltsick and I plunge, my only, with your arms—my cold mad father, my cold and feary father"—is Joyce's open statement of the dissolution of the soul into God—and the *Return*? No more than a dream returning on itself?

No wonder all Plurabelles are mentioned, they all under different names run to the same sea thru their careers. And all men are one earwicker Being fading into the Great Hive.

Blake's Mental Traveler also.

My world of metaphysical fancy has become identical with the world of life and death my body lives in.

But poetry can't touch Death, not poetry of normal consciousness.

Peru

And the old in senility going back to childhood, not wanting to give it up, knowing the ages will never come back again. All the beautiful events of love and consciousness.

Death makes everyman Saint, Christ & Buddha.

The great Nightmare I've always had from early Reichian times on is of being *discovered,* my emotions discovered—that I am an abstract child hiding in grown body afraid of life, adopting complicated protective memories to insure my isolation from Invasion from forces of life beyond my control.

"Father, into thy hands I commit my spirit"—Them's the right words.

Christ took on God as a dare, with enormous hopeless courage.

Have fear that all my successes, my evasion of anxiety, work, my poetry, my loves, my travels—have all been a plot—Orrellana, ran ashore & bought soap—my very being born and swimming to 34—a plot the dream-universe conspires in—to prove what?—

(paranoia about the universe itself—The universe is a phantom out to get me (I'm anyone))—

Orrellana a large number of grey thatchroof houses along a grassy street on the riverbank and smoke come up out of the thatches getting toward sunset.

Peru

Still June 18, Friday night, docked near huge white tree fallen off bank of Rio—went up on top of the roof—passing

the smokestack saw the big horn—thought, what if they blew the klaxon while I was up here and—BLOOP—the horn blasted—urk—my fault—a rope I pushed against, scared me, the noise—and saw shadows running around the deck—but no one came up to inquire—Later saw a shadow as huge as King Kong projected on the brown muddy nite water—Someone moving between the light and the rail—And the electric bulbs swarmed with legion of minute insects, flying mites, whirly like myriad stars around the Death-Illumination—but no death there, just more big moths & strange dragons.

Then lay back and looked up, the night black and all the stars, clean and clear and was huge foggy black holes in the Milky Way that runs over the whole field of the sky.

We're at the beginning of the human age—two years old—beginning to walk off earth—too bad I won't see the great maturity of the Universe of the old age and Death?

Rewarded with a glimpse of oblivion. A whistle song heard on instant by some Being over the Divine radio—just to reassure him, in his swift passage thru that all is O.K.

June 19—Woke at dawn, across the river the jungle floor cast over with red, and faraway purple-red clouds on the transparent air, the sun not yet come up throwing its rays before, stillness in the sky except for many mosquitos hovering silently outside my hammock.

Peru

But I myself am vanity, I am vanity.

The snell-nosed Elephant-faced God—looks like the Chavin-Raimondi Stone in Lima Museum.

Or perhaps—worse horror—after more "hallucinations" I will finally reject them all, including Harlem vow never to disavow the Light I see— and be left with realization of half my life passed in madness and returned with my 5 senses to the (Disneyland) of Here & Now.

And either way (or another thru Christ or another thru Jews or another thru Gas) will I ever know the "Truth"?

The preying Mantis is one outpost of sentience. Sitting in the sunlight, pale blue sky, bluish clouds assembled forward, he folds his arms and turns his head in all directions, perched on top of a rubber tube on the roof of the small ship going up Ucyali River June 1960—Earlier the turkey males, put in the same cage, fought and pecked at each other's bloody swollen combs. Got outraged, watching two turkeys put in same cage and poked it awkwardly behind wooden bars at head of big turkey, who incensed me by attacking all the little murderous roosters who bowed their heads and screamed. Half hour later when my righteous wrath was still in memory, I found before me a plate of cooked chicken— to say nothing of fried dried fish.

That duck I pitied was a murderer (they say).

Peru

♥

1 Corinthians 6:9—"homosexual" mistranslated.

♥

Is Paul a rat?

♥

The wound does not know itself, a spot [?] unnoticed on index finger of my right hand, skin peeled from the mouth of it—

Clouds like clouds in an old Jigsaw puzzle set I remember as a child on Haledon Avenue. The sky blue, the clouds opaque and 2-dimensional bluish frogs in the sky, sperm spirits, animals, with each on anima—the procession of clouds—as if seen before, [?]—1960—"Jigsaw puzzle sensation"—as if the clouds were cinema mounted and transparent moving over across stage set of forest on river bed. The blue.

Dream on Shipboard June 19—1960. Condemned in a toy Freddie Bartholomew Protected dreamworld, to have my car and nice home in modern orphan asylum, but always try to escape to the supermovies— everytime I go to the supermovie enter another world-dimension of an asylum, where I rescue a little boy trying to climb wall and help him escape.

Go visit Frisco, Whalen's studio, I have an appointment with him but Robt. La Vigne[42] and Walter Lima are there, waiting for me on stairway in Gene's apt, cause I have an appointment with them too—I had been

42. A San Francisco painter, Robert La Vigne introduced Ginsberg to Peter Orlovsky.

Peru

in a bus, and been painting it—rang the buzzer to get off one block be-
fore (in Rome) but couldn't as I had to gather together my canvasses
and paints—the white tube on the roof shelf—a girl helps me—I do get
off—Back at "Gene Whalen's"—on downstairs landing—tho I had said
to Whalen or Gene we would spend a quiet evening contemplating to-
gether—Robert is waiting for me—so finally I solve it by asking Whalen
for one stick of hashish and bring it down to Bob, saying O.K. I have
time to spend short time, one hour with thee, then return upstairs—
leaving Whalen in lurch—and Bob too—Later I explain to Whalen, tak-
ing a walk to forest on roof—that it's my vanity makes me promise spir-
itual excitement to everyone and make important dates contradictory,
dates which I am not fulfilling and always breaking.

Then I wake up in hammock after we see and hear a huge grunt of
combat, two beasts, being in combat, one sort of giant mouth-squid ele-
phant, versus some kind of bodiless turtle—the mouth grunts & gulps
down, or gulps up, the turtle—It's a short ugly struggle like vomit. The
struggle is similar to my struggle with hammock to stay balanced in
place, I wake, also similar to turkey quarrel.

Dream same morn—on top of cliff, interviewing Raymond Weaver—
talking to him, explaining my feeling for him as a sort of Prophet—a
presence—to him personally in the dream having a chance to go back
and question him.

Then talking to Trilling[43] and Barzan, they have their offices on top
of the clip, enquiring.

43. A critic, essayist, and teacher at Columbia University, Lionel Trilling (1905–
1975) was one of Ginsberg's most trusted and valued advisers throughout his early
development as a poet.

Peru

"I'm the Secty of the Alumni Org. and would like, finally, definite information on postgraduate scholarships to present at next meeting or in paper—but also (ahem, kaf) would like to make use of that information myself." As I talking I feel I'll fall off cliff, so I fell and hang on to the desk drawer handle of Barzan's immense side-desk. Trilling sitting nearby has disappeared. At the orange-juice stand several hungup graduate students are still at it, inquiring for gossip & info as to who's got what "in" where.

The Reply[44]
(Pucallpa, Several days ago)

God answered with my doom! That I am doomed and don't know my life from Death, don't know what's Beast or Hallucination, Mad, I must die, I am annulled, this poetry blanked from the fiery ledger.

That my lies be answered by the worm at my ear, my Jest of the Call of God by the Beard that covers my face like the skin of a monster, by the trembling of the cheek jaw flesh that covers my unrecognizable skull, by my hand falling over my eyes to cover them from the sight of the skeleton, my stomach vomiting out a death too near to God, my body in a swoon and the noise of the Drone of Creation adoring the Slayer, the yowp of birds in the Infinite, the dog bark like the sound of vomit in the air, frogs croaking death at trees,

Christ poor Hopeless lifted on the Cross between Life & Death! There is no one but the Ever Unknowable—lives forever! None but the Dead Gong that shivers thru the flesh! And this is no illusion,

None but the Presence be mighty to Record None but the Presence in Death! None but He before whom I am helpless! None but He by

44. First annotation for "The Reply," *CP*, 265–66.

Peru

whom I know I am Lost Soul, taken to Death! None but He who I weep & despair!

He haunts me, will not let me live! None but he who forbids my onan. Makes me change from Allen to the skull!

Who knows and Searches out my Soul—My soul that is not mine! I cannot keep! My soul that belongs to the Dogs! To the Serpent Death.

Old one-eye of Nightmare, one Eye God of Dreams in which I do not wake but die O world of ministering angels helping me to Death. Women, women, whom I have rejected, who bade me bear babe and not live forever! Not Challenge God his onan scream of Infinity.

God is one-Sex and I who am imperfect must reproduce myself to cling to earth the Being.

Old Artaud who refused to shit! Is this Allen who wanted to be God? Yes, this is Allen on his mortal bed, bodyflesh crawling with its own impermanence, hands perishing afraid—pulled in by the Frightful Hand of the God of the Dark—legs moving away with their own life, like a worm's blind wriggle, cut—the plough is God himself! And this is no illusion!

And I can blank out this Consciousness, escape back to my own life, and will, poor worm, poor pitiable Christ afraid of the Foretold Cross, never to die—And I can escape but not Forever! The Time will come, the Consciousness will come, the hour will come,

The strange Truth will enter the Universe again, the Death will show me its Fang Face as before—and I despair that I *forgot*! To know that this Truth would come again, tho I must die of it.

Sacred! What's Sacred when the Thing is all the Universe? Creeps to every soul like a vampire—organ singing in the bearded stars! God, that God, my God of dreams & visions, is None but Death himself! And we the Beings hatched to His out of our bodies, be absorbed. I'll die to horror that I die! And this is no illusion!

Peru

Recognize his Might! I watch the sacrifice of my skull, as on Aztec pyramid the prisoner youth gave up his heart to the frightening sun.

For I chose self-love—my nose, my frightening hands, my beard, my ass, my cock, my soul—and now the Faceless Destroyer of myself!

Death makes me cry! The Bacteria of Death have invaded my mind—the slower the worse—the longer I'm damned with Illusion of Self.

When the mighty burst of music comes from out the Inhuman door.

You're up against it, kid. But aren't we all? It's not just Death, it's the spirit behind death, Death Himself, Itself—and I am full of Shit! Poor being come home to life to squat in a dark field & drop my load.

"You get finished—I don't know—some say your spirit has to stay down here below till Judgment Day.

"And Christ? I seemed to see he was just another one of us beings."

"Yes, Christ is not God, just a man dying"—

"We are all Christs then, that is we are all Sers (Beings) that have to go on the Cross of death"—

"Yes, that's right, Christ is Nobody but himself, dying like everything dies—nothing values, except God himself."

"But all this life is worth nothing then?"

"No, worth nothing at all, after death, it is all thrown away, all thrown away & you go to God."

"What is God? He seems to be inhuman."

He nods.

"—a combination of an elephant and a snake and a man and a mosquito and all the trees."

Thus the plumed serpent & all the Hindu animal deities—but Paul says, "no Image."

Finally I said (after second cigarette), I'm going upstairs to write.

So it does seem Final, that Vision Not so horrible this far away.

Peru

June 21, 1960—Dream—in long house, apartment, modern, well furnished, with Auden—we are having a long rapport, conversation, he is taking an interest in me—like a Turkish Bath—but very sweet, wants to make me, I say to myself, why not encourage him, let him fuck me for that—we are talking, he looks down on me with kind eyes at last—then a troupe of Bohemians ring the bell & enters—I am amazed that he knows them, they visit so familiarly—one especially who looks like a black-haired Harpo Marx, the character in the Connection, the father—a devil for that matter, with horns of hair—the boy who played in *Goodman's* play as the father (not the Connection)—Some Joker plus several girls shuddering with peyote, and Tessa and Peter Van Meter & who knows—so they all pass in the door & he shows them thru the house & out the back door, just like that So I'm relieved he has no great commerce with them & can pay attention to me, only.

God is the Blob & we his food. The more we die the bigger he gets. He cultivates us to eat—like the mouthsquid-elephant trunk eating the armorless turtle of dream a few days back. So the ultimate in religious Ecstasy—the moment of Death—will be a huge grunting struggle to escape being eaten by a huge Demonic Being that runs the Universe?

History of Visions—a list
- In bed on pentagon, 1944 in Joan's[45] apt., dreamed of music playing celestially from family phonograph.

45. Joan Vollmer.

- High on benzedrine, thought I saw the curtains move, the nite of the Wolfeans & nonWolfeans.[46]
- High on marijuana, with Brigit Oflynn and Norman Schnall, the telepathy of drumsticks tapping out communicative rhythms of practice pads in her apt.
- In Harlem with Neal in Apt. 104th St, heard the red sound of Eternity in Illinois Jacquet's Flying Home, high on marijuana, 1945.
- Hitch-hiking with Neal from Denver to Texas, the mountains seemed like painted stage settings, 1946.
- In apt. in Harlem, with no drugs, the 4 visions of Blake, 1948 and the Terror on Campus.
- In car crash 1948, the Jehovah chain of guilt and necessity leading me to jail.
- Home in Paterson 1949–50, the tremblings of the veil—the trees seem alive.[47]

(All this time, many dreams: Is This Not Great Gentility: The Shrouded Stranger:[48] A Crazy Spiritual)[49]

* 1954—Pact of love with Peter—the lamb between us in Foster's or Stewards in S.F.

    * 1955—Peyote sensations with Sheila & Peter

    * 1958—Recognition of Bill as Lamb in Paris hotel room.

    * 1959—Lysergic acid Dancing God in Stanford.

    * 1960—Ayahuasca Death Vision

46. Legendary evening in Beat Generation history, during which Jack Kerouac and Hal Chase (Wolfeans) and Allen Ginsberg and William Burroughs (non-Wolfeans) debated the state of literature and its future.

47. See "The Trembling of the Veil," *CP*, 22.

48. See "The Shrouded Stranger," *CP*, 55–56.

49. See "A Crazy Spiritual," *CP*, 83–85.

Peru

(All this time, Dreams—the Eye in the Black Cloud, the music in Huanco on my birthday Singing in afternoon dream)

Also: Laughing Gas 1958–1959 series
    Ether in Lima-1960.

Others coming out of moviehouses—(from childhood pictures)—later on Times Square—the transiency of buildings—
    Peyote in Paterson 1950—The solidity of space.

    Paintings—Cezanne, Klee, Rembrandt, Bellini, El Greco, Angelico, on "T" the Triumph of Death.

    With Peter at Assisi the clouds afright over the Umbrian plains in moonlite; cocksucking in darkness on the grass in front of Cathedral doors.

    Seeing Naomi last time in hospital.

    First nite in Santiago where I drank Coramonal bottle and later nites of codein—the Universe as a transient phenomenon, a dream disappearing.

    Death—Leave *All* behind—love of Peter, my history of my soul's loves Paul, Jack, Hal, Neal, Peter—leave Bill & Gregory—leave my father and

Peru

brother and the memory of Naomi—leave Peter forever, leave my child-
hood, leave my college, leave my travels, leave the world to oblivion for-
ever. All in vain and to be forgot—and forgetting myself, to be absorbed
and become a huge inhuman being that is everything from mosquito to
elephant at once and has all the intelligences in It-Him, and all the dif-
ferent feelings from Murder to Delicate Angelcy—All be in Him—

And if the

Buddha b right, and

him Nothing at all, so *All* song, even the God

The cup of coffee with milk in the kitchen at Paterson, which Louis,
I, and Edith drink, cozy and family, will be the first to pass.

1 Timothy 6:16—from Paul "who alone has immortality and dwells in
unapproachable light, whom no man has ever seen or can see" The
moth's approach.

Monday afternoon, on the muddy river, huge white trees washed
down the bank and lying askew in the mud and water, at table on upper
little deck, they're playing cards or sitting around staring, I'm lost in
Testament reading in stockings, all the chickens are walking around
dispassionately in their cages—they're monsters w/no mercy who don't
learn—and the clouds are thin behind the ship, the sky blue above, the
motor throbbing, and voices calling the cards and ringing of money on
the table. The passengers—Carlos Mustache with net shirt who's an ac-
countant in Iquitos, young father Carlos also who has green shirt and

kid and is proofreader on Iquitos Daily News. The fat young captain with his genitals abulge in thin pants, the brown sailor with white teeth smile who played tomtoms; the short Bosun who's always naked, who tied up the ship to trees; and a dozen big breasted smiling girls.

In Requena, the cantina, the men passengers, youths and aged with white pimples on their noses, *salud,* and all drink at once, gossiping about Brazil—with a local acquaintance, Indian affairs govt. rept., who in his yellow silk shirt bordered with conjunct brown triangles, white sox, brown shoes, neat, and brown pants, looked exactly like Lester Young,[50] lacking only longhair—but had the Chinese eyes and gold teeth and strange ears.

June 21, 1960

God is a big hairy armpit. Guy in bed near my hammock.

"green armpit" poetry as Clellon Holmes[51] said of Gregory 1952.

"All the comforts of home"—the book snitches of N.Y.—going down from apt. to supermarket, to buy turkey or hamburger and tomatoes and spinach—the USA is a huge fat dream—

50. Jazz saxophonist Lester Young (1909–1959).

51. John Clellon Holmes (1926–1988), a novelist, essayist, poet, and teacher, wrote *Go* (1952), considered the first Beat Generation novel. The roman à clef featured Ginsberg, Kerouac, Burroughs, Cassady, and others as thinly disguised characters.

Peru

The Llama Matches of Peru-Bolivia, with Made in Sweden sign—and almost Jap print simplicity of blue Andes, a spotted altiplano with one line, a long pink streak of clouds.

A yellow sky, and a Llama, furry and sentient on top of the world, staring and listening.

Entering the Amazon Sunset making the lake-like smooth glassy water blue, long clouds piled up blue-white clouds I've seen before—clouds I'd seen in Paterson—ship radio whistling and interrupting itself.

"The book of matches of N.Y."—Jack's constant sense of transience—special characteristic of his prose—constant suffering of awareness of stage-fadeout of all details.

Matadero-Iquito:

Can I look in the eye these creatures who are about to die?

Notes

Mystics & Magician in Tibet

Alexander David Neel—p. 139. "What becomes of these [mental] creations? , , , like children . . . separate lives . . ."

P. 139 Chdd (gchod)—Mystic Banquet—Red Meal and Black Meal—
1) Red Meal—"For ages in course of renewed births I have borrowed from countless living beings . . . Today I pay my debt, offering the distribution this body which I have held so dear . . . Shame on me if I shrink from giving my *Self*!"

2) Black Meal—The sacrifice was an illusion—"In fact, he *has nothing* to give away, because he *is nothing*."

p. 152 The Short Path—"Illness, Madness & Death" risks.

Deliver me from my ignorance. I wanted to be the Saint of Tenderness—

Tibetan sages sailing over the earth in silken ships, as interesting as going to London town with large ears and a green hat.

or an oaken bed at sea.

Life eats life.

(The first birds, whose feathers developed from quills developed from scales, turned back and ate their earlier form, the fishes)

Worms—Paeozic
Fish—Azoic
Reptiles—Mesozoic
Present—Cainozoic

Magic Wars—in which one existence encroaches on another by contact—and the victor makes the other sphere of existence disappear by his awareness of it.

Constant image—The void opening and shutting—a glimpse of lights going on and off . . . Morse code . . . blinkers—

The unwed [?] population of America.

Read James some Kant, Buddhist Tibet book, Wolfe, H. G. Wells
      The dusty birdsong in a tree—
Wolfe—Medusa—Sketch—"The clang of ice image, the clucking of a hen—and then time fading like a dream"—in Brooklyn, yet.

Coming from the ship, disappointed near dusk—the blue evening sky—the skin of God.

[. . .]

The awful invitation of a tall yellow door opening on a rainy nite in Iquitos—sitting in coffeeshop waiting for Ayahuasca bearded connection—the door was silent, but I saw it more like a snake to Invite me out.

Recollect—the look I gave myself in the hospital mirror in Stanford—in the blue-red bathroom light—seeing my living flesh & the corrupting face of my life—the skin draped over skull in this scary life, after passing for an instant's glimpse into another—now the face seemed bloodshot, flush on the meat, hung round the eyes, sweating, bald, fiery, burning, sick, ready, (really) to die, I saw it then as cocksucker's face—now in hindsight as face of vanity to die—the vain meat hanging on to its Incarnation, afraid to aware its doom. Like a worm that knows its flesh is dying.

Letter, Allen Ginsberg (in Lima, Peru) to Louis Ginsberg (in Paterson, New Jersey), June 21, 1960

Dear Louis:

Wrote two weeks ago or so—by now I've crossed over Andes & spent 10 days on Pucallpa, a small town on a huge river big as the Hudson—The Ucayali—which winds 1000 miles up to the Amazon—so took a small steamboat 6 days ago and, sleeping in hammock with mosquito net on passageway on dock, spent the week traveling up to the Amazon thru huge flat area of jungle—on riverside small grey thatch roof huts and every 20 or 50 miles a small cluster of houses and every 100 miles a little town, frontier towns, of several thousand gents. Cost of boat trip including 3 meals a day is $6—which is cheap—am now on last day of trip & just a few hours ago entered the Amazon proper—big wide flat brown shining water wide as a big lake with sticks & greenery floating on surface, balsa rafts and canoes paddling near shore—we dock at Iquitos this evening & I go find a hotel, stay a week, & then fly back to Lima, to catch plane home a week later. Iquitos is the river port at western-Peruvian end of the Amazon. From Iquitos one can take another steamer down thru Brazil and the Atlantic, 2500 miles, for $50—but I haven't the money or the time, & have to get back to Lima.

While in Pucallpa our main purpose was to look up a Curandero or witch doctor & try a native herbal brew called Ayahuasca which reportedly gives visions—similar to peyote, Mescaline, & Lysergic Acid—Well

Peru

I tried it 4 times with remarkable results as far as I was concerned sub-jectively—I certainly saw "visions."

What the drug seems to do is activate the unconscious without put-ting the regular consciousness asleep—so that you can both be awake *and* dream real solid dreams at the same time—a neat trick, but quite possible. The local Indians use it for curing illnesses, finding lost objects, communicating with the dead, religious visions, etc. and I'm sure they can do all that, from what I've seen. It was like stepping into a voodoo movie & finding it was all *real*.

Anyway, the main dream or vision I had was of the condition of my own death, i.e., how it feels like to do—and I don't think I've ever (except once before having "visions" in Harlem) been so terrified before in my life while awake. It seemed that Death was a *Thing*, not mere emptiness, a Living Being—and my whole life was being judged & found a vanity, as in *Ecclesiastes*—and I saw as in X-ray, my skeleton-head settling in fi-nal position on pillow to give up the Ghost—a *familiar* feeling, strangely —with the realization that I had known all along, but avoided conscious-ness, of the fact that I am flesh and that flesh is crass. The main after effect, aside from a desire to widen further the area of my consciousness, and realization that my life so far has been relatively empty, was reso-lution to bear children sooner or later before it is too late. The question is to be or not to be—and also, what *Thing* is beyond Being. I saw some-thing—a sort of great consciousness which was familiar, but unhuman— as if in one being were united an Elephant & Snake & Mosquito & Man—and all the trees—nothing like the terrible hidden God of Moses or *Revelations,* it felt like Whether this is vision or Hallucination makes very little difference—I passed thru several hours of intense suffering awareness of the Worm at my Ear. I thought of you and the whole fam-ily—everyone I knew passed thru mind at one time or another—with tears & love—realization that sooner or later, I, or everyone, enters a great solitude and give[s] up everything—which was painful to realize, which is why I said my life seemed a vanity, for I as yet had thought of it as semi-permanent & had not considered the inevitable. It also seemed that until I were *able* to freely give myself up, entrance into some great Joy (in life or beyond life) would not be seen—but that there is some kind of Inhuman Harmony yet to come. But this is speculation. In any case the universe did seem like one Being.

Well that's enough of that for awhile—I wrote a great deal this month, huge ranting wild poems, psalms, notes, sketches, drawings, a whole book actually—I'll have to reread it in a year to see if it's still hot. But poetry doesn't seem enough—in the vast strange & middle of the night.

Also bought a lot of native poetry—hand-painted ceramic ashtray types for souvenirs which I'll bring home—and a hammock & mosquito net.

I thought of poor Williams, living so long on the edge of death—"for this is the first—and last—day of the world"—he wrote. Had a dream of him entering Non-Being with huge snowy-feathered angel wings And saw you Louis as a sort of Elephant-nosed seraph or Deity with old human eyes. Well the Indians in the jungle certainly don't lack a huge metaphysical inner Civilization, half the town of Pucallpa drinks ayahuasca every week & has its own secret life aside from radios & movies of the A-Bomb. So that's I suppose the proper poetic climax of my trip down here—it's been almost half a year & I am nostalgic to get back to N.Y.C. & see everybody & see you.

Love
Allen

June 25

Chinese Restaurant, Iquitos—I have just eaten Death—(looked up from my musings on the Void to see a plucked chicken hanging dead from a hook in the huge kitchen—and my empty plate which had contained cooked pig flesh).

What is this, the belly of the whale?—a dark night sky, white ribs of clouds flashing in its depths as I lift my head for an instant—on the mud road—and several hundred croaking chirping and utterances of grunt, the sound of running water, music straying out of a house from radio— I go home to face my host, The Evangelist. Leaning against a lamppost to write in yellow light, a moth strikes my head—and the creaking and sawing of frogs and mites in the grass, in the trees, throughout the air continues.

Later on the road, a spot of high grass near the athletic field wall, the black pozo corner, where I usually hear water running—a louder noise, the snoring of 3 or 4 frogs within 10 meters of each other—I stopt with closed eyes to listen a few minutes—suddenly disturbed that one of these conversational rackets might be a snake—come out to get me and draw me in what I was listening to—my mind dissolved into this whirlpool of consciousness.

Which is what I hope and fear.

They are calling me from the backdoor of the hut.

Sitting crosslegged on pole on ground back of hut—looking at fogged sky star, my face felt like the face of the cross-legged skullfaced uplooking aghast warrior in Mochica pottery.

"Where can I connect for some G?"

A conscious phantom—jazz riding it out gaily.

Peru

Some joke metaphysical being, eyeless, taken to invading my life, all the dead details come alive with secret significance that awaits me—sneaking into popular songs, frog croaks, my cough, my stray thoughts, my very death to come.

"What will be, will" says song—or it croaks in Bach.

The Beat Generation, a decisive moment in American consciousness—henceforth the horses' heads are herded toward eternity/ No group as weird before. Weird in sense of Lamantia's[52] paraphrase of Poe's Wier—The elements were resent before in Poe, Dickenson, Melville, Whitman—then Crane—An evolution of human consciousness—"Widen the area of consciousness."

Farewell, Hitler Dear,
    sang 6 million
    Jews
      in the symphony
    of life and death—

[...]

Recollect—a state of complete confusion and fear, in which I finally covered my eyes and wanted to escape from the vision, for the problem seemed to be:

Realizing that my conscious existence was an empty deceit

That my skeleton lay on the floor waiting

That that deceit that was "I" would be annihilated

52. Surrealist poet Philip Lamantia (1927–2005) read at the Six Gallery reading in San Francisco in 1955.

Peru

That I had the choice of exchanging my present "I" consciousness for a terrible strange one I'd been avoiding all my life, or

giving up altogether and willing the total annihilation of all consciousness.

Accompanied by the fear that if I consent to annihilation of *all* consciousness I would lose out on the Main Chance God Monster.

And that the Main Chance God Monster consciousness I was seeing and fearing, was nothing but another illusion in which I could be permanently trapped—a hell—if I made the wrong decision—might be what they call "Satan," i.e. permanent entrance to another monstrous illusion in which I (believing it to be real) would be reborn according to whatever this Karma Monster disposed for me as a new form—probably a mosquito or a Serpent.

Accompanied by the suspicion that this *was* the way of God, total acceptance of being any and all of his forms, and suffering all his deaths.

So that the way (to wisdom) might be to accept whatever hideous suffering was in store.

But not knowing whether this all was an illusion.

Or whether if I did accept entrance to the matter,

I might actually die as Ginsberg there and then as a result of Supreme Decision which reduced my old Earth world to a fragment of my old Allen Imagination which I was now, finally, choosing to leave, my body died,

Accompanied by fear that this whole illusion might result in my literal death, yet still be illusion.

Accompanied by the fear and realization that on deathbed one day I would literally be confronted by this choice as final

Accompanied by fear that if I tried to will Blackness void and total disappearance, I might lose out on all Being—

"Also be or not to be"

Peru

Or that I might not *escape* the wheel that way out but merely will myself a more cowardly new torture form till I had courage to face Being—the Being Itself—

and the Being died literally then and there re-manifest the living presence in my sight—leaving the free will to enter it, and die and be It eternal, or

Continue the deceit of Being "I"—always in future faced with the same inescapable problem

reborn over and over to more and more human and animal torture and deceit as my cowardice continues—and that perhaps I had been faced with this choice before and chosen wrong, for here I still was in the old situation of Death.

And that thru continued wrong choice I might find myself further and further away from the center of being, way out in the illusory outskirts of torment and doubt—torture and death—

Or right now chose to leap out of myself, free myself from the deceit of Allen and this Earth World and Time, and send my hidden soul forth to Eternity—

Leaving my corpse back here to be horrified over by Peter and Louis and this world—

They assuming I had died of bad drugs and hallucinatory accidental misfortune premature, some John Hoffman scandal—and that was way to have my cake and eat it—(this world and the next both)

was to have children—

and that this leap into life and the Feminine creative seeding,

was the same leap—change free of my old life self that was demanded of me in corresponding later physical death—

that the spark of another Allen soul be seeded and left on earth to find its way

While my own self, free of its selfhood, rejoined its Maker, dies.

All this the apparent problem confronting me in Ayahuasca II Pucallpa.

This is the best summary so far of the actual problem as it appeared.

And the horror knowing that I could choose to forget it all entirely—but that it might—it would certainly—reappear on deathbed.

Thus "A Wasted Illness"—

And my skull turning left and right on pillow till setting still in final resignation—"In Thy Will" etc.

I am not God.

Who was Naomi?

[?] & Snowflakes

H. G Well's History on Infinity of Wars.

Thos. Wolfe—New Year's eve with Starbuck—his 24th year—Starbuck's song Chile Bon Bon, & Ca C'est Paris—But the doom's there—and Wolfe's Betrayal of Starbuck.

Thos. Wolfe I am a rich homosexual Jew come back to haunt you now, suck your cock correct yr prose, admire your genius and wail at yr stupidity.

Peru

Oh! the artificial
  conversations! In
  which he's all confused—
At least he wrote it
  down with shame,
But proud! proud!
    The fool.
And Esther's mad herself!
Poor Starbuck, beaten in
  the Paris Night,
The Friend—and where did
  Starbuck die?
Two mad ones screaming
  in a room
But he's a great poet with
  Blue gates and bones.
Unconscious prophecies
  of mad Fate.
Didn't he ever read Whitman and get
  Sympathetic for the
  sweat-lip'd defeated one?
    That He is I, the Christ?
And Esther's right, he thinks,
  To deny "the stayless Doom?"
Poor Wolfe, Poor Esther when
  Doom shows a Human Face
  —More wise than they,
        More Just, More Kind,
more stayless than his Memory,
  more rich in graves.

"A shout of hatred" at the
    Night? old Father Nite?

Poor Wolfe on deathbed
    brought to Judgment—
as I'll be—too—for all
    that Raving against
        Him
Whose power Wolfe never
            Guessed to be—
Wolfe the Atheist—
      Proud Self! to die—
There's the Great Betrayal—
    that he never met in Books.
    In the Morn,
    the Vomit! The
    Unbeatable Egoist—
    raving on.

In Iquitos

Reading Wolfe and Commentary in Chinese Restaurant
    till Midnight—
out to continue in the park—a dark place—
    except a kiosk of bright light & benches
The bandstand—I walked to it and went up—on
    bench a pool of water on tile floor—
disturbed—on the benches sleeping people—

Peru

one negro youth in blue shirt

and another in pants—I pored over my book, regardless—

   Wolfe in his agony

"I lost my squeal"—a cough from the negro—

   I looked up

an apparition on the bench,

a woman with long black hair and thin cotton dress,

Her legs up on bench in classic Greek profile,

Hair falling down over her head, poverty, solitude

What hope at all—breathing in the nite, hands clutched

   over her breast eyes closed—

and the Negro farting, I smell in the tropic breeze,

and rocking on his hip rapidly in his dream,

a baby sex rock, a palsy constant rock,

a trouble before epilepsy, dreaming—

The woman with Chinese red cheeks,

also swaying back and forth on thin hips—

 & 5 lights burning in the woodslat ceiling of the

   Bandstand in Iquitos—

and nothing I can do?

but go on reading Wolfe who lost his squeal?

She's on the nod like a junky—I fear she'll fall

   off the bench—

the junk is not willful, it's just poverty.

In the morn—Carlos my kid father host says they're the local mad people.

Peru

Dream June 27, 1960

Two letters in my pocket, written for "Ray Bremser"—I go with him to his apartment—he enters first—It turns out the police are there, too—hold him in custody—I wait, better dressed outside, when I glimpse police pants leg—but can't leave him—so go in, they seize me, I say "No need of that, I'm innocent & coming in the room knowing you're here"—It's a Pot pad that's the raid reason—

The stratagem to deceive the cops & get away is thru dream, i.e. give them ayahuasca—we all drink, all the ratty bohemians lying round on the bed, & the cops too—& take off our clothes to sleep together & dream—the cops on the nod leaning against the wall—

(Ginsberg—Did I think to escape the Nightmare after childhood by prosperity?)

Some creep tried to sleep next to me, but I fold up my limbs against Peter, or try to, and pull short silk cover, poorly scissored & too thin like a cross over me, plus other thin blanket—

I think & wait till the cops get hi enough so they dream & the situation lets me out—

To the bus which takes me down from Empire State Heights 5 miles to the UN 33rd St subway Labyrinth (old Dream image)—downstairs Coney Island stop A modern place with modern restaurants—my problem is how to get back up, back where I started on bus from, now—

Image also of a Dutch type open field grass plaza surrounded by low wooden 2 story gabled houses near the seaside—

I go in huge glassfront building to Penn Sta.—looking for restaurant end front of bus to get back on—much as scene at 33rd & Vreeland are when the bus pulls in to Paterson—front of bus with door & Bars of Aluminum—

So I get back up to the Hospital Room—She's got a gun & a baby, the wife—my wife? Joan? And the radio's telling her Crime—the cleanup woman in white is outside on the balcony way over the street—lying down—*She,* the heroine, decides to go, escape flight—leaves baby (newborn on dresser, and runs down thru elevator)—The Maid hears her go, into room, finds baby left, calls Hotel-Police.

Downstairs I see them enter strange bakery trucks, small opensided white trucks, stealing them, to make getaway.

Burroughs says, "When I heard those shots I almost ran away—remembering my own scandal[53]—but fortunately I decided to see it out with You"—They get on tram—as in Lima—

So the couple is sort of Burroughs & Joan, at times I'm Burroughs.

Last, in a private apartment in the wilds of 33'rd St.—her brothers & his gang have found him (Burroughs) & are giving him the once over—a confused scene—

Her brother is a sort of deadend kid, very sensitive & goodlooking, they back me—Burr against wall—He the brother's called the police to test Burroughs reaction to his sister—will he run alone or save her too—Burr goes to the cabinet (as Barbillion) to get pills, poison, to end their lives.

Seeing this the Brother pardons them, grabs pills & helps them escape I am questioned—what *should* they do?

1. Cool it, I say.
2. Hide out in brother's apt lost in Bklyn—he & his gang obviously are anonymous.

53. Allen Ginsberg was arrested in 1949 for allowing a group of petty thieves to store their stolen goods in his apartment. In lieu of a prison sentence, Ginsberg was sent to a psychiatric institute for observation and therapy. He met Carl Solomon during his stay.

3. She dye hair, he grow mustache & both *change* names & appearances.

4. On to England. The brother says, What?

   I say, if they change citizenship & go England & live there & take papers, it'll be hidden & finally free & alright.

Later in an office of investigation, I write to Central letter agency to have the letters of the person (whom I suspect of being the author of the whole villainy & cause of trouble)—sent to me first to the FBI office to investigate.

I have a set of them already, opened—She the girl I'm under working with, objects to my procedure, "Just order a list of mail—the mail itself not good to order"—but they've already sent me the mail & I've read it—

I wake [?]—sing the owls, chickens in the rainy dawn.

Earlier another dream I'm with Walter or Brad from Paris (Motorcyclist-Filmmaker-Narcotic Schizophrenic), (who went mad blaming Burroughs)—we ride out on lonely road, get chased by cops, flip & crash, run away from stolen motorcycle crash, the cops all over and looking for us, it's out on lonely road but populated (NY to Paterson—on Jersey Marshes)—I go on foot from restaurant to restaurant & evading cops sent out from nearby station.

Total anxiety all nite dreaming.

You know I've always asked to see God, since my early visions led me to believe that he was to be seen in Life, but finally I realized in later vision that No Man sees God Entire Naked & lives—and so what God showed me of himself was mysterious & unbearable—I saw as much as I could bear, but God included Death—but what I saw I could not bear to see more of.

June 28—

Setting out in dark tropic garden with bamboo door open behind me, in chair, my head bent up to look at all clear stars, a great swath of lights in the sky—even after 5 minutes saw a silent shooting star signal thru the high ceiling of soft air—my eye on a bright planet, then looking further at a foreign star—

If I take off my glasses the stars get fuzzy.

If I take off my mind they disappear.

We are a special set of conditions, our senses & consciousness—not given this set of conditions we are what we see.

Or we see what we are.

Such pleasure to look at the stars—and be given this again before I disappear from what is. What should I begin to do now on earth, under the stars?—I feel like living again—

go forward to space to meet fate, the rain

as I go forward was in time to meet fate,

                    in Death.

Other sets of conditions would change

That is—What is, is what appears. What appears changes, i,e, stars & tables. Back to Laughgas insight.

Each star is precious—I saw one on the horizon, solitary.

And a firefly winking over the same tree.

And 2 crickets vibrating back & forth across the garden, sometimes in unison, sometimes opposed, sometimes the chirps half-overlapping, the sound like knife scraped against stone 200 feet away.

Maybe stars burn sending out rays of light that push each other further away, expanding till the energy's spent & leveled out & the stars disappear before they reach infinity—and all the energy starts flowing in together to the center again to one beating heart where God is alive and complete for an instant before he blows up again, to create the worlds.

Peru

Space (then) doesn't exist & god is a single point of total Being in
the Void—that exploding sets out to spread in the Void—

yang-yin, each side—

Life with the hole of Death

Death with the protrusion of life.

Does either side ever get completely spotless,
Life or Death—Total? once total, would
there then be change?

The Void (Space) does not exist, so there's no problem of what's
infinite.

Matter does seem to exist in the void—a limited amount of mat-
ter-consciousness-stuff.

"Infinite" means, "non-existent"

Given a Void, the only opposite would be something that knows the
Void—(i.e. Being-consciousness)

That opposite, by the Nature of things, by its own nature, could ap-
pear & disappear always returning in the same way—like a blinking
light—knowing it would disappear once it knew it was void, and would
reappear again once it didn't know it was void.

The void knows itself.

He minute Being dies, I has to reappear.

i.e. it has all the properties or attributes or behavior of a phantom
that doesn't exist becoming aware of that fact, and of the special non-
existent conditions it don't exist? in

Like a ghost that suddenly realizes it's a ghost, pure.

Morning 28th June.

Still in Iquitos a week already, waiting to connect—sitting in Carlos family house—arid woodsmoke from kitchen—in the middle room the radio on too loud forbidding conversation, tuned to Evangelical station which plays hymns and debile lassitudinous chants with violin and accordion and piano and bored-sounding sad girls saluting the Seignor— The old man the church-pastor reading the sportpage of yesterday's *Commercio* in underwear sleeveless and towel wrapped round neck, his eyeglasses perched, chicken pecking on the dirt floor, hammock slung across room, 3 beds hard around the walls, they all sleep together in one room, I guess—A mirror half mildewed, the lady's umbrella and scarf and belts hanging from a nail—The radio announcing birthdays of individuals in the block, Carlos leaning over it bored, waiting for breakfast, bricks under the bed, a shovel against the wall, laundry hanging from a cord, a fly crawling over a bone on floor, one red slipper for small feet, sneakers and football pumps luxurious on floor, in come white dog asniff, long dusty wire stretched from centerpole to light hanging 3 ft. from floor at wall—And over the 7-foot wall, the living space of the next door house too separated only by that short board white-washed wall— Now Carlos reading his hymn book—they are all sitting around, waiting for Doom, like me—but. But they make me sick of bibles and radios and hymns—and their sanctity.

8:15 a.m.—the radio comes from Quito.

"Ben and I, here by the City Hall, the Bank, the grocery store," he thought "Why here? In Gath or Isphahan. In Corinth or Byzantium. Not here It's not real." Aryfemidorous Farewell.

♥

    If there's a War—WW III—it's fire and rain of blood—
and that's apocalyptic—

    If no war, it's miracle after 5000 years of war.

    Mankind is swamped by stupid Death.

The world in the

    belly of the whale

    as well as I—

as my inward apocalypse—

    the death of old self

    and the living death to come—

and the world's new change

    to turn the Universe

    inside out, or burn,

are both the same extremes—

    Dream—June 28—

    Killed 2 serpents—with stick as they came into door—evil look on
faces—

    One after other, saw the 2 snake faces in door, rising & looking on
me—with hallucinatory spectral evil eyes.

    Later dream. Duncan,[54] talking about death, nodding his head &
agreeing to it, accepting, half frightened, wise.

♥

54. Poet Robert Duncan.

Peru

Depression in morning—Duncan disturbs me, and all S.F. seems shabby, myself posturing about visions shallow, finding open field to assert nothing but my Will or Self.

"Crosssticks bored ten old household
      With rackrent clap"—awaking dream
Twilite sleep—verse

Sleeping in mosquito net while I'm still alone alive.
But the worms will get me later, rain.
      "and the fire & the rose are one"

1 July 1960—
      Ayahuasca V
"A permanently existing Ghost"—Spencer
      Sitting with head bowed down 9:30 PM in a hut by the corner in a chair in a field of vegetables outside Iquitos on road to S Juan under the mothy stars with huge dark black clouds thru which starlight rayed—as in my old dream—after an hour of waiting after drinking from small gourd cup 3 swallows of different tasting mix—again the accumulation of consciousness of Another—or another world—or many worlds, many dimensions, all closed off from each other—the theory of probability mathematics—at the center of which closed structure, honeycomb of dimensions, and outside them all, another sphere or Area of the Invisible Permanently existing spirit that has neither dimension nor Time, that feels very old—like baby god of winds or ancient maps blowing from the Netherworld to create & push this existence along in time—at one point

Peru

the veil lifted and I saw, rolling thru a strange black chaotic dimension, a vast serpent, an endless Dragon, huge as dream—ocean liners—rolling thru dream oceans—whose face I saw and the rolling forepart of the body but whose middle & tail if any were lost in time so far back, impossible to see.

The Brujo tapping his foot (as if in time to an electric motor I heard later somewhere on the horizon—in town)—and whistling softly and evenly into the cup—and another later taking up the whistle, which I listened to—a plaintive varied repetition of some small faraway theme— but the Spirit outside the universe whistles just so thru material lips— and had the sensation of this disembodied endless spirit outside Dimensions, signaling its Eternal presence at all places & times—in fact this whistle is as his universe, we are a song on the lips—a song which he will resolve the harmony of at our personal death, when we'll enter outside our dimension into his Spirit, and understand the incomprehensible faraway sensation of the whistle tune of existence—because it comes from *outside* this dimension, is not a part of it.

Oh Mathematician, can you break thru the Science-fiction Dimensional walls and communicate with some creature in another Dimension who is also simultaneously perhaps working on the same formula— mathematically seeking which of all infinite Probabilities is one of the other probabilities that might coincide with ours and communicate.

A vision of some Golden Age Dimension, of permanently goldlike corporeal golden Olympiads.

A project for a painting: of Dimensions, a creamcolored canvas with bright red rubber (moving) lips, whistling a tune Behind canvas a [?] a phonograph, in which a record is whistling, the machine having been devised

[. . .]

Mona Lisa's smile is perfect expression of the significance of a spirit outside the Landscape, revealing itself thru lips, or whistle. Da Vinci! What did he *mean*? That's the whole point, the meaning of the Mona Lisa smile—"enigmatic"—"all things to all men"—but personal, more than insinuating knowing & saying so—tells everything—it is the sense of the outside God, it has the same purpose as Him. Mona Lisa is god, at least. Big lips anyway—a portrait of the Tranquility. I hardly looked at it in the Louvre, it was stereotype, didn't know what to read into it— Da Vinci's picture of consciousness,

Again, my life-seraph—arguing with me—"But you don't love *me*," he says. "Don't you understand?" Perhaps pointing with his finger at the ceiling of the Apartment—to say I mistake his transient form & get hung on it, which is going to rot, as I will & my love will if it's fixed on that mortal object—if it's being on him & not what's behind him, behind women, behind the life process, behind the veil of Death—the permanently existent Smile & Whistle of Life behind life.

Outside on bed in fields, the clouds folded and black over the stars, with some starshine floating them the puffs of smoky heaven—lay back & stare at the universe, imagining the Space and extent of it, the far Beings and the union to come.

July 3, 1960

Death is a breaking thru the blood, skin, eyes, & bones, a breaking & cracking of the teeth—not an airy brilliant Golden ray or wire floating out freely.   Such pain, the "Spirit" has to escape from its transient self, to rejoin the X.

Peru

Take this consciousness (Allen)—
lying on deathbed
    and suddenly subtract from it bodily functions,
paralysis, & realize the body will never move again,
and it goes to another fate.
    Then, with this anxiety & growing awareness
Of another fate,
    Subtract memory of where it came from (this
Body, Allen, this world)
    So that the past & future (future predicated on past
knowledge of Allen growing, in life, sick, & now dying—
that not remembered, so no future death is in mind either)
are removed from the consciousness—
    There you then have pure consciousness
without individualism,
    which will be located in eternity (without
awareness of past & future)
    which will seek another consciousness or,
which will perhaps meet another consciousness, &
battle for knowledge between the two, or battle for
existence, one or the other—
    A battle for existence between 2 consciousnesses
(as the drawing of the snake)
    and this is my anxiety, & fear to leave the
habitual consciousness, to be another, I know not *what*—
and continue on thru a series of changes of consciousness
toward what end? What horrible end? or What
"Good" end.
    A fear not to be one, anymore

" "   to be *another*.

" "   to lose this identity, this feel, this existence.

A fear of wandering eternally from existence to existence.

Therefore preferring (rather than continue

Existing same old identity)

to die, to not exist.

But I *will* lose identity in death—and either die,

or become another.

Afraid to become another—afraid of being trapped

In some awful wheel which will take me thru endless

Torments, each seemingly real.

Yes that's the formulation; Some other

Consciousness of whose nature I am not (& can't

Be) sure is trying to displace my consciousness and

I am afraid to give up

July 4, 1960—

Ayahuasca VI—renewed urge to procreate, stronger "down to deep reaches of my being."

Reading Boehm's Fundamental Statement

"A craving in nothing"

This is like the Laugh Gas sensation, i.e. the sense of return to the first event in the Void, which led to all the other events logically and according to laws of Events, once a first event appeared.

Q, Exactly what's the nature of the first event?

Q. Exactly what's the law of event?

The first Event is Magic ("what creature gives

birth to itself")

Peru

The general law from last Ayahuasca in Lima (#6) is, Being extends itself in every dimension, and the number of dimensions, and the space-time inside these dimensions, are lordless, since they are all Magic, arbitrary, and limitless by nature of existing in a void, with tendency to infinite expansion since the void has no limits, so that the event will "fill it" entirely, i.e., existence has no more limit than void.

At one point or other knower existence must extend to its limit and annihilate the void, "extend to its limit" here means create or Be in another new dimension which "Magically" includes or resolves or crosses with the void & contradicts it.

Existence to be completely limitless must also contradict itself, so as to have no limitations or boundary. Thus, perfection of Being its own Death? In some manner this situation probably already exists, i.e. The Universe. Universes are probably *both* the flash of a second an event that never existed

and, within that second, event, an infinite series of dimensions of time & space.

And this is only *one* of the accidents in the void, there are a number of accidents, all happening at once and yet at "different times,"

In the same spot (nowhere) yet stretching out in different dimensions of Being

And each Being Creating & reproducing

itself endlessly in its own dimension-system—

[. . .]

July 9—Last nite in Lima—woke dreaming at 5 AM, grey blue sky outside big window, govt. palace milky & huge across street—rooster calls—

Dreams—Meeting Peter, in bed together in a R.R. car, embracing, talking—I explain my new feeling of Death to him, get worked up, lean on his shoulder crying "What will happen to me when you're gone"—

he seems to know, feel it's alright, gets on top of me to fuck me, I avoid it, my ass has tumors—he screws my mouth, but I can't take it, my face is covered with snot & tears & saliva, I have to turn away & wash & spit & blow my nose—

Dream shifts to cabin in Arctic woods, I'm married, wife knitting by fireside, dog sleeping restlessly at end of couch under window that faces on the bleak unknown nite—the dog suddenly bristles & barks hysterically—

"He never does like that place by the window—there's something out there that disturbs him"—

The window suddenly smashes thru, the frame half falls out, it's some hairy bear monster—

I go to the window (coming in from kitchen door) (near fireplace in small cabin room) to look out—It's *still there*—and attacking again, I glimpse a human face outside, the man puts a huge folding bearskin for power over his shoulders & face—and pushes his huge leaden paw against the house window again—at my face—I open my mouth to bite the finger coming at me, horrified—I have no gun, no knife—no protection—and this thing is bent on entering the peaceful house—wake with mouth snapping to bite—

Later remember Peter dream & calm myself with thought, acceptable, that I'll die first—but the bleakness after Peter's joy goes & he becomes aware of the unanswering joyless end of life?

Death is a truck that comes in the garden.

Read in Iquitos: Kant, parts of *Story of Philosophy*—parts of *William James Reader*—*Tibetan Magicians* David Neel—*Portable Thos Wolfe*— *A Short History of World*, H. G. Wells—James Jeans, Article on *Size and*

Age of Universe (Smithsonian 1936?)—Some of John Burroughs on Nature—*New Testament* (on ship).

Muddy bamboo fronts on houses, dark thatch roofs.

30 Junio 1960.

Cabin on outskirt of Iquitos—waiting for Julio Maldonado, slightly high with acrid alcohol smell, to arrive at house and drink—

. . . His mescla for Ayahuasca as follows: Ayahuasca, Toe, Tobacco, Ayahuman, Pucalupina, Yoraculpuna, Huygacaspe, Quillorenaca, Cumacefa, Palo de Sangre.

Sitting in movie—
The universe has begun to frighten me—
The Green Mansions, but—the angel is too sweet—
Thus far, came hoping and with companions
But—crossed the frontier of Peru
Saw the ruins of Machu Picchu looming aloft in the mist—
drank my magic potion—shuddered
This not what I expected, Death—
Thus far, companioned, with music, food, lovers.
Thus far, Poetry—but now at last
Come to the place I prophesied where all the symbols come True
"All the myths are real"—as Snyder said in his Hallucination
Portland 1950—Peyote the inspirer—
in that green hell I trembled

and now the Universe is that green hell
where I've already begun to disintegrate—
The cough at morn, tumor at my sphincter,
Solitude for five months, the hungry poor—
And a God—if a God—more vast than I can remember
And if no God, I'm mad and halfway thru my life
lost in a fantasy that ends with my skull—
And if a God—my life is broken up by this Dread Miracle
That chills my self in amaze and makes vain
    as the scraping of a chair on tile floors in Chinese
    Restaurants in Jungle towns
All this scribbling of 16 years
and praying after Joy and when all along I knew the black Dread
                    Night would end the game.
Now at the end of the road of the mind
Another country looms, the place of death,
a border I have never seen before
and a curtain of darkness where the world ends.
If I only knew there was anyone or anything to pray to—
I was given a god, young, but never expected him to come true
and been playing with his Names since 1948
And now stept off in chaos—and I can't escape except in dying.
And the games of the middle class America
from which I innocently came
is only a game to escape the coming Death and the consciousness
                                it implies.

Peru

Can't yet focus it in "particulars" except a constant
sense of dread as if caught in conspiracy like Oedipus, which
drags me to blindness and ruin.

"Our privilege is to have perceived it as it moved"—
Santayana re spirit.
   The universe is disappearing sez Laugh Gas.
   God is an action not an idea. i.e.—alive, it is alive.

The universe intermirrors its own dimension, the sky is a mirror of
our mind, but God is outside the Mirror.

July 2—flying over Amazon to Pucalla—The black little lakes mirroring
the clouds and sky.

The struggle of the fittest—only eternal creatures survive—but man
is not quite yet (boom!) an eternal creature.
   Over the Andes—Nobody lives here, nobody, nothing.

Re memory of LSD.
   Damn! I always do that—forget the feeling and substitute another
image for it. Then I begin to think in terms of the image and the whole
point gets lost—the whole feeling.
   Like what I saw on LSD and Music was a vast inner Mouth, a Thing,
ever-Triumphant in Glory—and it's reduced in my mind to the image of
a Hindu statue dancing on its own body.

Music—to feel beauty entirely let it take possession of you.

Everytime I realize something new I assume others know it too (or can know) or know more and thus the tone of the poetry. Good advice for beginners, avoids paranoic-jejune.

(The relaxation of the dead body)—as the life goes out of the hand.

_____o_____o_____

Lima, July 2, 1960—Who's the dreamer? We are the thoughts of Eternity. This is our relation (See Boehme Divine Intuition, III, 8) or, we are thoughts of eternity, nothing but thoughts of eternity.

If I attach myself to the reality of the thought, I miss the thinker, I mistake the thought for the one Mind, the thinker, Eternity—and, as the thought is transient I perish with the thought.

By this paradox I understand eternity contemplation itself thru me, thru my discrimination and/or ascendency to pure thought.

In this pure thought I am eternity contemplating Myself.

Otherwise, believing our thoughts real in this Earthly dimension— we are the thoughts of Eternity, the thoughts of What is Not. We mistake our condition for what is.

Eternity, thinking of what Is, is ourselves, thinking of what Is, and *not* mistaking our realm of Being for that which Is.

Eternity in thinking of the Myriad Which Are Not, thinks of What Is.

We are the Myriads which Are Not. This is our realm, until we realize we are not and realize what is.

Eternity, thinking of Inexistent Myriads, creates us.

We must realize that our Existence (dimension—however seeming—vast) is merely an elimination of what is Not in Eternity.

Realizing this, annihilating ourselves, we realize eternity, or we are eternity realizing itself in another flash.

This flash is the mystical Illumination, or known as such to us.

The Mystical Illumination is Not the Contemplating God, but God (or eternity) contemplating Himself.

God uses our Eyes, which don't exist.

Death is the breakdown of this dimension, which is of its own nature unstable, since it (even to itself) finally doesn't even exist.

[. . .]

Ayahuasca VI

I only want to leave the world—is first my realization—a few minutes before drinking and contemplating.

Blake's—"We are led to believe a lie/When we see with not thru the Eye" means:

We, the interior central self, the Being-Sentience is not to be identified with the physical eye (the physical eye) (the physical body) which sees only material in this Dimension—

for the true-being-sentience is inside the head, is a noncorporeal spirit dwelling in the body and using this body to see the world of dimension in which this body exists. Therefore look *thru* the eye, as a window, an instrument, to observe the world—but don't let your eye trick you and make believe you (self) are the eye.

Peru

Old Father Fisheye—the eyes of a fish swimming in the ocean of my imagination, are the eyes of Louis my father.

The old brown violins of Europe—brown with age—listening to Beethoven op. 135—

5 Metros De Poemas—Carlos Quendo de Amat.

July 9, 1960—Limactambo

Into the great airport chanting singing sea-mass of light—into thy lands lord I give my soul to disappear—in plane rising over the plane of light of nite time Lima, the structure of the streets in skeleton—the myriads of lamps under the fog, vanished—not unlike the Unknown, George Capriota Leslie Less, Max Brown's sister and Leslie's cousin seen me off—up over the clouds into the full blue moonlight—the ghastly clouds a floor—and black rifts above—I am in the bearded space, over my own head, with the roar of ears in the air, and cough in chest, beginning a homecoming cold, an ache in chest presage of some debilitation near my heart.

Talk with architect Calderon—and how vast the earth below—a lonely light on what must be desert or coastal plain—he says drugs N.G. because change the body, show the enter light—but then no integral permanent change—so true—tho I didn't want believe it before—must be—

So set out on the lonely road that knows where go—black road—and

The star in sky, the coast, the moon, SA below, 6 months from misty Isles thru lakes and Machu Picchu and mud markets and lunar Puno to cities and jungle and the dread bones of my skull in the hut—now flying home to life again. N.Y—all like a predestined old drama, old Path—that must be—toward Doom—and

The confusion of the scare, which way to go in Doom—need a teacher, need a wiseman who knows, between fire and fire which is God and which is Death? or is there even a God to look for?

"Immovable kind of the roads that are gone."

I cannot turn back, for where can I turn to, before I was born? And that's the same again—there's no place to hide but in death itself, and I am trapped within this Doom.

And it is coming: it's coming—and I don't know who I am, and yet I don't know who Death is yet either—I'm afraid of the minute I have to break out of my skin at last, I have to leave my body, leave my soul, my memory—and become a—what shining mass of strange unconsciousness forever rolling and reborn in tricky worlds of death—and what great central blackness rolls my bones? and gives me suck of dimension?

I'm poet, I've striven to record Beauty—all gone—yes, let this life pass, I hope I give up my memory without screaming.

And no love there? Another thing—I don't know, beyond my dimension, beyond my limit—a limitless beast—a bear-skin with human face as in last nite dream.

As the plane rides on over cities spotted on the coast—that It might come any minute.

I'm an accident, a skull with a beard, riding on a big lane—going?— where?—Home?

The romance is over.

It would be enough to rest in death and forget it, except that there will come a moment where I will have to know—where maybe I will have to know—when I flee, in what direction—what choice to make between the strange consciousness of death, and the old consciousness I had of both—and what other that might come claim me by default? What other that might be rebirth as Allen, as a worm, or unimaginable hell, or

Heaven, or nothing at all. Things I can't imagine, which'll suddenly be Fate—and I might lose Faith and panic at oblivion—shrivel at the touch of pain—passing thru bone—and reject the Fire of death—prolong the agony—another lifetime in another universe of Be, without memory of what I went thru before, without learning—or is there as they say an instant's flash to grasp at, enter, and be lost forever in the Huge? or miss and be another self, another me in other pitiable form, wanting a separate self to continue.

And I don't know—and even want to know, to grasp beforehand—to keep control of my own consciousness—which may be Hell itself.

So I shake my head back and forth confounded and lay it back in desperacy fatigue and sigh and will my soul to Whoever or Whatever made it. Hoping at last moment I won't fight back

For the soul goes out of the body, I go out of my body even now sense it, I will have to *leave* this body, and it will never see this body again, or all the bodies I ever knew, and all that's waste and foregone—except whatever Babe I leave behind a babe—and stay in this existence. Is that right? This life to die? or eke another life, forgetful of the change? and whose my babe gonna be? another Me? or someone else, and I get nothing left—the last cheat of death—a total loss. No someone else, he won't remember Louis or Jack Kerouac or Peter or dear ruins else, or even me.

And do I really want to live forever as me? Who's me? The best's not even Allen that I know of—tho the sweetest's been old love old me with honied breast, and bodies in a bed, and a transcendent joy at cock and balls in tenderness, and come all over Heaven in my mind Ya, that was good. But worth it?

Can't tell that the old father skeleton lifts his eyes and I know the truth at last, and suffer my soul to be unborn. And me see the octopus All.

Peru

All's an octopus. Who wants to be an octopus? But such an octopus: with all them living eyes! And God knows what the octopus is.

Panama City—Slept 3 a.m. to morn in Sta. Ana bandstand park— woken with rifleshot crack of drum and trumpet—all the bums got up to attention—and they ran up the flat in the Park.

Tonga—Panama-Colombia (Soma)—drug—pilde.

Dreams of amicable conversation with Duncan (last nite in Lima)— after reading Boehme and some of *The Field*.

N,Y, 1960—Schoenberg Verklertinacht last straining for human sentimental revolution—strain and sadness, of further hope, elsewhere. After the acerb cold reality of science.

O'Hara brings romanticist emotions and schmaltzy reactions to new cold language of abstraction in paint—

Nimrod—U of Tusa, Tulsa, Okla. Wants Poetry, Ted Berrigan.

Cockroach Man—

END

SELECT BIBLIOGRAPHY BY AND ABOUT ALLEN GINSBERG

Burroughs, William, and Allen Ginsberg. *The Yage Letters Redux*. Edited and with an Introduction by Oliver Harris. San Francisco: City Lights Books, 2006.

Ginsberg, Allen. *Collected Poems, 1947–1997*. New York: HarperCollins, 2006.

———. *The Essential Ginsberg*. Ed. Michael Schumacher. New York: HarperCollins, 2015.

———. *Iron Curtain Journals: January–May 1965*. Ed. Michael Schumacher. Minneapolis: University of Minnesota Press, 2018.

———. *Luminous Dreams*. Gran Canaria: Zasterle Press, 1997.

———. *Wait Till I'm Dead: Unpublished Poems*. Ed. Bill Morgan. New York: Grove Press, 2016.

Ginsberg, Allen, and Peter Orlovsky. *Straight Hearts Delight: Love Poems and Selected Letters*. Ed. Winston Leyland. San Francisco: Gay Sunshine Press, 1980.

Morgan, Bill. *I Celebrate Myself: The Somewhat Private Life of Allen Ginsberg*. New York: Penguin, 2007.

Schumacher, Michael. *Dharma Lion: A Critical Biography of Allen Ginsberg*. New York: St. Martin's Press, 1992. Reprinted by University of Minnesota Press, 2017.

———, ed. *First Thought: Conversations with Allen Ginsberg*. Minneapolis: University of Minnesota Press, 2017.

ALLEN GINSBERG

(1926–1997) was an American poet, philosopher, and writer. He was a member of the Beat Generation during the 1950s and a leader of the counterculture that followed. His poetry collection *The Fall of America* received the National Book Award for Poetry in 1974.

MICHAEL SCHUMACHER

has written extensively about Allen Ginsberg and the Beat Generation. His books include *Dharma Lion: A Biography of Allen Ginsberg* and *First Thought: Conversations with Allen Ginsberg*, both published by the University of Minnesota Press. He is the editor of *The Essential Ginsberg* and *Family Business: Selected Letters between a Father and Son* (correspondence between Louis and Allen Ginsberg). He lives in Wisconsin.